TODDLERS

PRESCHOOLERS

INTRODUCTION

Welcome to the first six years of your child's life.
It sounds like a long time, doesn't it? It is.
And it isn't.

Everyone says that children grow so fast—a concept that's easy to understand before you have children because time goes by so quickly in your own life. But once your baby is born and you see how much she changes in the first weeks and months of her life, you will be absolutely astounded at *how fast children grow*. All of a sudden your baby is getting her first tooth. How did that happen so quickly? She turns one, starts walking and talking, and a couple of months later you've got a little kid in front of you. Your baby is no longer a baby.

Time goes too fast when you're raising a child. It's an incredible challenge! Are you making the right choices? Are you helping or harming your kid? What if nobody else seems to be doing it your way? Then, just when you get the hang of things, your child changes on you. This means that the rules you've been following no longer apply, and what you've learned and mastered doesn't necessarily work with your child anymore. She's moved on to a new stage and is in need of new guidance. You're back to learning how to do it again.

YOU CAN ENHANCE YOUR CHILD'S DEVELOPMENT

Child development is the process your child goes through to learn all the skills she needs to become an independent adult. Big skills like walking and talking. Seemingly small skills like stringing beads onto yarn or using a fork. In development, however, no skill is small. Each one is important, builds on your child's abilities, and makes it possible for her to reach the next milestone (and the next one, and the one after that).

In the following chapters, we have divided your child's development into four categories:

- **Developing Body** is your child's physical development, consisting of gross or large motor skills such as crawling, jumping, and riding a bike, and fine motor skills, which involve using the hands and fingers for picking up small items, using scissors, and writing.

- **Developing Mind** is your child's cognitive development, or how your child learns, processes information, and problem solves. It includes skills like exploring environments, learning to categorize, and doing math.

- **Developing Language** is your child's language development, which includes learning to comprehend and speak whatever language(s) your child is exposed to on a daily basis.

- **Developing Person** is your child's social and emotional development, which covers how your child interacts with others, expresses herself, values herself, and learns self-control.

Your child's development is an ongoing process, and she will be busy learning skills in all of these areas concurrently. And it's critical to remember that her developmental timeline is unique, just like she is. Your child is an individual, and she will develop at her own pace. She may be ahead in one area and behind in another at any given time. That's okay. As long as your child continues to show progress in a reasonable amount of time, you can rest assured that her development is right on track *for her*. What is a reasonable amount of time? It depends on the particular skill. We've highlighted "Red Flags," or warning signs, of certain developmental delays within the chapters as guidance, but if you have any concerns about your child's development, bring them to the attention of your child's physician. If the doctor reassures you there's nothing to worry about, it will allay your fears. And if there is cause for concern, the earlier your child gets help, the better.

In each chapter, we cover the developmental milestones that are typical for that age range. A *developmental milestone* is simply a skill that is mastered within a certain time frame. There are general time frames within which most children master a given skill. Some will learn the skills earlier, some later, but most do it within a certain window of time. The many developmental skills we outline in each chapter are based on the general time frame of when they are commonly achieved.

You can enhance your child's development through myriad activities—none of which require special toys or equipment. Every chapter lists a number of developmentally enhancing activities for each area of development. Keep in mind that you will not be able to accelerate your child's development with any of these activities. That's because it's not possible to speed development, just enhance it. However, you can create a positive environment in which to learn skills.

HOW YOU PARENT MAKES A DIFFERENCE IN YOUR CHILD'S DEVELOPMENT

You cannot know what kind of parent you will be until you are in the middle of it. Over time, you will develop your own style of parenting based on what works best for you and your child. We all have different ways of doing things, and as parents we are all works-in-progress. We all make mistakes, and hopefully we learn from them and move on to do a better job. There is no one "right" way to parent. You will learn as you go on this parenting journey, applying what is important and what feels right to you.

On these pages, you will be introduced not only to your child's development for her first six years of life but also to a gentler approach to parenting— a more respectful way of treating your child. This

approach helps create a strong bond between you and your child, giving you a deeper understanding of her, and in turn making the experience of being a parent more enjoyable and easier in many ways. The better you know and understand your child, the better you are able to meet her needs and solve or avoid behavior problems.

Before you jump into learning about your child's development, we'd like to share some simple ideas that govern our philosophy on raising children.

You are the expert on your child. No one knows your child better than you do. Even if you are a first-time parent. Even if your child is only a week old. You are the one spending time with her, getting to know her, loving her, holding her, comforting her, and studying her. Your doctor is not the expert on your child. Neither is your next-door neighbor, your mother, or your sister-in-law. You are the expert on your child.

If this is your first child, you may feel as if you do not know what you are doing. But you have within you all you need to be your child's parent. You will know what to do—figuring it out—as each new situation arises. Which leads us to our next point...

Trust yourself. Trust your instincts. They are usually right. If you feel that something isn't right with your baby, seek out help, and keep seeking it until someone listens to you. If a strategy you try with your child doesn't feel right, then don't do it. If it feels wrong, it is wrong. If it feels right, it is right.

Trust yourself. Listen to that voice inside. Give yourself time. Be kind to yourself. You will figure out everything you need to know. You have all the answers, even if they're hard to find sometimes.

Trust your child. Even your newborn. If your baby cries, pick her up. Believe her when she tells you (whether by crying as a baby or with words when she's older) that she needs you. She does! Be there for her. She knows what she needs and wants. She has desires, likes, and dislikes, just like you do. Trust that she is telling you the truth, and treat what she has to say as important.

Treat your child with respect. Your child deserves the same respect you give your friends, family, and even strangers. We can teach our children what they need to learn while treating them respectfully. They deserve to be treated as such for the simple fact that every child is a person. They may be little people, but they are no less important than adults.

Children are innately good. They want to do good and be good. They are naturally social beings, which means they want to be a part of things, helping, contributing, participating. Social creatures do not try to cause trouble or act up simply because they can or to upset others. If they show disruptive behavior, it is because something is not right in their world, but they do not know how to express what it is. So it comes out as "bad" behavior. Children are not innately bad, nor are they manipulative. When they behave in a way that we don't like, we need to figure out what is causing the behavior and try to fix the problem. When the problem has been addressed or solved, the undesirable behavior

disappears. This approach, instead of punishing the child for behaving badly, shows her that we respect her as a person. She is important enough to help her feel right again, so she can be social again, which is right where she wants to be.

Children can feel the difference. They know when they are being treated with respect, and it positively affects their behavior.

Think long term. If you consider that you are actually raising a future adult, rather than raising a child, then you start to think long term. What do you want for your child? Who do you hope she will become? What traits to do you hope she'll have? How do you want her to approach life? Think about these questions, and consider whether your parenting style is helping you achieve your goals. If you want your child to be independent, but you tightly

control your child's every move, are you helping her? Check in with yourself once in a while to make sure your parenting techniques are consistent with your goals for your child.

Be the person you want your child to be. This is perhaps the most effective thing you can do as your child grows. You are the model on which she will base herself. She learns how to do everything from you, including how to treat others, how to live life, how to be in the world. To make the greatest impact in guiding her, you must embody those qualities you hope she will have. You will see this idea woven throughout the book. As a parent, you must consciously and consistently model the behavior you want to see in your child because she will imitate you in every way.

It's so very simple, though not very easy. Luckily, you have time to grow into the person you hope your child will become. As your baby grows, you'll grow with her. When you make mistakes, you'll learn and do better the next time. You don't have to be perfect. You are not perfect. Nobody is. (And remember that as you watch your kids grow. We all make mistakes— both parents and children.)

Figuring out the kind of parent you will be is something you cannot accomplish before your baby arrives. You can start formulating opinions and ideas about parenting, but you won't discover your baby's personality or what her needs are until you get to know her. She may turn out to be more easygoing or more needy than you expected. You also do not know how parenting will affect you or how your overwhelming love for your child will affect your approach to parenting.

Keep an open mind to all ideas, and adopt those that work for you and your baby. Think of yourself as a work-in-progress. Allow yourself to make mistakes and then learn from them. Give yourself and your baby the best start on this new journey by meeting her needs and treating her with respect from the beginning. You are the expert on your child. Listen to, trust, and follow your instincts when it comes to your child. Think long-term results rather than short-term solutions. Be the person you want your child to be. Do the best you can with what you have each day, and your child will have the best of you—which is precisely what she deserves. You can make all the difference in your child's life and development.

Your baby is programmed to breastfeed, and so he comes equipped with a *sucking reflex*. He will suck a nipple (breast or bottle), your finger, or his own thumb. You may have seen him sucking his thumb on an ultrasound when he was still in utero.

When your baby isn't hungry, you can offer him your finger to suck on to soothe him if he gets upset. To do this, put a clean pinky finger into baby's mouth with the pad of the finger facing up and the fingernail against the tongue. If you stroke the roof of his mouth with your finger, he will start sucking and pull your finger into his mouth up to the first crease. You may be surprised at how much suction one awfully little person can create! When he's sucking, there should be significant resistance to pulling your finger out of his mouth. If he stops sucking or tries to push your finger out of his mouth, gently wiggle your finger and stroke the roof of his mouth again. That will usually get him to start sucking again, which helps calm him.

Another primitive reflex that you will notice right away is the *rooting reflex*. This reflex is triggered when you stroke your baby's cheek. Whichever cheek you touch, he will automatically turn in that direction with an open mouth ready to latch on and feed. A mother can use this reflex to initiate breastfeeding by touching her finger or nipple to her baby's cheek. He will open his mouth wide and turn toward the nipple, ready to nurse.

TIP   Avoid Nipple Confusion

You can soothe your baby with a pacifier, but we don't recommend using one during the first few weeks of life. Occasionally, a baby will develop "nipple confusion," which means he has problems switching between the nipple of Mom's breast and the nipple of a pacifier. This can delay the establishment of solid breastfeeding and has been linked to a shorter total duration of breastfeeding. Once your baby is nursing well and gaining weight without difficulty—usually around three to four weeks of life—you can introduce a pacifier to satisfy his sucking needs.

Your baby comes programmed with a sucking reflex that not only allows him to eat but also to comfort himself. Sucking at the breast, on fingers, or a pacifier is very soothing to your baby, and can be a way for you to calm him when he gets upset.

Another very noticeable reflex is the *Moro* or *startle reflex*. When a baby is startled, he will throw his hands and legs wide open and then slowly recover his normal resting position. He can be startled by motion or sound, and he may cry in response. Unfortunately, the Moro reflex can occasionally wake a sleeping child. Many parents find that swaddling their baby will prevent the arm and leg motion associated with the reflex and make it less likely that their baby will wake up.

Other primitive reflexes relate to baby's hands and feet. The *palmar* and *plantar* grasps involve a hand or foot curling around an object. If you put

Put your finger in your baby's palm and he will immediately curl his fingers around yours—and hold on tight! Your newborn baby will use his grasping reflex to stay attached to you, and keep you attached to him as well.

RED FLAG!

The presence of primitive reflexes is an important clue to a well-functioning nervous system. Your baby should demonstrate primitive reflexes when he is born and should gradually grow out of them over the first several months. If he is missing some of the reflexes at birth or they do not disappear at the appropriate time, your physician may want to investigate further.

your finger in the middle of your baby's hand or foot, his fingers or toes will curl around your finger. The *hand-opening* reflex triggers the opposite motion. Touching the back of baby's hand leads him to uncurl his fingers and spread them wide open. Finally, the *stepping* reflex demonstrates a primitive first step. If you hold your baby upright under his arms and let the sole of one foot touch the floor, tabletop, or your lap, he will move his legs in a way that looks like he is walking.

Protect Your Baby's Head and Neck

Your baby develops muscle control over the first year along a logical progression: from head to toe. At birth, the head and neck are very wobbly, able to stay up for a second or two before falling to one side. This instability occurs because he hasn't yet learned to control his head and neck muscles and because he hasn't developed the muscle strength to hold up his very heavy head. Compared to an adult's head, which is only 5 to 10 percent of our total body weight, a newborn baby's head makes up around 25 percent of his total weight. Imagine holding your head up if it weighed 30 to 40 pounds (13.6 to 18 kg). You might wobble a bit, too!

Over the first two months of his life, your baby will gain strength and develop better control of his head and neck muscles. His head will continue to wobble occasionally, but he will be able to hold it up for longer amounts of time before it flops to one side. When on his tummy, he will be able to lift his head off the floor and move it from one side to the other. By four months of age, he will have almost complete head control with little to no wobble as he looks around at the world.

Babies this age are so cuddly and snuggly. Hold your baby as much as you want to—let him sleep in your arms or on your chest—keep him with you all day long if you like. Lying on your chest makes him feel less stressed. He will grow faster and breathe more regularly.

During the first few months of your baby's life, **you need to keep an extra close eye on his head and protect it from flopping around unnecessarily.** Its relative heaviness makes it easy for the head to fall in one direction, pulling the body with it—down the stairs or off the changing table. With a newborn, this means making sure you have one hand on baby's head and one on his body when moving him from one place to another. *Always* be sure to support his head with your hand when you lift him to your shoulder. You should also be careful when putting him down, because his head may descend more quickly than you anticipate and can hit the surface harder than you expected.

Use Your Face to Help Baby Track with His Eyes

Six muscles control the movement of each human eye, plus another muscle that allows the eye to focus. At birth, each eye is controlled separately, and you may notice that your baby looks cross-eyed or that his eyes are staring in different directions. After two or three weeks, however, he will develop conjugate gaze as he learns how to use his eyes together. **By eight weeks, he will have enough control over his eye muscles that he will be able to track you as you move across his field of vision.** His tracking will be jerky at first. When he reaches sixteen weeks of age, his head and neck control will complement his control over his eye muscles, allowing him to smoothly follow you with his eyes all the way around the room.

It also takes time for a baby to learn how to focus his eyes. At first, his eyes act like a poorly operating camera, sometimes focusing too close and sometimes too far from the object being studied. The distance at which he can focus best is 12 to 18 inches (30.4 to 45.7 cm), or the distance from the crook of your elbow to your face. This means that your face is in focus when you are holding him in your arms or when you are breastfeeding.

Hanging toys above your baby's face gives her practice learning to focus her eyes. She's working on her eye muscles! Try to hang items about 12 to 18 inches (30.4 to 45.7 cm) above her.

Over time your baby will gain control of the focusing muscle in his eyes and be able to see things more clearly. Remember that "more clearly" is a relative term. Newborns have much blurrier vision than adults do. Recent research suggests that a newborn's vision is worse than 20/100. That translates to a reading ability just below the big E on the eye chart. This is not due to a problem with the lens but rather the result of an immature retina. Even with that level of vision, however, your baby can appreciate facial features such as your eyes, nose, and mouth.

Hang Toys in Front of Baby to Stimulate Use of His Arms and Hands

While your baby is learning to control his head, neck, and eyes, he is also learning to control his arms and hands. At first, his arm motion is random, which is why he may occasionally hit himself in the face.

By the time your baby is eight weeks old, his movements become more purposeful, and he will stop hitting himself and start hitting things around him. This is an excellent time to place hanging toys within his reach. He will learn that if he moves *this* muscle, then *that* toy moves, and he will repeat that motion over and over again. Over time, he will develop the hand-eye coordination he needs to grasp a toy, and by sixteen weeks, he will be able to bring it to his mouth.

By the way, if you are wondering, his torso and legs are still undeveloped at this stage. Remember that his physical development moves from head to toe. He will develop skills in those areas of the body in the upcoming weeks and months.

Touch your baby. Massage this perfect little person. He has the softest skin you've ever felt! Give him hugs and kisses and blow raspberries on his stomach. Physical contact is the best way to connect with him.

TIP   **Protect Your Baby's Face**

It's a natural impulse for newborns to bring their hands close to their faces, but if you find that your baby is scratching himself, try putting newborn mittens on his hands. Also, be sure to use a nail file or nail clippers to keep his fingernails trimmed short.

Activities to Enhance Your Child's Physical Development

- Touch your baby. It builds your connection with your child and stimulates him to move those parts of his body that are touched. Give him hugs and kisses and blow raspberries on his stomach.

- Learn how to give your baby a massage. Rub his back or his belly, and stroke his arms and legs.

- Play with your baby! Place him in different positions—on his back, on his tummy—and help him move his arms and legs around. Gently stretch out his arms and legs. Find a baby yoga book for other exercises to do with your newborn and infant.

Newborns Can Move with Purpose

Despite all our talk about random and unplanned movements, you should know that babies are capable of having purposeful movements as well. A newborn is able to push and crawl up his mother's chest to find a breast and start nursing. All on his own.

An entertaining activity for you and your newborn is to watch him mimic your facial expressions. To try this, you need to catch him in a quiet, alert state—perhaps after nursing when he is full and content but not yet sleepy. First, stabilize his head so it doesn't wobble. Try lying him on his side or his back with good support for his head. Next, put your face 12 to 18 inches (30.4 to 45.7 cm) away so you are in focus. Finally, make slow, deliberate changes in your face, such as raising your eyebrows or opening your mouth wide. If you are lucky, he will respond with the same facial movements several seconds later.

For more examples of newborn abilities, including wonderful pictures, check out *Your Amazing Newborn* by Marshall and Phyllis Klaus.

- Make eye contact. Smile at your baby. Give him lots of love and attention. You can never give him too much.

- Hold your baby. Wear your baby in a sling or front pack while you do household chores, go for a walk, shop, or work on the computer. It's especially useful at the grocery store because your baby stays happy longer when he's being held.

- Help your baby have a sense of movement. Gently bounce, sway, and rock him. Dance with him!

- Give your baby objects to reach for and play with. Best choices are colorful toys that are easy for your baby to hold and can be washed in the dishwasher, or everyday items such as wooden spoons, metal bowls, and measuring cups.

- Shake a noisy toy and let your baby turn his head to look and then reach for it.

- Strap bells to your baby's wrists and ankles and let him discover that his movements cause the jingles.

- Give your baby freedom to move around. Put him down on the floor so he can look around, kick his legs, and wiggle. Don't leave him in a swing, car seat carrier, or bouncy seat for long. They are too limiting for movement, and he needs to move to develop!

- Give your baby some tummy time, where you lie him down on his stomach to play. Talk to him so he will lift his head to see you. Or hold a bright or noisy toy in front of him so he'll try to look at it. Your baby will learn to lift his head and push up on his arms. He might even learn to scoot around on the floor. He will strengthen his back and neck muscles that he will need in the future to help him crawl.

DEVELOPING MIND

It used to be thought that babies are born as a blank slate, or as Aristotle called it, *tabula rasa*. In truth, your baby was born with more cognitive skills than you might realize.

Sound. Your baby already has the ability to hear well and to localize sounds. He will turn his head toward a voice or music. More important, he has the ability to distinguish between voices.

Immediately after birth, he shows a preference for his mother's voice over other voices, and he will turn his head in his mother's direction. He will also recognize other familiar voices besides Mom's by the time he is one month old.

Smell. A newborn can recognize certain smells. He will almost immediately learn his mother's scent. Studies have shown that babies prefer clothes that their mothers have worn to clothes used by other people, including other nursing mothers. That means he knows what his mama's breast milk smells like. He may even start to fuss when his mother walks into the room, and he smells her. He's already saying, "I want you, Mama!" He also quickly learns to prefer sweet smells and tastes and to avoid acidic or bitter tastes.

Sight. Your baby's vision is primed to recognize patterns. It takes several weeks for him to learn to control his eye movements; think of it as learning how to properly aim a camera. However, once the camera is aimed correctly, he will prefer certain patterns over others. His favorite will be a facial pattern; he would rather look at eyes and noses than at other objects. He will also be drawn to contrasts. It is true that babies prefer bold black-and-white patterns, but they also have the ability to distinguish between subtler contrasts. By eight weeks, their sensitivity to contrast is almost as good as an adult's!

Even young babies need tummy time. Your baby might not lift his head very high at first but over time he will strengthen his back and neck muscles, and be able to look around the room and even up at the ceiling. He's working up the strength to be able to crawl someday.

Activities to Enhance Your Child's Cognitive Development

- Read to your baby! Yes, even to your newborn. Show him picture books with bright colors and high-contrast patterns. He'll love looking at the pictures and listening to your voice.

- Talk to your baby. Look at him, smile at him, and engage him in conversation from the day he is born. He will love listening to you.

- Hang a mobile with high-contrast patterns above the changing table or in his crib, if you use one. Alternatively, create a floor gym with several hanging toys for him to lie beneath, look at, and reach for.

- Place an unbreakable mirror in the crib or next to the changing table for him to see his face and movements. Position a large mirror low on the wall so he can see himself when he is playing on the floor.

- Provide toys that make different sounds, including musical toys that make noise when touched. Your baby will learn that hitting the toy will make a pleasant noise.

- Play music. Sing! Don't restrict yourself to kids' music simply because you have a baby. Your child will love whatever music you play for him, so choose something you like to listen to as well.

- Engage your baby's sense of smell by putting fragrant things near him, such as flowers, lemons, oranges, vanilla, cinnamon, grass, dirt, and tomato plants.

DEVELOPING LANGUAGE

It might seem strange to be talking about language at this age, but a large part of your baby's intellectual development involves communication. Within the first few months, he will start to babble and coo and develop intonations and inflections, with sounds rising and falling as if they're being used in a sentence. Try mimicking these sounds and intonations back to him. In its simplest form, this is the beginning of conversation, where one person says something, and the other person responds.

At this early stage, your baby's language takes the form of crying. It will develop into a more sophisticated system as he grows and learns to cry

Let your baby look at himself in an unbreakable mirror. Although he won't yet realize that it is him in the mirror, he will enjoy the other person who is moving around, smiling, and looking at him.

in different ways to express his different needs. The only way your baby can tell you something is not right is by crying. By consistently responding to him every time he cries, you are encouraging him to communicate with you as he grows. (And, no, you're not spoiling him. You cannot spoil a baby!) You are showing him that you are there to help fix whatever is wrong and to meet his needs.

Your baby will learn to cry in different ways, in different tones, for different needs. It may be hard to make the distinction at first, but over time you should be able to tell the difference between cries of hunger, frustration, pain, and fear. When your baby can communicate his needs with different cries, you will be better able to respond to his needs, reinforcing the benefits of communication.

Activities to Enhance Your Child's Language Development

- Talk to your baby! And look at him when you are talking to him; let him see your face. Keep up a running conversation whenever you change his diaper or feed him, whenever you take him shopping or out for a walk in the woods. Talk to him just like you would talk to an adult, telling him about your plans, showing him a bird's nest, and asking him questions. He will learn about the inflections and intonations of conversation and over time will respond to you in kind.

- Sing to your baby—whatever songs you like. It can be a lullaby, kids' song, show tune, folk song, or rock 'n' roll. If you sing the same song every time you comfort your upset baby, he'll start to recognize it and be soothed when he hears it. This

TIP   Babes Are Meant to be in Arms

Hold your baby as much as you want to, or as much as he wants to be held. You cannot hold him too much! He's been inside your body for nine months—He instinctively wants to stay in touch with your body. Your heartbeat, smell, movement, and voice soothe him and let him know he is safe. Many babies do not want to be put down. They are happiest, cry less, and take longer naps when they are held or in contact with Mom or Dad. Slings and other infant carriers are made especially so you can hold your baby as much as you want and still have free arms to get things done.

can be useful in the car when you can't physically comfort him, but you can sing your song to help him relax and calm down.

- Read books to your baby. Your newborn will love listening to your voice. Choose picture books with bright colors and contrasting patterns. He'll enjoy looking at the pictures as he grows.

- When you touch parts of baby's body like his nose, toes, and belly button, name them and make up rhymes like "toes, nose!"

DEVELOPING PERSON

A baby's first few months set the foundation for a life of social interaction. He learns that when he is hungry, he will be fed, when he is wet or his diaper is soiled, he will be changed, and when he is scared, you will comfort him. By consistently responding to his needs, he learns to trust that you will take care of him. This trust gives him a belief that the world is a safe place in which to grow up.

Create a Healthy Attachment with Your Baby

Forming a healthy attachment with your baby gives him a strong sense of security as he grows. **By being there for him whenever he needs you —day or night—you lay the foundation on which he will build his independence.** Children need a secure "home base" that they can trust to always be there. That home base is you. It gives them the courage and confidence to venture out on their own when they are ready, to become independent, and to grow and explore. It also gives you a strong and close relationship with your child.

Building a healthy attachment involves many instinctual parenting actions. The first is skin-to-skin contact with your baby, something that nursing moms naturally enjoy whenever they nurse their babies. It is also a great way for dads to get in on the attachment process. Dad can take off his shirt and lie his diapered (but otherwise unclothed) baby on his chest for snuggling and bonding time. Your baby will love listening to your heart beat (the same heartbeat he listened to for many months—he loves

Smile at Your Baby, and He Will Smile Back at You

Babies learn to smile in the first several weeks of life. At first your baby's smile is a response to inner pleasure, such as a full stomach, but by several weeks of age, he will begin to express social smiles. The social smile may reflect his ability to see your face, recognize your smile, and respond with his own smile. Enjoy this smile; it is a treasure. It is a smile that says he truly knows that you are his parent.

You may melt into a puddle of mush the first time your baby smiles at you. By the time he is several weeks old, he may start to smile at you whenever he sees your smiling face.

that sound!) and to your voice as you talk to him and touch him.

Consistently respond to your baby when he cries. Go to him. Pick him up. Try to figure out what he needs and meet that need. (Is he wet/soiled? hungry? lonely? hurt?) Learn his cues and respond to them before he cries. He'll start to tell you ahead of time, before he gets upset, that he needs something. When you begin to recognize those cues (something you learn as you go), it becomes easier to meet his needs before he cries. Maybe he'll start to squirm and fuss when his wet diaper is bothering him. Or he'll start sucking on his fist when he's hungry.

Kiss your baby! All the time! All over! Shower him with love and attention; you can never give too much. There is no such thing as spoiling a baby, so don't let anyone tell you that you're spoiling him (see page 31). You're not. What you are doing is building a strong and healthy connection with your child.

Play with your baby, read to him, and talk to him as if he's a person. (He is!). Engage with him. If you move beyond his line of vision, keep talking to him from wherever you are. Use your voice to let him know that even though he can't see you, you are still nearby. (When he's older he'll actually understand that concept and be comforted when you call from another room. You're building up to that by starting to do this now.)

Hold your baby as much as you can and want to. Wear him in a sling or front pack. He loves to be held close and touched. Keep him with you, near

your heart so he can hear that comforting rhythm. Look at him when you are feeding him, changing his diaper, and bathing him. He will stare right into your eyes every time you feed, change, and bathe him, so talk to him and look directly into his eyes. Connect. Bond. Attach.

Adjust Your Parenting Style to Complement Your Baby's Temperament

This is a good time to discuss your baby's temperament. We all know that some children are born flexible and easygoing, while other children are slower to warm up to new people and situations. For whatever reason, the latter group has greater difficulty with transitions and becomes easily frustrated. If your child is in the "slow to warm up" category, he may cry more and smile less often. He may be more hesitant with new experiences and more unwilling to change his routines. He may have stranger anxiety that makes him uncomfortable around new faces.

One temperament is not better than another. There are many aspects to temperament beyond those mentioned above, and there are benefits to every type of temperament. However, it is fair to say that some temperaments are easier to parent than others. An easily frustrated, slow to warm up child requires more patience, more attention, and more comforting than other children do. If you have a child who requires more energy from you, make sure you take care of yourself and find ways to replenish your energy.

Activities to Enhance Your Child's Emotional and Social Development

- Have fun with your baby. Play with him! Revel in his presence and make him feel loved and cherished. The knowledge that you just enjoy being with him is one of the most wonderful gifts you can ever give.

- Love your baby. Unconditional love is one of the greatest gifts you can give him. If he truly feels loved and appreciated just for being who he is, he will develop a sense of self-value, a sense that he is worthwhile.

Nursing your baby provides many benefits. It provides skin-to-skin contact as well as eye contact with your baby, allowing for excellent bonding time. Nursing also provides the perfect food at the perfect temperature and shares your antibodies with him, thus protecting him from many infections.

- Wear your baby in a sling or front pack. Hold him as much as you want to. He loves being held close and touched.

- Always respond to your baby when he cries. Do it with love. He needs your help to right whatever is wrong. Sometimes he just needs you!

- Touch your baby. Give him kisses, hugs, snuggles. Massage him. Do baby yoga together.

- Take time to read to your baby. He'll love the snuggling time with you, looking at the bright colorful pictures, and listening to your soothing voice.

- Continually talk to your baby. Tell him what you are doing, what you see. Point things out to him even though he won't understand enough to look. He'll be enthralled with whatever you tell him.

- Make eye contact. Look right into your baby's eyes when you feed him, change his diaper, and give him a bath. He'll be looking right back. It's a great way to connect and build trust.

- Join a playgroup or a mom's support group (where babies are welcome, too).

- Let other people hold your baby when he's happy. If he gets upset, take him back and comfort him. You are the parent and the greatest source of comfort for him.

- Take your baby out to see the world—on walks, errands, for lunch with a friend. Get out and do things with your baby by your side (or in your arms).

POSITIVELY PARENTING

Positively parenting is raising children in as positive a manner as possible. Positive attitude, positive attention, positive environment. Throughout this book, we will introduce you to methods of parenting in a kind and gentle manner. These methods will invest both you and your child with good feelings and dignity as you bring out the best in your child and teach him appropriate behavior through example, gentle guidance, and kind understanding.

You Cannot Spoil Your Baby

It's true. You cannot spoil your baby. A well-meaning friend or relative may urge you not to respond to every cry by comforting, picking up, or nursing your baby. They may suggest that you let him cry it out, let him learn to comfort himself, and that if you don't, you will spoil him. But it is absolutely impossible to spoil a baby.

Spoiling your baby implies that you are giving him something that's inappropriate, something that he wants but does not need. But babies are very simple; their wants and needs are the same. When they cry, they truly need something. They are hungry, wet, tired, or lonely. They are unhappy and are asking you for help, for a way out of an upsetting situation. Later on, perhaps when your child reaches a year, you can expect him to *start* to understand the difference between a want and a need. But for now, it is important to respond quickly to your baby's crying because he genuinely needs you.

Babies are totally dependent on their caregivers. They cannot fix problems on their own.

TIP Don't Let Your Baby Cry It Out

When you rapidly and consistently respond to your baby's cries, you are teaching him that you are there for him, that the world is safe, and that his needs will be met. Babies need to learn that the world will take care of them. If you let him cry it out when he is upset, he will lose trust in the world. And in you. If he can't be sure that you will respond to his needs—that the world is a safe place—he will always feel insecure and unsettled. And that is an unhappy way to live his life.

And they are not capable of self-soothing at this age. Their sole form of communication is crying. So the only way they can get their needs met is to ask for help. And the only way they can ask for help is to cry. At this basic level, crying is their way of telling you they need help.

Let's put this in perspective. Imagine you are a nurse caring for an adult patient who has suffered a severe stroke. He is unable to talk and is confined to bed. The only way he can communicate with you is to press a button that rings a very loud bell. When you hear the bell, you come to his bedside and try to figure out what he needs. Then you fix the problem for him. Would you talk about "spoiling" this person when you respond to him when he is hungry, lonely, or needs to be cleaned after a bowel movement?

Now it's true that the bell might be annoying. And it's true that if you don't respond to the bell the first time, the patient may ring the bell again and again and again until you do respond. But if this is the only way the patient can communicate when he really needs help, then this is what he has to do to get your attention. He is totally dependent on you for his care. In fact, he is totally dependent on you for staying alive, and he will do whatever he needs to do to get a response, even if it is annoying.

How to Discern Between Sleeping Noises and Waking Noises at Night

There is a difference between sleeping and waking noises. In the night, many babies will whimper and fuss and then settle themselves down to sleep. So if you hear a noise in the middle of the night, it is okay to wait and see whether it is just a sleeping noise or whether he is really waking up. If the cry seems to be escalating, then go to him. Don't wait too long, because the more he gets worked up, the longer it will take to calm him down.

Of course, it is possible for your patient to abuse the bell. He might call you when he *wants* something, such as changing the music on the CD player, as opposed to *needs* something to survive, such as eating. So, if you respond to all his wants with the same speed that you respond to all his needs, you might indeed spoil him. We expect adults to have the ability to wait for a response when it is not an urgent situation.

However, there is no difference between a baby's wants and needs. And developmentally, we don't expect babies to be able to distinguish between emergencies and routine needs; to them, everything is an emergency. So when you pick up your baby because he is crying, you are responding to his emergency. It is important for you to quickly respond to your baby's crying, and it is also developmentally appropriate because he truly needs you.

Another way of looking at your role as a parent is to see that when you rapidly respond to your baby's cries, you are meeting his basic needs. You are providing him with food and water, a secure place to sleep, and a stable environment. You are creating a loving relationship and giving him a sense that he belongs in this world. This is the foundation he will need to develop self-esteem as he grows up. Providing an emotionally and physically safe, secure, and consistent environment is key. When your baby learns that the world is safe and that his needs are being met, he will have faith in the world. That trust will allow him to direct his energies toward developing appropriate skills.

Don't Forget to Schedule Your Baby's Checkups

Your baby will need several visits to the doctor in the first three months of life. The **first scheduled checkup** will occur one to two days after you leave the hospital or around day three to five of life if he wasn't born in a hospital. The goal of this appointment **is to check the baby's weight, assess how much jaundice he has, and answer any parental questions.**

All babies lose weight in the first few days of life. Typically, they lose 6 to 8 percent of their birth weight and will reach their lowest weight on day four or five of life.

Jaundice refers to a condition characterized by a yellowish skin color that is the result of too much bilirubin in baby's blood. All babies develop jaundice, but some babies turn more yellow than others. If your baby is born premature or suffers from an infection, or if there is a family history of newborn jaundice, then he may have a higher level of bilirubin. Your baby's doctor will be able to gauge his bilirubin level by looking at him in the office, but if she is at all worried, she may order a blood test to determine the exact level.

At a certain point—based on how many hours old your baby is as well as other factors—the bilirubin level can become too high and dangerous for the baby. In the vast majority of cases, the treatment for an elevated bilirubin is to keep the baby for one or two days in the hospital under a special blue light. Typically, by day four or five of life, your baby's liver will be sufficiently mature to process the excess bilirubin. At that time, the light therapy

RED FLAG!

If your baby loses more than 10 percent of his birth weight, it is an indication that you might need help with breastfeeding. This is the time to see a lactation consultant and work on ways to make nursing more efficient and productive. You may need additional office visits, often every two or three days to recheck his weight until he is growing well.

is no longer needed, and the jaundice will fade over the next one to two weeks.

The final purpose of the first office visit to the pediatrician is to answer your questions. Remember that no question is too silly to ask. If you are unsure about something related to your baby, it is better to ask than to remain confused. We recommend that you keep a running list of your questions and bring it to your appointment. A designated notebook for medical questions to ask your baby's doctor is less likely to be forgotten than a list posted on the refrigerator at home—especially if you keep the notebook in your diaper bag.

The **second scheduled checkup** occurs when baby is two to three weeks old. By this point, the jaundice will have faded, and breastfeeding should be well established. The primary purpose of this visit **is to make sure your baby is gaining weight and to answer any new parental questions.** Your doctor may also discuss the recommended vaccines that are offered at the two-month well-child checkup.

The **third scheduled checkup** will take place near your baby's two-month birthday. Again, the **goals are answering your questions; measuring your baby's height, weight, and head circumference; and making sure his growth and development are on track.** He will also receive his first

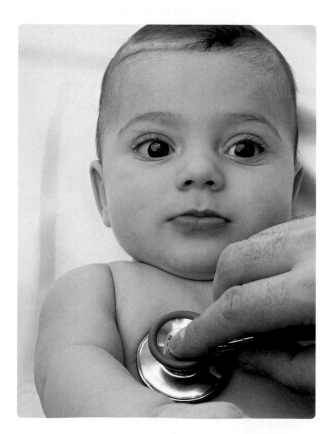

series of vaccinations if you choose to follow the recommended schedule, although he may have received a hepatitis B vaccination if he was born in the hospital.

It is beyond the scope of this book to discuss the pros and cons of vaccinations. In brief, if you have no concerns about vaccinations, we strongly recommend them and feel that the benefits of vaccinations outweigh their risks. (Be aware that most day care settings and schools require certain vaccinations before a child can be enrolled, although exemptions are available.) That said, we strongly believe in the right of parents to make their own choices about their child's medical care, including partially vaccinating or not vaccinating at all.

We encourage you to research vaccines ahead of time so you are well informed when you discuss the matter with your baby's doctor. If you want to explore these issues further, a good place to start is *The Vaccine Book* by Robert Sears, M.D., (www.askdrsears.com/thevaccinebook) or *The Vaccine Answer Book* by Jamie Loehr, M.D. The Resources and Recommended Reading section beginning on page 296 has information on how to find the most up-to-date list of recommended vaccines for children.

Your baby will have at least three medical checkups in the first three months of life: at three to five days, two to three weeks, and two months of age. In addition, if there are any concerns, he may need other visits as well to monitor his weight and development.

Supplement Breast Milk with Vitamin D

Breastfeeding is the best way to ensure that your baby will grow and develop properly. Mother's milk is made specifically to meet a baby's needs, providing the exact proportion of nutrients for his growing body and brain. Breast milk also changes as a baby grows and provides the correct balance of nutrition for later in life. In addition, breastfeeding protects your baby against infection; breast milk contains a number of antibodies and other protective mechanisms that prevent infection.

Although breast is best, breast milk does not provide an adequate supply of vitamin D for your baby's growth. Thus, breastfed babies require some sort of vitamin D supplementation. For some, the solution comes from sunshine: Exposing your baby's skin to the sun for fifteen minutes a day tends to provide sufficient vitamin D (although babies with darker complexions will need longer exposure times).

Some babies won't get enough sun exposure to make sufficient vitamin D. For instance, at certain latitudes, the sunlight won't convert the vitamin D precursor in babies' skin into usable vitamin D. (People who live on the latitude of New York City have between three and four months of the year where the angle of the sun's rays are unable to perform the conversion.) For this reason, it is recommended that all breastfed babies receive oral vitamin D supplements for the first year of life. Formula comes fortified with vitamin D, so formula-fed babies don't require any supplements.

TIP

Mind Your Time in the Sun

It should be noted that babies, like the rest of us, should avoid excessive sun exposure. Childhood sunburns are a leading cause of adult skin cancer. The three keys to responsible, moderate sun exposure are: Avoid the sun during the middle of the day, wear sun-protective hats and clothing, and use sunscreen when you are out in the sun. You may see recommendations against using sunscreen on children under six months old (based on fears that the chemicals might not be safe for infants). However, if you have no choice but to be out in the sun and you can't find shade or shield your baby's skin with clothing or another form of protection, it is okay to apply sunscreen. And despite the marketing, it is unnecessary to purchase a special "baby" sunscreen; any sunscreen with an SPF of 30 or higher will do.

Infants should ride in a rear-facing car seat until they are both 20 pounds (9 kg) in weight and one year old. The rear seat is safer than the front seat. If a child must travel in the front seat of a car, the car seat should still be rear-facing and any air bags must be turned off.

Install the Car Seat Properly to Keep Your Baby Safe

Babies should be in a rear-facing car seat until they weigh at least 20 pounds (9 kg) and are at least twelve months old. Make sure you adjust the car seat to fit your baby. All harnesses should lie flat (not twisted) and feel fairly taut. You should not be able to slide more than one finger between the harness and your baby. Ideally, the safest position for the car seat is in the middle of the backseat. Never install an infant or child car seat in the front seat of a car that has an air bag system. The air bag could seriously injury or kill your baby if deployed.

According to a government study, more than 80 percent of car seats are incorrectly installed. Make sure you review the owner's manual that accompanies new car seats and get assistance from professionals to make sure your baby's car seat is installed properly and securely. See the Resources and Recommended Reading section on page 296 for further information about car seat safety and where you can go to have your car seat's installation checked.

Keep Your Baby Healthy by Avoiding Germs and Smoke

A simple but effective way of protecting your baby from illnesses and infections is to wash your hands frequently. In addition, make it a rule that no one is allowed to touch or hold the baby without first washing his or her hands. Although using soap and water will do the trick, studies have shown that the many brands of alcohol hand sanitizer on grocery and drugstore shelves are equally effective at eliminating germs. And because the portable hand sanitizers are more convenient, people use them to clean their hands more frequently and thus spread fewer infections. We recommend that you keep a hand sanitizer in your diaper bag and several more scattered around your house.

Next, if you smoke cigarettes, the best thing you can do for your baby is to quit! Cigarette smoke in the house puts your baby at a greater risk of developing asthma and ear infections. A newborn can often provide the necessary motivation for parents to stop smoking. If you need help quitting, see your doctor or visit one of the many websites that promote smoking cessation, such as www. BecomeAnEx.org or www.smokefree.gov. If you can't quit smoking or if you have smokers visiting your home, make it a rule that all smoking occurs outside your home and car.

Pacifiers and SIDS

Recent research has shown that babies who fall asleep with pacifiers in their mouths have a lower risk of SIDS. Interestingly, the pacifier does not have to be used throughout the night, just while baby is falling asleep. So don't worry about reinserting the pacifier if it falls out during the night. Note, however, that if you are breastfeeding, we don't recommend giving your baby a pacifier until breastfeeding is well established, usually around three to four weeks of age.

A common way for newborns to fall asleep is on your chest. This type of skin-to-skin contact is a wonderful way to bond with your baby. However, remember that babies should only sleep on their tummies under supervision. At all other times, babies should sleep on their backs.

"Back to Sleep" to Prevent SIDS

Sudden Infant Death Syndrome (SIDS) is the sudden death of an infant under one year of age that cannot be explained by another medical cause. There are several major risk factors for SIDS. A baby who is exposed to secondhand smoke after birth or whose mother smoked during her pregnancy is at increased risk. The same is true if the mother uses or used illegal drugs such as cocaine or heroin. Premature and low birth weight babies have an increased risk. And a primary and preventable risk is allowing a baby to sleep on his tummy.

In the 1990s, the American Academy of Pediatrics (AAP) recommended that all babies sleep on their backs. (Side sleeping is not recommended by the AAP because babies who sleep on their sides may roll over onto their tummies.) Since then, the SIDS rate has decreased by around 50 percent. It is true that SIDS can still happen when babies sleep on their backs, but it is clear that babies are safest sleeping on their backs.

It is also recommended that babies do not have loose, soft bedding, or soft toys in their sleep areas because these items are associated with an increased risk of sudden death. It has also been shown that it is safer to have your baby in the same room with you rather than in a separate room.

Guidelines for Safe Sleeping

Sleeping in a Crib or Bassinet

- Put baby to sleep on his back.

- Use a tight-fitting sheet on a firm mattress.

- Keep your baby's sleep area free of soft bedding, toys, and pillows.

- Make sure baby's sleep clothes are appropriate for the bedroom temperature.

The slogan "back to sleep" means that babies should sleep on their backs instead of sleeping on their sides or stomachs. Sleeping on their backs, with no stuffed animals, pillows, or soft bedding nearby, significantly decreases their risk of SIDS.

- Keep blankets at baby's chest and below.

- Do not use comforters, quilts, or heavy blankets.

- Never put baby to sleep on a waterbed, sofa, pillow, or any soft surface.

Co-Sleeping

Co-sleeping is when you fall asleep next to your baby, whether you're taking a nap, sleeping through the night, or catching some extra sleep in the morning before you start the day. Most parents co-sleep in some form, whether they realize it or not. Please practice it safely.

In addition to the safety guidelines mentioned earlier, you should:

- Keep blankets at baby's chest and below.

- Do not use comforters, quilts, or heavy blankets.

- Never co-sleep with your baby on a sofa, recliner, waterbed, or any soft surface.

- Do not co-sleep with your baby if you're overtired.

- Never co-sleep if you smoke, have been drinking alcohol, or have consumed legal or illegal drugs that impair you or make you drowsy.

- Never allow anyone besides Mom and Dad to co-sleep with baby.

- Use yourself as a buffer between baby and his siblings if the siblings still co-sleep with you.

- Replace your headboard if it has cutout designs.

- Eliminate space between your headboard and mattress. If you can place two fingers between the mattress and headboard, it is unsafe for baby.

Most parents co-sleep with their baby at one time or another, whether it is all night long or just bringing the baby into bed for a few extra minutes rest in the morning. Waking up to your baby's smiling face is the best way to start each day. If you do find yourself co-sleeping, please adhere to the safety guidelines listed here.

In this case, consider placing your mattress on the floor.

- If possible, sleep on a queen- or king-size mattress if baby is sharing the bed with you. The bigger the better when it comes to mattress size and the family bed.

Nurture Yourself So You Can Better Nurture Your Baby

Nurturing your baby can be wonderful. It can be an absolute joy to calm his crying by nursing him, to tickle him and make him laugh, and to talk to him and have him coo back to you. But taking care of a baby is hard work. It is tiring to feed him eight to ten times a day, change countless diapers, and carry him around in your arms for much of the day. All parents are sleep deprived at this stage of their baby's life, and it is common to feel overwhelmed. First-time parents have the added stress of feeling like they do not know what they are doing. (They do know, instinctually, but it's sometimes difficult to believe that.) One of the hardest years for parents is the first year they spend taking care of their child.

To combat all the difficulty, stress, and sleep deprivation, it is important to follow several simple rules. First, sleep when the baby sleeps. We know this can be hard to do. Adults don't usually take naps in the middle of the day or go to bed at 7:00 pm. And when your baby falls asleep, that's when you can straighten the house, take care of email, make phone calls, or finally take that much-needed shower! Those early evening hours are perfect for some alone time, couple time, just zoning out in front of the television, or curling up with a book. But remember that sleep is a basic human need, and you will function far better when you are well rested.

Second, accept help when it is offered. People want to help and are going to offer their services. Learn to say, "Thank you very much, that would be lovely," and take them up on their offers. Better yet, have a list of minor chores that they can do for you. They might walk the dog, clean the kitchen, or go food shopping. If you have older children, encourage friends and family to pay extra attention to them and take them out of the house on a special date.

Third, scale back your expectations. You will not be able to accomplish as much during your baby's first year as you have in the past. So let the garden go, postpone renovating the house, and don't accept new projects at work. Your focus this year is on your baby; he is your main accomplishment.

Finally, find small ways to nurture yourself. The simplest method is just taking three deep breaths when you feel overwhelmed. Or you might sit in a rocking or other comfortable chair and not do anything for five minutes. Attend regular yoga classes or go to church or synagogue if that is meaningful and restorative for you. Find other parents with young babies and meet for a playgroup. These families could become some of your closest friends as your baby grows. Whatever you do, remember to take care of yourself. You will be a better parent if you do.

Baby Blues and Postpartum Depression

Some parents feel overwhelmed caring for a new baby, and some don't have the resources to care for their child. If you are having problems caring for your baby, please get help. That help might be medical assistance from your doctor, financial assistance from your local government, or child-care coverage from your religious community. If you think you might need it, seek out counseling so you can have someone to talk to and help process your feelings. With the right support, you can get through these tough times with help and enjoy a happy, warm relationship with your baby. Both you and your baby deserve that.

You may have heard the terms the *baby blues* and *postpartum depression*, and it's important to understand the difference between them. The *baby blues* are short-lived episodes of feeling overwhelmed during the first few weeks of your baby's life. Many moms experience crying jags a few days after their babies' birth when they are sleep deprived, nursing isn't going well, and they feel like they can't cope with the new responsibilities in their lives. Fortunately, the baby blues usually resolve quickly with some sleep, support from friends and family, and extra tender loving care.

Postpartum depression is a more serious condition. Affected mothers say that the world seems gray, unfriendly, and lonely, and their babies bring them no joy. This usually occurs several weeks after the baby is born but can start as late as six months after childbirth. This is a medical condition, similar to depression that occurs at other times of life, but that arises following the birth of a child. Severe postpartum depression can require medication. **Many medical organizations feel that postpartum depression is under-recognized and are recommending that mothers be screened for it at the baby's two-month well-child check.** So don't be surprised if your baby's doctor asks about your mood at your baby's checkup; he or she is just making sure that the whole family is healthy and supported.

A yoga class is a great way to relax, renew, and rejuvenate. You may even find a baby and mom/dad class where you get the refreshing benefits of yoga while bonding with your baby.

2

INFANTS

3–6 Months

Reaching and Grasping

Can you believe your baby is already three months old? The period from three to six months is a terrific time in your baby's development. She is much more alert now, studying faces, toys, and her hands. She is so much more interactive—and therefore lots more fun in the sense that she's a full participant in your play. She wants to touch things with her hands and put them right into her mouth. That's how she explores things and learns about them. She smiles, coos, giggles, and babbles. She loves to be held and snuggled. She's starting the journey toward mobility as she learns to roll from her tummy onto her back and vice versa. Hold on for an exciting ride!

As you read through this chapter, tracing the development of the average infant from three to six months of age, remember that your baby's development is still partly determined by her birth process. A premature baby may not have reached her "due date" yet and can't be expected to have the same skills as a full-term child. And children acquire skills in different ways and at different speeds. Your child may be right on track with the information we present here, or she may be ahead of or behind it. If you have particular concerns about your baby's development, discuss them with her physician. But remember that babies, like older children, grow and develop at their own pace. Relax and enjoy your baby's expanding abilities!

As your baby matures, he will become strong enough to push himself up on his arms, raise his chest off the floor, and hold his head up by himself for several seconds. The more often you do tummy time, the stronger he gets, and the more he will enjoy it.

Watch as Your Baby's Primitive Reflexes Disappear

You might recall from chapter 1 that your baby was born with many primitive reflexes. As she learns to purposefully manipulate certain parts of her body, her active control over these muscles will replace the primitive reflexes. In the case of her hands, by four months old, her palmar grasp will be replaced by a deliberate grasp, a conscious decision to open her hand, touch, and then close her hand around an object.

Other primitive reflexes will also disappear during this stage. The rooting reflex will be gone by four months, while the Moro or startle reflex might last until five months. As you might expect, the plantar grasp, where your baby's toes wrap around an object that touches the sole of her foot, takes longer to go away. Because she doesn't develop full control of her legs and feet until much later, she won't lose her plantar grasp until after six months.

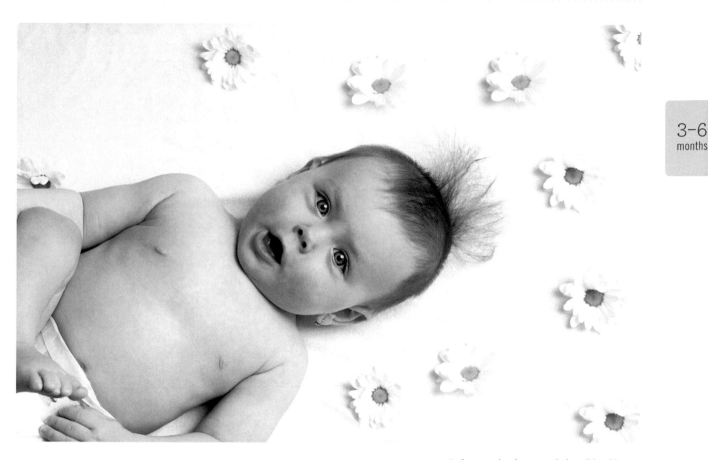

By four months of age, your baby will be able to control her eye muscles well enough to follow you around the room. Her gaze becomes less random and more purposeful, as she seeks to keep you within sight at all times.

DEVELOPING BODY

Your Baby Is Learning to Control Her Movements

At three months old, your baby is a mixture of reflexes and purposeful motions. She is learning to control certain muscles. Some motions are still random (for example, her legs), but she is able to move other muscle groups deliberately in the way that she wants (such as reaching to grasp a toy). The muscle groups that she will learn to control during these three months are her head and neck, her eyes, her hands, and her torso.

Hold Her Upright to Strengthen Her Head and Neck

By the time your baby is three months old, her head and neck have progressed from being mostly wobbly to mostly stable. Her head will still wiggle from time to time and will still flop over when she is tired or tilted too much off the vertical. The majority of time, however, she will be able to keep her head aligned in a straight line when upright.

A simple way to test neck strength is to do a "head lag" test. When newborns are lying on their backs and pulled up to sitting with their arms, their heads fall back, or "lag," as they come up to the vertical position. At two months of age, your baby will still have a slight lag, but her head will not fall back as far as a newborn's will. By four months, there should be no discernable lag at all; the head should stay perfectly in line with the torso as she is lifted into the vertical position.

Another way to see the increase in neck strength is to put your baby on her stomach. As a newborn, she was barely able to lift her head off the floor to turn it from side to side. By three months of age, however, she will be able to raise herself up on her elbows and hold her chest off the floor. She can hold her head up, sometimes all the way to ninety degrees, allowing her to look around the room.

By four months of age, her head and neck will be strong enough to stay upright with no wobbles, or at most an occasional wiggle, as she is shifted from one position to another. Her head lag should disappear, and she will be able to turn her head in all directions, looking at things all around the room. As her head and neck muscles strengthen, you will not need to protect her head as much when picking her up or carrying her.

Move Toys from Side to Side to Help Her Track with Her Eyes

As your baby grows, she is learning to track with her eyes. At first, the tracking is jerky, jumping from spot to spot. However, by four months, she will smoothly follow an object 180 degrees around the room. She will no longer have a preference for objects at a fixed distance. The muscle that controls her eyes' ability to focus has developed enough to be able to zoom in and out, and she will be better able to focus at varied distances.

Your baby's visual acuity will also improve. At birth, she was able to see slightly better than the big E on the eye chart; by around four months of age, she can see the third line of letters, or 20/60. This means that she is seeing twice as clearly as she did at birth.

Gazing into Those Baby Blues… or Browns

You may look into your baby's eyes and wonder what color they will be. Eye color is determined by melanin, the same pigment that adds color to our skin. In general, the darker your skin, the more likely you are to have darker colored eyes. There are also basic genetic rules that help determine eye color. Brown eyes are dominant to both green eyes and blue eyes, and green eyes are dominant to blue eyes. This means that if a baby has the gene for brown eyes and blue eyes, her eyes will be brown because brown is dominant. However, eye color does not follow perfect genetic lines, as evidenced by hazel eyes or by people with two different colored eyes.

One way to encourage your baby to use her arms and hands is to place soft toys within arm's reach. She'll also work harder to lift her head to look at you if you lay down on the floor with her during tummy time.

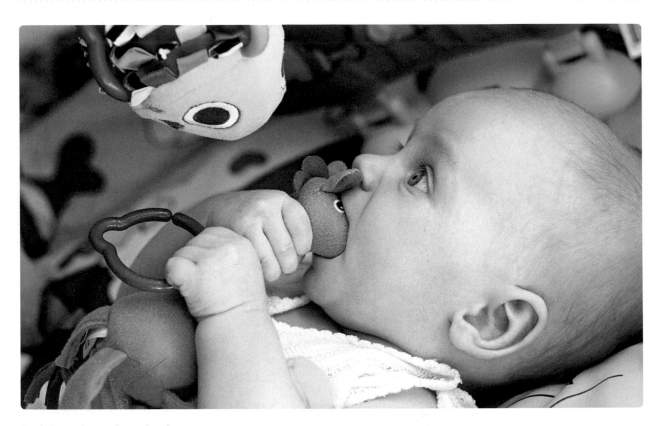

Your baby uses her mouth to explore objects. She's actually learning about her environment when she puts things into her mouth. Be sure to keep anything that could be a choking hazard well out of her reach.

Your Baby Puts Everything—and We Mean *Everything*—into Her Mouth

By two months of age, your baby started gaining control of her arms and hands. Instead of hitting herself or poking herself in the face, she began to hit nearby objects. One way to encourage your baby to use her arms and hands is to put soft toys in front of her. By three months of age, she will have the hand-eye coordination she needs to grasp a toy. And by four months, she will develop the necessary skills to bring the toy to her mouth.

Babies are born with either blue-gray eyes (in more fair-skinned populations) or brown-black eyes (in darker skinned populations). In some cases, a baby's eyes will retain their original birth color. Usually, though, over the first several months, a baby's eyes will darken as she gets older and gets more exposure to sunlight. Some eyes can change after twelve months of age, but most eye colors are set by six months.

At this age, everything goes into baby's mouth. She will develop a conscious desire to hold things, to look at them closely, and to taste them. And taste them again, and again, and again. Along with the hands, the tongue and the lips are great tools for exploring objects. The sense of smell also comes into play as she brings objects to her face and sniffs them. Babies use taste, smell, and texture to categorize objects—something we continue to do as adults. When we come across an unfamiliar substance, we touch it, smell it, and occasionally use our teeth or tongue to define the taste and texture.

Make sure your baby can't put anything into her mouth that she could choke on. An easy way to protect your baby from accidentally choking on small objects is to follow this simple rule: Any object that can slide through a cardboard toilet paper roll holder is too small for your baby to play with. Older siblings can be especially helpful when it comes to putting this rule into effect. Plan a craft day and decorate several cardboard tubes that you

Teach older children that it is not safe for babies to play with small objects. If something can slide through a cardboard toilet paper roll, it is a potential choking hazard and should be kept away from your baby.

TIP

Don't Reach for the Syrup of Ipecac

It is no longer recommended that you keep syrup of ipecac at home to help your child vomit up ingested poisons. Here's the current wisdom: If it is necessary to induce vomiting, it should only be done under the supervision of a physician in the emergency room.

leave in every room in the house. Then siblings can use the tubes to help them figure out which of their toys their baby sister or brother can play with safely.

A major hazard of mouthing everything is that your baby may unknowingly swallow dangerous substances. Keep the poison control phone number prominently posted near every phone in your house. See the Resources and Recommended Reading section on page 296 for your national or local poison control phone number.

Call poison control for anything your baby ingests that you suspect might be dangerous, whether it is Aunt Jane's medicine, cleaning fluids, petunias, or potting soil. They can tell you whether the substance poses a threat to your baby's health and whether you should go to the emergency room. Never be embarrassed about placing a call to them. They have heard everything and won't make you feel silly for calling. It's better to have your mind put at ease than to worry about the unknown.

Teething pain can turn your happy little love into a fussy, needy, terrible sleeper. If your baby is suddenly showing these signs and biting down on things a lot, you may want to offer her some sort of pain relief—either homeopathic or medicinal.

illnesses will cause her to spike a fever. So while it is very likely that your baby will sometimes be sick with a fever at the same time she is teething, the fact that the two happen at once is merely a coincidence.

Your baby's teeth will come in according to a certain order. The first four teeth are the upper and lower central incisors, followed by the four lateral incisors. Although these teeth usually arrive in pairs, some odd combinations are possible, such as

Your Baby May Start Cutting Teeth

If you are wondering when your baby's first tooth will arrive, watch for clues such as drooling and chewing on objects. However, your baby may be drooling and chewing simply because she is between four and six months old, so these aren't definitive signs of an emerging tooth. **On average, the first tooth arrives around eight months of age, but the range extends from birth (yes, some babies are born with teeth!) to fifteen months old.**

It's just a myth that teething causes fevers. It's possible that teething may occur at the same time as a fever, but it does not *cause* a fever. Your baby will develop twenty teeth by the time she is two to three years old. In that same time period, she will also have ten to fifteen illnesses, such as a cold and cough or vomiting and diarrhea. Many of these

RED FLAG!

One caution as your baby's teeth start coming in: Do not let her fall asleep with a bottle in her mouth. The concern is that the formula or pumped breast milk will pool next to her new teeth and lead to tooth decay. If your baby needs a bottle to soothe herself to sleep, fill it with plain water.

having three teeth in the middle along with one of the lateral incisors. After the first eight teeth come in, your baby will get her first molars. The four canines follow, filling in the holes between the lateral incisors and the first molars. By the time your baby is twenty-four to thirty months old, her last teeth will come in—four more molars, which are often called the two-year molars because they tend to erupt around the time children reach their second birthday. That's all twenty of her teeth!

Protect Your Baby from Falling as She Learns to Roll Over

Your baby needs to learn to coordinate the muscles in her torso with the muscles in her arms and legs in order to roll over from stomach to back or back to stomach. As she practices this new skill, she will probably get stuck halfway over with her shoulder caught underneath her. By six months, however, she should be able to roll over at least one way, and usually both ways. **When your baby can consistently roll from her stomach to her back, her risk of Sudden Infant Death Syndrome (SIDS) decreases dramatically, because she can roll herself out of trouble.**

Most babies learn how to roll over—the beginning of mobility—after four months of age, but a few are able to do so earlier. Sometimes it's a slow, deliberate learning process, and you can see her building up to it. She will twist onto her shoulder and back again for several days in a row. Then, *voilà,* she rolls over. Or she may suddenly surprise you (and herself) with the new skill. One day you may find that when you put your six-month-old baby down in the middle of the room to answer the phone, you return to find her under the couch putting dust bunnies in her mouth!

Now that your child is rolling over—or at the age when she will master it at any moment—you should never leave her unattended when she is up off the floor. You can't leave her on the bed, couch, or changing table for even a minute. You may think she can't reach the edge or you may feel secure because she hasn't learned to roll over yet, but you never know. It's best not to take any chances.

Chewing on fists and fingers can be a sign that your baby is teething but is also a common phenomenon in children 4-6 months old.

Your Baby Learns to Sit Up by Herself

By six months, your baby can probably sit up on her own for a few moments at a time. Sitting is a more complicated skill than you may realize. It requires a degree of strength in the torso muscles to hold the upper half of the body upright *plus* the appropriate amount of balance to stay steady. So not only is your baby strengthening her torso so she can sit up steadily, but she's also learning to establish the right balance to stay there. When you see her almost falling backward, think about the coordination she needs in her abdominal muscles to pull herself upright again without overcompensating and falling forward.

It takes many weeks to learn the skills necessary to sit up, and while your baby is learning, you need to protect her in case she falls over. If she falls forward or sideways, her arms or hands may break her fall. (Be ready to catch her just in case.) However, without the proper protection in place, she could really hurt herself by falling backward onto her head. In order to provide this protection, you should position her in a C-shaped pillow, place pillows behind her to cushion her fall, or sit on the floor with her between your legs so your body can buffer her.

Activities to Enhance Your Child's Physical Development

- Bond with your baby by touching her. Give her hugs and kisses and blow raspberries on her stomach. Physical contact builds a connection with your child, and it also stimulates her to move those parts of her body that you touch.

- Give your baby a massage; rub her back or her belly and stroke her arms and legs.

- Begin your day with play. Place your baby in different positions—on her back, on her tummy—and help her move her arms and legs around. Stretch out her arms and legs gently. Find a baby yoga book and try the exercises with your infant.

- Smile at your baby. Look into her eyes. Give her lots of love and attention. You can never give her too much!

- Keep your baby in your arms. Wear your baby in a sling or front pack while you do chores, go for a walk, shop, or work on the computer. Baby wearing is perfect at the grocery store because your baby stays happy longer when she's being held.

After a baby learns to roll over, you need to be especially careful that she doesn't roll off the changing table. Always stay with her when she's up off the floor. It's not safe to leave her unattended even for a moment.

3-6
months

A floor gym with hanging toys and a bright colored mat is a great place to let your baby play on her tummy. Put her down several times a day every day, even if for only a few minutes.

- Gently bounce, sway, and rock your baby to give her a sense of movement. Dance with her in your arms!

- Arrange interesting objects for your baby to reach for and play with. Choose colorful toys that are easy for your baby to hold and can be washed in the dishwasher, as well as everyday household items such as measuring cups, wooden spoons, and nonbreakable bowls.

- Shake a noisy toy to entice your baby to turn her head to look and then reach for it.

- Strap small bells to your baby's wrists and ankles and let her discover that moving her arms and legs causes the bells to jingle.

- Allow your baby to move around. Put her down on the floor so she can look around, kick her legs, and wiggle. Don't let her spend much time in a swing, car seat carrier, or bouncy seat. These limit movement, and she needs to move to develop.

- Dangle safe toys in front of or above your baby. Set up a floor gym where the toys hang over her while she is lying flat on her back. This will encourage her hand-eye coordination as she learns to focus on an object before reaching and grasping it. She may also randomly kick the toys as a prelude to more deliberate leg motions.

- As your baby is learning to roll over, place toys just beyond her reach so she'll need to roll over to get them. She will learn that rolling over will help her grasp the toy.

- Give your baby some "tummy time." Lie her down on her stomach to play and talk to her so she will push up on her arms to see you. Or place a bright or noisy toy in front of her so she'll try to get it. This helps strengthen her back and neck muscles, which she'll need when it's time to crawl.

- As your baby gets more comfortable sitting up, place her in the middle of several supportive pillows or a C-shaped cushion. This will allow her to practice making minor adjustments, using her torso muscles, without risk of falling over and hurting herself.

DEVELOPING MIND

Your Baby Is Learning Cause and Effect

The developmental changes in your baby's mind are not as dramatic or as obvious as those taking place in her body. She is continuing to refine the skills she was born with. She can localize sounds and still prefers her mother's voice to other voices.

Babies love to be carried in slings or other carriers. They are kept close to Mom or Dad—exactly where they want to be—getting to see the world in a safe embrace. Wear your baby as often as you like. You may find that your baby naps better there than she does lying down on a bed.

3–6 months

Your baby loves to reach for dangling toys—especially bright-colored ones with good contrasts. A mobile is extra fun because she sees it whenever she's in Mom or Dad's arms. Of course she has such a good grip that she's likely to pull the toys off when she gets a hold of them.

But she now recognizes other familiar voices, such as her dad, siblings, and caregivers. She still recognizes her mother's scent and prefers sweet smells and tastes to bitter ones. And she still prefers certain visual patterns, such as high-contrast pictures and pictures of faces.

Your baby is also in the process of learning the concept of cause and effect. She learns that when she moves a particular muscle, her hand opens up and she can grab a toy. She realizes that when she cries, someone comes to pick her up. And she finds that if she smiles, Mom and Dad smile back at her and pay more attention to her.

Cause and effect will drive your baby's learning for the rest of her life. It's a boon to have it start so early. As she learns to be more deliberate in her actions and explorations, she can begin to count on things happening a certain way. It also gives her a sense of security to have a measure of predictability in her play. And it makes her want to practice over and over again to see the same results, to know that things are predictable.

Your baby is learning to anticipate upcoming events. She will recognize the signs that it's time to nurse when Mom places her in a nursing position. She may start to wiggle, kick her legs, and make happy little noises to express her delight that it is time to eat. She will open her mouth in anticipation when she sees the breast or bottle.

One thing that your child does not yet have a handle on is object permanence, or the understanding that objects continue to exist even when they are no longer visible. For example, it is obvious to an older child that a rubber duck still exists even if there is towel covering it. She will just reach under the towel to collect the toy. However, to an infant, even if she sees you put the rubber duck under a towel, she will not look for it there because it is no longer visible. For babies, it is truly a matter of "out of sight, out of mind." Object permanence is something she will start to learn over the next three months.

Turn off the Television!

One thing that will not enhance your child's cognitive development is television. Medical experts and organizations strongly believe that children under the age of two should not watch any television at all, including videos made specifically for infants. There is no evidence that these "educational" videos are beneficial to your baby's development because they turn your baby into a passive, noninteractive observer.

What is proven to be highly effective at enhancing your baby's development is human interaction. Talk, sing, and read to your baby. Play with her. Engage her in conversation. These are scientifically proven to be the most beneficial approaches to stimulating your child's cognitive, language, social, emotional, and physical development.

Do your child a favor: Turn off the television and recycle any baby videos you own. Then scoop her up and spend time playing together.

Activities to Enhance Your Child's Cognitive Development

- Read colorful picture books to your baby! She'll love looking at the bright colors and bold, contrasting patterns while listening to your voice.

- Talk with your baby. Engage her in conversation from the day she is born, being sure to maintain lots of eye contact.

- Place a mobile with high-contrast patterns above the changing table or crib, or set up a floor gym that has several hanging toys that she can look at and reach for.

- Attach an unbreakable mirror to the crib or next to the changing table so your baby can see her face and movements. Place a large mirror low on the wall so she can look at herself when she is playing on the floor. Your baby won't understand that she's looking at her own reflection, but she will enjoy seeing that person moving her arms and smiling at her.

- Provide toys that make music or different sounds, especially those that make noise whenever your baby touches them. She'll learn that the cause and effect of hitting particular toys is getting to hear pleasant sounds.

- Show your baby how different objects have different sounds by comparing a bell to a rattle or a drum.

- Give your baby easy-to-clean objects with different textures that she can feel and put in her mouth.

- Play music and sing! You are not limited to kids' music simply because you have a baby. Your child will love whatever music you play for her, so choose something you like to listen to as well.

- Explore new environments with your baby so that she has new things to see and watch. Go to the park to look at trees, flowers, and birds. Go to the mall to show her colors and motion. Visit an aquarium or find a fish tank where she can see fish swimming around.

- Engage your baby's sense of smell by putting things near her to smell, such as flowers, lemons, oranges, vanilla, cinnamon, grass, dirt, and tomato plants.

Your baby will enjoy colorful and easy to grasp toys. It is very helpful for development to give her a variety of textures to hold and chew on. Over time, she will learn the difference between how different materials taste and feel.

3–6
months

DEVELOPING LANGUAGE

Your Baby Uses Crying and Body Language to Communicate

Your baby's verbal language is developing slowly at this stage. She is babbling and cooing, developing intonations and inflections, with sounds rising and falling as if they form a sentence. Mimic some of her sounds and make new ones for her to try out. This is the beginning of conversation!

Your baby is already learning a few words. By around six months of age, she will recognize her own name. Probably the best way to help your baby's language development is by talking to her. Isn't that wonderfully simple? She learns language by listening to it, learning to understand it, and eventually forming the words herself.

At this point, your baby's primary form of communication continues to be crying. However, you've probably noticed that she is learning to cry in various ways, using different tones to correspond

Your baby's body language clearly tells you how she feels—happy, upset, hungry, delighted, or in pain. You have been reading her body language naturally from the day she was born.

TIP

What's with the baby talk?

When you talk to your baby, you should use both adult conversation and baby talk. Adult conversation teaches babies about the inflections in language and about the give and take of language between two people. Baby talk is useful because it exaggerates articulation and intonation, which helps your baby separate out sounds and words.

to each of her needs. Over time you may be able to tell the difference between her cries—identifying which one signals hunger, frustration, pain, and fear. Remember to trust yourself and your instincts; you are the expert on your baby. This understanding will allow you to respond appropriately to different cries, making her feel heard and understood.

Your baby is also using body language to communicate with you. We all do. She will smile, frown, or look puzzled, scared, interested, bored, and more. She will reach out to you to be picked up, push you away when she doesn't want contact, close her lips when she doesn't want to nurse, and maybe even turn her back on you. You've probably been reading this type of language without even thinking of it as a language. But babies' bodies and faces can be just as expressive as spoken words.

Activities to Enhance Your Child's Language Development

- Talk to your baby! Let her see your face when you are talking to her. Gaze into her eyes and talk to her whenever you change her diaper or feed her, whenever you take her shopping or out for a walk in the neighborhood. Talk to her just like you would talk to a friend, telling her about your plans, showing her something in a store window, and asking her questions. She will learn about the inflections and intonations of conversation and will eventually respond to you in kind.

- Sing your favorite songs. Your baby will love whatever you choose, whether you prefer lullabies, show tunes, folk music, or rock 'n' roll. Pick one song to sing whenever you comfort your upset baby because she'll start to recognize the tune and calm down as soon as she hears it. (This is especially helpful when you're driving in the car and can't physically comfort her.)

- Read to your baby all the time. Look at picture books together, ones with bright colors and high-contrast patterns. She'll love listening to your voice and looking at the illustrations.

- Name the parts of your baby's body when you touch them, such as her nose, toes, and belly button. Make up rhymes like "toes, nose!"

Crying is another means of communication for your baby. Over time, you will learn the difference between her whimper of loneliness, her wail of frustration, and her shriek of pain or fear. Responding to all her cries, no matter what the cause, will teach her that the world is a safe place to be.

- Name objects in your baby's environment. This includes people (Mama, Daddy, Grandma), animals (dog, cow, horse, bird), objects (tree, flowers, chair), and body parts (hand, tummy, ears).

- Make up stories for your baby. They can be simple or elaborate, but as long as they are told in your voice, they will engage and entertain her.

3–6
months

DEVELOPING PERSON

Respect Your Baby's Temperament by Taking Cues from Her Mood

By the time your baby is three months old, you will see her personality begin to emerge. She may be a flexible, happy-go-lucky child or one who needs more time to warm up to a situation. Every personality type is wonderful, and the important thing is to recognize and respect your child's particular personality and innate person-ness.

If your child needs space and time and doesn't do well in confusing, chaotic situations, don't force them on her. As a slow-to-warm-up child, she won't

---

TIP   Let Others Hold Your Baby When She's Asleep

If your baby is at the stage where she cries anytime you try to hand her to someone else to hold, then keep her in your arms while she is awake. When she falls asleep, it's a good time to let Grandma, Grandpa, or a beloved friend hold her. They will get the joy of snuggling your little love in their arms and she won't be traumatized by being unwillingly passed around.

---

enjoy a family reunion with lots of noise and new faces and will cry if you allow her to be passed around from relative to relative.

So, what should you do in such a situation? Go to the reunion, but hold your baby in your arms. Do not pass her to relatives. Listen to her cries to stay with you, her home base, her safe place. Don't worry about what your relatives will think if you say, "I'm sorry, she wants to stay with me. But we'll stand real close so you can talk to her." Your baby is a person, and her comfort level comes before anyone else's desire to hold her.

Even though part of your infant's social development is preset, part of it can be learned as well. If you come from a large family and your child is going to spend time with lots of relatives on a regular basis, you can try to expose her to bigger groups of people for short periods of time to build up her tolerance level. Take her to the mall or your church or synagogue for ten to fifteen minutes, and leave before she starts to melt down. As your baby learns that group events don't last forever, she will start to adjust to longer visits.

Thumb Sucking and Pacifiers

Your baby is learning how to calm herself. Perhaps the best soothing mechanism is sucking her thumb or a pacifier. If you recall from chapter 1, sucking is a primitive reflex that fades over time. However, most babies find sucking to be incredibly comforting and continue to do it as a habit.

Which is better—sucking a thumb or a pacifier? Honestly, it really doesn't matter. A thumb never gets lost, and it is easier for your baby to find it in the middle of the night. But you may worry about how you'll get your baby to stop sucking her thumb when she's older. You may have a battle either way—thumb or pacifier—if you choose to break her of the habit before she is ready to give it up. Keep in mind that your baby won't be doing it forever, and that when she's ready, she'll give it up quite easily. So try to follow her timeline, if you can, rather than setting an arbitrary deadline for when she no longer needs that source of comfort.

Activities to Enhance Your Child's Emotional and Social Development

- Enjoy your baby. Play with her! Bask in her presence and make her feel loved and cherished. The sense that you just enjoy being with her is one of the most wonderful gifts you can give your baby.

- Love your baby. By showing her unconditional love, you are contributing to her sense of self-value, a sense that she is worthwhile.

- Hold your baby as much as you want to! Wear her in a sling or front pack. She loves being with you, held close and touched.

- Consistently respond to your baby lovingly when she cries. She needs your help to right whatever is wrong, and sometimes she just needs you.

- Give your baby kisses, hugs, snuggles. Touch her. Massage her. Do baby yoga.

- Read to your baby every day. She'll love to snuggle with you, look at the beautiful illustrations, and listen to your calming voice.

- Talk to your baby all day long. Tell her what you are doing, what you see. Point things out to her. She'll be mesmerized by whatever you tell her.

- Look right into your baby's eyes when you are feeding her, changing her diaper, and bathing her. She'll look right back. It's the perfect time to build trust and connect.

- Join a playgroup. Introduce your baby to other children and adults.

- Let others hold your baby when she's happy and willing. If she gets upset, take her back and soothe her. You are the parent and her greatest source of comfort.

- Take your baby out to see the world—on walks, errands, or coffee with a friend. Do things with your baby by your side (or in your arms).

3–6
months

POSITIVELY PARENTING

Help Your Baby Develop Good Sleep Habits

You are most likely wondering: How can I get more sleep? How can I get my baby to sleep longer at night? Every child sleeps differently, from the deep sleeper who can easily fall asleep by herself to the light sleeper who needs to be next to an adult to feel safe enough to sleep. If you are in need of more sleep (and who isn't?) maybe we can help.

First some background. Adults and babies have certain sleep patterns in common. Everyone has the same basic sleep cycle. We start out in a light sleep, move to a deeper sleep, and then return to a lighter sleep, sort of like riding a roller coaster. The lighter sleep after the deeper sleep is usually associated with rapid eye movements and is called REM sleep. Babies have shorter sleep cycles than adults do. Whereas adults have cycles that might last ninety minutes, babies have cycles that tend to last thirty to forty minutes. Older infants and toddlers will have longer cycles, maybe forty to sixty minutes, and older children slowly approach the ninety-minute cycles of adults.

We all, babies and adults, have our own individual sleep cues. We have rituals and talismans before going to bed that help prepare our bodies to fall asleep. Perhaps you read or listen to music or a noise machine to get to sleep. Or maybe you fall asleep to the television. You might need absolute silence and a pitch-black room to be able to fall asleep. These are all sleep cues.

Finally, we all wake up in the middle of the night—not just once, but several times. As adults, we simply adjust the pillows and blankets, roll over, and go back to sleep. Babies must learn to make this transition. They have to learn to turn the corner and slide down the slope back into deeper sleep.

You can use this newfound knowledge to help your baby develop good sleep habits. **First of all, create rituals and habits that set the stage for falling asleep easily.** You might nurse your baby, change her diaper, read a book, and then cuddle to sleep. Whatever pattern you choose, be consistent by using it every night.

Be Realistic about What Constitutes a Good Night's Sleep

From a medical perspective, the definition of a baby "sleeping through the night" is sleeping five hours in a row! By this definition, even a great sleeper will wake up at least once a night. More likely, your baby will wake up every three to four hours during the night. Her tummy is tiny, and breast milk is easily digested. This means that she will get hungry on a regular basis. Most babies this age wake up three times during the night to feed.

Think about the cues you are using to help your baby fall asleep. If she falls asleep at 8:00 p.m. while you walk around the house, holding her in your arms, then when she wakes at 2:00 a.m., she will probably need to be in your arms while you walk around to fall back asleep. The same is true if you nurse or rock her to sleep: She'll want to do the same when she wakes during the night at this age. If you don't mind doing these things in the middle of the night, then there is no reason to change what you are doing. But if you don't enjoy these activities at 2:00 a.m., you need to define a new sleep cue for your baby.

Realize that your baby won't always need your help to get back to sleep. It could be a relatively short period—perhaps just twelve months— or it could be as long as eighteen to twenty-four months. And the way you help her fall asleep at six months may be different than what you do when she reaches twelve or eighteen months old. What she needs in the middle of the night when she's older may simply be your presence. Perhaps a snuggle, followed by a rub on the back, and she'll drift back to sleep.

However, if you want your baby to learn to fall asleep on her own, then it's essential that you allow her to get drowsy while you cuddle together but then let her fall asleep on her own without any physical contact from you. Put her down so she can spend the last few moments of drowsiness by herself. She then may be able to fall back asleep in the middle of the night on her own without any help from you. (Except when she's hungry, of course.)

The phrase "sleeping like a baby" probably doesn't hold the same meaning for you as it once did. Most babies at this age sleep for only three to four hours at a stretch during the night, waking a few times to feed.

Not all babies will be able to do this; some need a parent next to them to get to sleep. We do not advocate letting your baby cry it out—at this or any age. So if your baby cries when you put her down or cries in the night, pick her up. Calm her, let her get drowsy again, and try putting her down once more. It may take weeks or months for her to learn to do it on her own.

Another option is to put a mattress (her crib mattress or a bigger one) on the floor in your room and lie down with her to get her to sleep. (You can move the mattress to her own room after she's a year old, but it's safest that she be in your room right now. Plus it's more convenient because she's waking at night. You won't have to go far to reach her.)

When your baby wakes in the night, you can feed her if she's hungry and snuggle back to sleep. This way she learns to fall back to sleep while lying down and without motion (such as walking or rocking), but she has the added calming benefit and security of your presence. As your baby gets older and is sleeping through to the morning without waking, your presence won't be needed during the night anymore, only at bedtime to get her to sleep.

Try to be flexible. Recognize the cues your baby gives when she is tired. She will begin to yawn, rub her eyes, and become more cuddly and quiet. When you see the cues, take advantage of the situation and help her fall asleep when she is

naturally tired. Do it right away! If you wait too long, you will miss the window of opportunity. So be ready to jump at the chance, even if you have to rearrange your schedule or cut short the night-time rituals.

Make sure your baby gets regular naps during the day. When babies miss their naps, they sleep worse at night. So, schedule your days around her naps to make it more likely that she will fall asleep easily in the evening.

Make sure her environment encourages sleep. Keep the room dark. Buy blackout shades for the summer when it stays light later to make it easier for baby to fall and stay asleep. Is there any background noise in the baby's room? Many babies sleep better with white noise than with music or complete silence.

Make sure your baby is sleeping in a room with a comfortable temperature. This is an issue both during the summer, when she might be too hot, and in the winter, when she might be too cold. When it's cold, put her in a warm sleeper rather than under blankets to avoid the risk of suffocation. If a blanket is necessary, tuck it in tight and make sure it does not go higher than the middle of her chest.

Creating a peaceful bedtime routine at a regular time each evening helps your baby learn to settle down for sleep, even at this young age. Appropriately dress your baby for sleep, making sure she is not too warm in the winter or too hot in the summer.

Remember to Schedule Your Baby's Well-Child Checkups

There are two scheduled well visits at this stage of your baby's life: the four-month and the six-month well-child checkups. The format for these visits is similar to the two-month checkup. First, your baby will be measured to make sure that she is growing well. This will include her weight, height, and head circumference, which will be plotted on standardized growth curves.

Remember that the pattern of growth is more important than the actual numbers. Your child can be just as healthy if she is the thinnest or chubbiest baby in her playgroup. However, if she is crossing growth percentiles, that might be a point of concern. For example, if she was on the 95 percent curve for weight at two months and then drops to 50 percent at four months and 10 percent at six months, she is crossing percentiles. She might not be losing weight, but she is not growing as she should. The reverse is true if she is gaining too much weight too fast. Your physician will explain her growth pattern to you and discuss any concerns that come up.

After the growth checks, your physician will discuss your baby's new skills and make sure she is developing normally. Your doctor will ask whether you have any questions, so don't forget to bring your list! And finally, your baby may get more vaccinations. If you are following the recommended schedule, the two-month vaccines are repeated at the four- and six-month checkups, with only minor exceptions. If your baby turns six months old during flu season (October to April in North America),

your physician will recommend a flu vaccine with a booster dose one month later. The current recommendation for the flu vaccine is for all children ages six months to eighteen years old. See the Resources and Recommended Reading section on page 296 to find out where you can get the most up-to-date list of recommended vaccines for children.

Avoid Starting Solids Until After Six Months of Age

Continue to breastfeed your baby during these three months. **The World Health Organization recommends exclusively breastfeeding your baby for at least the first six months of life, adding other food but continuing breastfeeding until your child is at least one year old, and breastfeeding after that for as long as it is mutually desirable for mom and baby.** There are ongoing nutritional and immune system benefits from breastfeeding for as long as you do it; don't let anyone tell you that your baby doesn't need it anymore.

It is recommended that solids should not be introduced until after six months of age. One reason is that infants who start solid food sooner than six months have a higher risk of food allergies. In addition, starting solids can interfere with breastfeeding, which is still the best source of nutrition for your baby at this age.

Even so, many parents start solids before their babies reach six months of age. Although we don't recommend it, we can give you some clues that suggest that your baby is ready to start other food besides breast milk or formula.

First, your baby should be really interested in food. You can usually distract a three- or four-month old baby away from the mashed potatoes on your plate, but she will be harder to distract as she approaches the six-month mark. Second, she should have lost the primitive tongue thrust reflex that automatically pushes food out of her mouth. Next, she should have sufficient coordination to feed herself with her hands. She needs to be able to pick up the food on her high chair tray and put it into her mouth. Finally, she should have enough torso strength to hold herself up in her high chair without slumping over. She may not be able to sit alone, but she should be able to use the high chair as a support.

Once you have decided to introduce solids, we recommend starting with the blandest of foods. Try ripe banana, applesauce, mashed potatoes, or sweet potatoes. Avoid cow's milk until after your baby's first birthday. In addition, if you have any concerns about food allergies, you may want to delay introducing all other dairy, wheat products, and peanut butter until then as well. Honey should be avoided until your baby is a year old.

Baby Health and Safety Tips

Continue giving your baby vitamin D supplements for the first year of her life. In addition, the car seat should still be facing backward, you should insist that everyone wash his or her hands before touching the baby, and you should stop smoking if you haven't quit already.

As mentioned previously, be sure to avoid excessive sun exposure. Childhood sunburns are a leading cause of adult skin cancer. The three key steps to moderate sun exposure are avoiding the sun during the middle of the day, wearing sun-protective hats and clothing, and using sunscreen when you are out in the sun. Even though you will

RED FLAG!

Baby walkers are downright dangerous. Baby walkers are like exercise saucers except they have wheels that allow your baby to move around the house. If she walks to the edge of a stairway, she can tip over and fall down an entire flight of stairs because she is strapped in. Accidents like this are the major reason Canada has banned the sale of baby walkers.

Protect your baby from the sun by keeping him in the shade as much as possible and using hats and long-sleeved clothing when you have to be out in direct sun. Other important tips are avoiding the mid-day sun and using at least SPF 30 sunscreen when you can't avoid being out in the middle of the day.

see recommendations against using sunscreen on children under six months old, if you have no choice but to be out in the sun and you can't find shade or protect your baby with clothing or a towel, it is wise to use sunscreen.

As your baby develops strong head, neck, and torso muscles, you may consider giving her new toys that allow her free use of her hands, such as jumping harnesses that hang from a door or stationary exercise saucers. These products are fine at this age, although they will not enhance your baby's development. If you use them, make sure your baby spends most of her time completely free to move around on the floor. She needs to be able to move her body to develop properly.

How to Help Your Colicky Baby

Colic, a condition that typically shows up when a baby is two months old and can last until she reaches six months, is defined as "persistent crying without any known cause after a thorough investigation." **If your baby can't stop crying and you are sure she is not wet, hungry, or in pain, it could very well be colic.** Be sure to check for unusual causes of pain or discomfort. Take off her clothes and diaper and examine her thoroughly from head to toe, looking for possible problems. Perhaps she has a bug bite or some hair wrapped around a toe that is bothering her. Changing your baby's clothes will also tell you whether the outfit she was wearing was uncomfortable.

If you have checked everything and you have decided that your baby is suffering from colic, you will have to live with her tears while trying to comfort her as best you can. Stay with her, hold her, and try to focus on helping her feel better. It can be so upsetting not to be able to calm your baby, but don't take it personally. It doesn't mean you're a bad parent. Try not to get frustrated or angry with your baby. She's not doing it on purpose; this is something that's out of her control. If you can focus on your baby's discomfort rather than on your frustration or exasperation, then you will be better able to feel compassion, and hopefully your negative feelings will melt away.

The good news is that the crying doesn't last forever. It usually starts in the late afternoon and continues for several hours into the evening. In addition, although colic can continue for weeks to months, it usually passes by the time baby is six months old.

There are things you can do that may help. Changing the baby's diet (if formula feeding) or the mother's diet (if breastfeeding) might alleviate the problem. Many mothers have reported that excluding broccoli, cauliflower, and dairy from their diets helped. Second, stay in motion. This might mean carrying your baby in a sling, or it might mean infant massage or burping your baby more frequently. Finally, seek help. It is very normal to be frustrated when you can't soothe your crying baby. Find other people to hold her for you. If there is no one around to help and you find yourself getting angry at your baby for crying, it is okay to put her down in a safe location, such as a crib, and to collect yourself in another room. Remind yourself that it's

RED FLAG!

If you are worried that your baby's persistent crying is not merely colic but the result of a more serious underlying condition, see your doctor for an evaluation. Some medical conditions such as esophageal reflux can mimic colic and are very easy to treat.

not her fault and she's not doing it to upset you. It is happening *to* her. Try to bring your focus back to your baby to ease your frustration and feel more empathy toward her.

Nurture Yourself So You Can Better Nurture Your Baby

To be the best possible parent for your baby, you need to take care of yourself. The first year of a baby's life is one of the hardest years on parents. It is full of joy and wonder, but it is also exhausting. You may be sleep deprived and feel overwhelmed, as if you are being pulled in multiple directions at once.

So remember: Sleep when your baby sleeps, accept help graciously ("Thank you, that would be lovely"), and scale back your expectations. And nurture yourself. Find those parts of life that ease your mind and make your heart sing and put them in your schedule. Whether it is coffee with a neighbor, an exercise rotuine, or a prayer group at your place of worship, make sure you take time for yourself.

It's also important to take time for yourself as a couple. Nurture your relationship with your partner or spouse. Go out and spend time together as adults *without* the baby, if you can.

This can be particularly difficult for parents who don't want to leave their baby. And that's okay. If you're not comfortable leaving the house without the baby, then don't. Spend some couple time together in the evening once the baby has gone to sleep. Watch a movie, snuggle, talk, and get romantic.

3-6
months

Regular physical activity reduces stress and also leads to more restful sleep. (You could probably use some of that these days.) Remember to take care of yourself as you take care of your baby.

Some parents can't afford to hire a babysitter. If that is the case, ask relatives to help or find other young couples with children and arrange a babysitting swap. Some parents don't want to "waste" a night out and would rather get something accomplished. If that is the case, go grocery shopping as a couple and stop for a romantic picnic on the way home.

Whatever you do, be sure to make time to check in with each other. Reconnect and make a point to talk about how much you love and appreciate your partner. Saying it out loud to each other is very important. We need to hear that we are valued, that we are good at what we do, and that someone recognizes the big and little things we do to help each other. Don't assume that your spouse knows how you feel. Tell him or her. Often.

3

6–9 Months

Rolling, Scooting, and the Beginning of Language

At six to nine months of age, your baby is more engaging, more alert, and more fun! He's like a little person! He *is* a little person. He is able to sit up on his own so he can look at you from across the table like an adult or an older child. He can sit in the seat of the grocery cart (which you may think is the most adorable thing ever when you see him sitting there for the first time, swinging his legs, and looking so big and cute). He is increasingly interactive, and he's rolling, scooting, and crawling around. He is able to explore more with better control of his hands and head and is so interested in the world. And his language takes off as his babbling turns into recognizable sounds. Who knows? His "ma ma ma" could be nonsense syllables, but it might really mean Mama!

As you read through this chapter on the general development of six- to nine-month-olds, remember that each child is unique. Your baby's development will happen at his own pace, and though you can certainly create environments and opportunities to enhance his development, you cannot actually speed it up. He'll do things when he's ready to do them. Your child may be right on target with the information we present here, or he may be ahead of or behind it. If you have concerns about your child's development, please raise them with your family physician or pediatrician. But remember that children will develop in their own time. Relax and enjoy your baby's expanding abilities!

DEVELOPING BODY

Your Baby Is Sitting Up Steadily and Ready to Explore

At six months of age, your baby is sitting up on his own for a few seconds at a time. If he reaches too far to one side or leans a bit too much off the vertical, he will tip over. Most of his falls will be soft as he lands on outstretched arms or his shoulder, but he will occasionally bump his face or, worse, the back of his head. A C-shaped pillow is useful for protecting him from hitting his head when he falls backward.

Incredibly, in just a few weeks, your baby will have much more control of his torso muscles and will have enough strength and balance to sit steadily without toppling over. He will also be able to push himself up into the sitting position. By maneuvering his arms and twisting his torso, he will move from his stomach to a solid sitting position.

This is a giant developmental leap for your baby and leads him down the road to independence. He has been limited by having to sit in a chair or someone's lap. Sitting by himself opens up more of the world to him and leads to more exploration. It frees his hands and shoulders to become more active in exploring as well. A slouching baby needs to use one arm or shoulder to keep himself upright and balanced, but now that your baby has both hands free, he is ready to test out new skills.

Sitting up by herself is a great accomplishment for your baby. She's upright like everyone else and suddenly her hands are free to explore. Think of all the new things that can go into her mouth!

Encourage Your Baby to Transfer Objects from Hand to Hand

Your baby is learning to transfer objects from one hand to the other. Think about the skills needed to accomplish this task. It requires a certain level of coordination to grasp an object with one hand, move both hands together, and then simultaneously release the object with the first hand and grasp it with the second. Amazing! It is easier to put the object down and pick it up with the other hand. If your baby wants to hold two objects at once, at first he will prefer to pick up each object separately, one in each hand.

You can encourage your baby to transfer objects by putting two desirable toys on one side of his body. He might just twist and pick up each object in separate hands, but sooner or later he will pick up the first toy, transfer it to his other hand, and then pick up the second toy.

Your baby will also learn to rake with his fingers, pulling an object toward him. He will then grasp the object in the middle of his palm and wrap his fingers around it. This is the deliberate palmar grasp, as opposed to the primitive palmar grasp he had when he was born.

If your baby wants to explore the object with his mouth, he might need to loosen his fingers to get his lips around the object. With smaller objects such as cereal circles, he risks dropping the object before it gets to his mouth. To prevent that from happening, he might grasp small cereal circles in the crease between his pinky finger and palm and then suck them out with his lips. He's starting to feed himself!

By nine months your baby will be able to pick up food and feed himself. Be sure to offer foods that dissolve easily or are soft so he won't choke. He will love to be feeding himself, no matter how long it takes for him to pick up one piece of cereal!

The *pincer grasp* is more delicate and advanced. It involves holding a small object in the tips of the fingers to eat it or look at it closely. The three-fingered pincer grasp uses the tips of the thumb, index, and middle fingers, while the two-finger pincer grasp uses only the tips of the thumb and index finger. Most children develop the three-fingered pincer grasp by nine months of age and the two-finger pincer grasp by twelve months.

6-9 months

RED FLAG!

Your baby should not be showing any type of hand preference at this age; he should be using both hands equally. Most children do not start to show hand preference, such as when feeding themselves or scribbling with only one hand, until they are about two years old. If your baby seems to be using one hand much more often than the other, please talk to your physician as soon as you can to explore the possible reasons.

With the increase in his fine motor skills, your baby is able to hold his own bottle. Make sure you still hold him when you are feeding him a bottle. Don't just prop him up somewhere on his own. Feeding is a special time to connect with your baby in your arms; he looks right into your eyes, and you look right into his. It's a trust-building and social activity. So let him hold his own bottle while he's in your arms!

He also likes to pick up things and shake them or bang them together. He'll love playing with pots and pans, banging on them with a wooden spoon or simply banging them together. (And, wow, does that make a lot of noise! He'll be thrilled; you, however, may need earplugs.) He's getting strong, too. He can bang hard, and he can bounce up and down all by himself, working out his leg muscles, when you hold him up to stand on your lap.

Your baby can get around a room by rolling over (and over and over), so don't mistakenly think she's not mobile yet if she isn't quite crawling. She can still get into plenty of trouble simply by rolling.

Your Baby's Hands Are Made for Exploring

Your baby loves to be touched and tickled. He is discovering his own body parts, especially his feet. When lying on his back, he will touch his feet and play with his toes. And, yes, the toes will go right into his mouth like everything else! Talk to your baby about what he is doing to help him learn the names of his body parts. "You've got your feet! And these are your toes. Wow, look at how you can wiggle your toes!"

Your budding chef will love cooking on the kitchen floor, though perhaps at this age he is more of a budding drummer. What could be more fun than making a terrific racket with a wooden spoon and some metal pots?

Crawling, Standing, and Climbing... Oh My! It's Time to Babyproof

This is an exciting time in your house as your baby learns to crawl and pull himself up to stand. Crawling is another very complicated set of motions. It will take your baby quite a while to coordinate his arms and legs. He has to lift one arm up and balance on his other three supports while advancing his hand and placing it safely in its new position. Then he has to repeat that motion with his other arm and then with both knees. With time, he will learn how to move one arm and one knee at the same time, speeding up his rate of travel, but that requires more balance.

Soon your baby will start pulling himself up to standing on couches or coffee tables and in cribs, where he can use the slats as support for pulling himself up. Although some children learn to pull up before nine months of age, most actually don't learn this skill until they are ten to twelve months old. Don't panic if your baby is slower moving into toddlerhood. You will still have lots of time to chase him around when he finally gets going!

Not All Babies Learn to Crawl

Ever since it was recommended that parents put their babies down to sleep on their backs, a very small minority of babies, less than 5 percent, bypass crawling and move straight to walking. Experts theorize that because some babies spend so little time on their stomachs, they never get the experience on their hands and knees that is necessary for learning to crawl. This is why regular tummy time for your baby is so important.

If your baby never crawls, that doesn't mean that he won't be mobile. Rolling around the room is a form of mobility, as is scooting around on his back or bottom. And all babies will learn to rotate while sitting, another form of mobility, which allows him to face a new direction.

Crawling and pulling up expand your baby's horizons and introduce new safety concerns. It's time to babyproof! To do this most effectively, you need to see the world from his point of view. Get down on your hands and knees and crawl around your home. (We're not kidding.) You will find the missing puzzle piece under the cabinet, and see why electric cords and outlets are so fascinating. They are exactly at eye level! Look at objects that are 1 to 2 feet (0.3 to 0.6 m) off the ground, because that will be your baby's eye level when he is standing. Check out good places to pull up to standing and see what your baby may be able to reach and pull down onto the floor. The magazines on the bedside table, the VCR and DVD players, and plants are now all fair game.

Childproofing your house does not simply mean moving tempting objects out of reach to a higher shelf or behind a gate. That isn't fair to your little explorer. If he sees these items, he will still

Turn Your Home into a "Yes" Environment

The goal in babyproofing is to change your house from a "no" to a "yes" environment. In other words, you should remove everything you do not want your baby touching, either for safety or sentimental reasons. Turn your home into a place where you never (or very rarely) have to say, "No, don't touch that." Babies touch things. That's what they do. It's how they explore and learn about their environment. If you keep things around that you do not want your baby touching, it's unfair to him and incredibly annoying to you. He's likely to get frustrated when you keep saying "No touching!" and you're going to get irritated that you have to repeat yourself over and over. So it is in everyone's best interest to take all forbidden items out of view, so you can say "Yes!" all the time.

One reason electrical cords are so irresistible to babies is that they are right at eye level, just hanging out of the wall waiting to be pulled or chewed on. If your baby is mobile it's time to babyproof!

TIP Don't Put Everything Under Lock and Key

We suggest that you leave some drawers and cabinets unlocked in the kitchen. If your baby knows he can get into the Tupperware cabinet or pull out some old pots and pans, he will not be concerned that there are cabinets and drawers he cannot get into. You can put his plates, bowls, and cups on a low shelf in the kitchen, so as he grows he can take out what he needs when he's hungry or thirsty. Be sure to have baby toys and activities on low shelves where your baby can easily reach them.

Teach your baby how to safely go down stairs as soon as you possibly can. He will love climbing up the stairs, but also needs to learn how to come back down, going backwards with feet first.

want to get to them. It's better to remove these temptations altogether, either by hiding them out of view behind cabinet doors or by storing them elsewhere in the house for several months. Alternatively, if you can't remove the dangers, such as the corners on the fireplace hearth or electric outlets, make them safer by putting cushioning on the sharp corners and plastic protectors in the sockets. It won't be forever. In just a few months your baby will have moved on and will no longer be interested in tipping over your plants and eating the dirt.

If you combine crawling and pulling up, you get climbing. (Isn't he too young to start climbing? Nope!) Your baby can learn how to go up and down stairs or climb onto a small chair at this age. **Because a baby climbing up might fall down, it is very important to teach your baby from the start how to climb down safely.**

Show your baby how to get down by helping to move his body while you describe what you're doing. Turn him around, put his feet over the edge, and help him slide down on his tummy. Once your baby knows how to get down from a couch or chair safely, he will be safer on the stairs. Even though you should have gates at the top and bottom of the stairs, you may occasionally forget to latch the gates. If your baby knows how to go down stairs safely, he will be safer if he tries to do so when you are not around.

Activities to Enhance Your Child's Physical Development

- Touch, hug, and kiss your baby to strengthen your connection with him and to stimulate the parts of his body that are touched.

- Massage your baby. Rub his arms and legs, and his back, chest, and tummy.

Make your baby's environment a fun place to explore. Provide lots of interesting objects nearby that will encourage him to roll or crawl. Balls, blocks, and spoons—things he can hold and put in his mouth—offer hours of entertainment and skills practice.

- Get on the floor with your baby and play! Talk about the toys, colors, and shapes you are playing with. Roll a ball over to him and show him how to roll it back to you.

- Lie down and let your baby crawl all over you. (He'll do this naturally, without need for encouragement, and he'll do it for years to come!) He'll also use you as a support to pull himself up to standing.

- Do baby yoga. Find a book that suggests exercises you can do with your infant.

- Look at your baby. Smile at him. You can never give too much love and attention.

- Wear your baby. Keep him with you in a sling or backpack while you do things around the house, shop, or take a walk. It's convenient to do at the grocery store—plus your baby will be happy longer if he's being held.

- Encourage your baby's sense of movement. Rock, gently bounce, and sway him. Dance with him in your arms!

- Have toys with openings that your baby can put smaller objects into—such as a shape sorter (though he'll need help with getting the right shapes into the holes). You can make your own from an empty wipes container and clean frozen juice lids. He can slip the lids into the wipes container and open it up to dump them out again. That's hours of fun and development right there!

- As your baby is learning to crawl, place toys just out of his reach so he'll need to crawl over to get them.

6-9
months

Playing outside is good for your child's physical development at any age. Let him play in the grass and feel the texture of grass and leaves. Take him for walks in the woods. Get out and explore together!

- Give your baby colorful toys that are easy for him to hold and can be washed in the dishwasher, or hand him normal household items such as wooden spoons, metal bowls, and measuring cups.

- Make your home a fun place to explore. Put lots of interesting objects in safe locations so your baby will want to roll, scoot, or crawl over to them. Put them at various heights so that he will see different objects when crawling, sitting, or pulling up to stand. Remember that you don't need fancy toys. Just make sure the objects are big enough that he can't choke on them.

- Provide some noisy objects, such as pots, pans, and wooden spoons. They are fun, and as your baby keeps banging because he loves to make noise, he's also enjoying cause and effect!

- Be sure your baby has the freedom to move around. Don't leave him confined to a swing, car seat carrier, or bouncy seat. They limit his movement too much, and he needs to move to develop.

- As your baby learns to sit up with more stability, continue to place him in the middle of supportive pillows or a C-shaped cushion. He can practice making minor adjustments to his torso muscles without hurting himself if he falls over.

DEVELOPING MIND

Your Baby's Learning Is Taking Off!

It is amazing what your baby is learning right now. He knows the differences in the tone of your voice, and your soft, soothing voice can calm him when he's crying. He knows familiar objects—such as his toys and household objects he sees or plays with—and he recognizes familiar people. His understanding of cause and effect keeps growing, and he will babble to get your loving attention.

When your baby drops a toy from his high chair, he will briefly look for it. Object permanence is starting to creep into his understanding of the world. He will even search for out-of-sight toys. And he's taking a closer look at things, turning toys upside down to see them from another angle, as he tries to understand objects better.

By nine months of age, babies are not only interested in new objects but are interested in new people as well, especially other babies. Join a playgroup to get your baby out with other kids and adults.

Expose Your Baby to a Wide Variety of Interesting Objects

The key words for these three months are curiosity and exploration. Your baby wants to know how things work. He has mastered cause and effect (I shake this toy, and it rattles) and now is learning the rules of the world. But the rules are confusing! As adults, we take so much knowledge for granted and forget that what is obvious to us is not obvious to a baby.

For example, why should water be hot in one circumstance, cold in another, and room temperature in a third? It looks the same in all three situations, but not all are safe to touch and can be harmful. And why is the carpet soft but the wooden floor hard? We know the answer, but your baby has to touch and taste and smell everything to find out for himself.

As your baby explores, he will use all his senses to learn about the properties of objects. He will hit the wooden spoon against the pot and hear a terrific bang. He will then hit the pot with a metal spoon and hear a different clang, learning that different items make different noises. He will hear the ringing noise when keys jangle and want to shake them, too. He loves making noise and discovering what sounds he can make.

Your baby will smell and taste as many objects as he can, putting everything in his mouth. He will realize that a plastic ball tastes different from a rubber ball, which tastes different from applesauce. He will use his tongue to explore, finding which things have a rough or smooth texture and which are sweet, sour, or salty. Your baby will learn about different smells and develop preferences for certain foods.

Your baby will explore with his sense of touch. He will learn that both wooden and tile floors are hard but feel different. He will find that a carpet can be rough or soft. He will rub his nose in your clothing or a pillow to see how it feels on his face.

6–9
months

RED FLAG!

In rare circumstances, you may notice that your baby does not seem to hear or see things that other children his age see and hear. He may not repeat sounds that you make or notice the bright red wagon a few feet away. In more extreme cases, he may not turn his head when a dog is barking or may not follow your face with his eyes. If you have any concerns regarding your child's hearing or vision, be sure to discuss them with your doctor, either at a regular well-child checkup or by making a special visit.

And finally, your baby will explore the world with his eyes. His vision has improved dramatically, and his sense of color has sharpened so that the world will be a visually dynamic place. He will notice different patterns and shades of colors and will no longer need bold contrast to be interested in an object.

Encourage your baby to explore and learn about the world in a safe manner. Make sure all the objects he has access to are big enough not to be choking hazards and are located in a safe and accessible place. Give him enough to play with so that he won't be tempted to explore less safe areas such as kitchen counters. Watch him play outside with a bucket of water to splash in but keep the toilet cover locked down so he won't play in there.

Activities to Enhance Your Child's Cognitive Development

- Look at picture books with your baby! Talk about the pictures and read the stories. He'll love hearing your voice and looking at the bright colors on the page.

- Engage him in conversation. Talk to him. Look at him. Smile at him. He loves listening to you.

- Put your baby on a quilt made of different fabrics or with different patterns. He will be able to see and touch the differences.

- Hang an unbreakable mirror in the crib or next to the changing table for your baby to see his face and movements. Securely attach a large mirror low on a wall for him to see himself when he is playing or crawling on the floor.

- Provide toys that make different sounds, such as musical toys, and especially those that make noise when touched.

- Let your baby discover that different objects have different sounds by giving him items like a bell, rattle, xylophone, or drum.

- Fill a box with objects made of different materials, such as metal, plastic, and wood. Let your baby dump out the box and explore the contents. He'll notice they feel different, and when he hits the objects with a wooden spoon, he'll listen to the different sounds they make.

- Play cause-and-effect games, such as filling a container with objects, water, or sand, and then dumping it out or building a tower with blocks and knocking it down. (He may never tire of that game!)

- Partially hide an object under a blanket and ask your baby where it is. At this age, children are able to mentally re-create the whole object even if they can see only part of it.

- Give your baby a pile of differently textured clothes and linens. Let him explore the difference between smooth cotton sheets and nubby cotton towels, between leather and cloth belts, between rubber sandals and canvas sneakers.

- Play music for your baby. Don't limit yourself to kids' music simply because you have a baby. Choose something you like to listen to; your child will love whatever you play for him.

- Expose your baby to new environments so he has new things to observe. Look at trees, flowers, and birds in the park. Go to a café to show him other people laughing and talking. Visit an aquarium or pet shop where he can see fish swimming around.

- Engage your baby's sense of smell by letting him sniff flowers, lemons, oranges, vanilla, cinnamon, grass, dirt, and tomato plants. Save empty spice jars (made from plastic) that still have the scent of the spices and let him play with them.

DEVELOPING LANGUAGE

Your Baby Begins to Imitate the Sounds You Make

Your baby is beginning to make recognizable sounds. His conversation will change from babbling to simple sounds such as nonsense syllables. He'll start using consonants, including *n, m, b,* and *d.* In English, the most common sounds are mama, baba, and dada. Very rarely, your baby will use these sounds consistently enough to consider them a word, but that skill usually doesn't arrive until close to a year.

Your baby is starting to comprehend more and more. He will begin to recognize his own name as well as people around the house, such as Mommy, Daddy, and the names of his siblings and any pets. This is also the time when he learns to point with his index finger. The combination of those two skills makes it the perfect time for him to learn new words. When your baby points at something, name it for him.

Your baby will also begin to imitate at this age. He will try to make the same sounds that you do. Repeating the sounds in his environment is how he learns a language. You can encourage this skill by repeating sounds back to him that are part of your native language.

At about nine months old, your baby can start to learn sign language. If you begin to use signs when you talk to her, as soon as she can coordinate her muscles she'll be doing the signs to communicate with you. Start with a few simple and useful signs like "more," "hungry," and "all done."

6-9 months

Read to your baby for at least 20 minutes every day. Talk about what you see in the illustrations and point to specific objects on the page, naming them for your child. She'll love reading with you.

Children are innately programmed to learn language. Your baby's brain is hardwired to recognize and repeat sounds that he hears in his environment. This means that he can learn any language that he is exposed to in the first few years of life. So if he hears "thank you" and "milk," he will be learning English. But he will learn French if he hears "merci" and "la lait" or Spanish with "gracias" and "la leche." And yes, if he hears all those words, he will learn all three languages.

Teaching Your Child to Sign

If you want to teach your baby sign language, there are many books and websites on the subject. Sign language can be a lifesaver if your child has any sort of verbal language delay, allowing him to communicate even if he has difficulty making himself understood with spoken words. In that kind of situation, it can substantially reduce your child's feelings of frustration while his verbal skills catch up.

When it comes to languages, children are like sponges and will learn to speak whatever they hear, as long as they hear it consistently. So if you want your baby to learn Chinese, he has to be exposed to it on a regular basis. We're not talking about one hour a week but daily exposure. You have to show him the pretty flower, point out the barking dog, and ask whether he wants more to eat—all in Chinese.

Another language that some parents introduce at this age is sign language. Most children can learn to sign before they can learn to speak. Signs give them tools to communicate, lowering their frustration over trying to communicate but not being understood by Mom or Dad. Pointing only gets you so far. Your baby understands so much and knows what he wants to tell you, but he physically can't without signs. This is true for months to come—well into his second year of life. He'll continue to sign even as he begins to speak because the signs give him a larger vocabulary while his vocal mechanisms catch up.

Because your baby's hands are quite dexterous, he can learn many, many signs starting at about nine months old. The trick is to do the signs consistently when you are talking with him. If you always touch the tips of your fingers to your lips when you ask him if he's hungry, he will learn to associate the sign for "food" with the concept of being hungry or wanting to eat. And soon he'll be able to tell you himself when he's hungry without you having to ask him!

6–9
months

Activities to Enhance Your Child's Language Development

- Have conversations with your baby! Respond to his babbling. Give him time to talk and then respond to what he said. Talk to him just like you would talk to a good friend. Show him something you're working on, ask him questions, and recount a memory. Hearing the inflections and intonations of conversation will help him learn to respond to you in kind.

- Sing a variety of songs, from childhood lullabies and kids' songs, to pop and rock music. When you consistently sing one song every time your baby needs comforting, he'll soon recognize it and calm down when he hears it. This can help in the car when you can't pick him up to comfort him; sing your song to help him relax and calm down.

- Read to your baby as often as you can. Choose books with bright colors and simple illustrations. He'll love looking at the pictures and will start interacting with the story. He may point to pictures or do hand motions that go with the story.

- Make up rhymes as you name the parts of your baby's body that you touch, such as his nose, toes, and belly button.

- Name everything in your baby's environment. People (Mama, Daddy, Grandpa), animals (cat, duck, pig), objects (cup, bowl, flowers), and body parts (fingers, mouth, ears).

- Tell make-believe stories. Simple or elaborate, they'll delight your child as long as they are told in your voice.

DEVELOPING PERSON

Lessen Your Baby's Anxiety by Keeping Him Close to You

At this age, your baby loves to watch and observe other people, especially other children. He will smile at his own reflection in the mirror, and he will really enjoy watching that person he sees looking back at him. He recognizes familiar people and will play games with them. However, if he encounters an unfamiliar face, even if it's Grandma's, he's likely to cry if she gets too close.

Your baby still loves to be held and carried much of the time. She will feel more secure and more comfortable exploring the world in your arms than when she is being held by a less familiar person. Slings, wraps, and other carriers are a great way to keep her close and happy.

Stranger anxiety, or the fear of unknown people, shows up somewhere around eight months of age. Your child is at the age where he knows some people. He sees them on a regular basis and is comfortable in their presence. That comfort does not extend to anyone he sees only occasionally.

Stranger anxiety manifests itself as crying when someone unknown to your baby approaches him. Even when your baby is safe in your arms, a stranger talking to him, moving in too close, may scare him and make him cry. This is not the time to hand him around to people at the office party or family reunion. Keep your baby in your arms and talk in a low, soothing voice, reassuring him that you're right there and he's safe. Walk him away from people if he's getting upset. This will help him calm down and feel secure again. Always stay close throughout this phase. And remember that he will outgrow it by the time he is two years old.

This is also the time that separation anxiety appears. Your baby will cry when you walk out of the room or if he notices that you are not within his sight. He suddenly recognizes when you are not there. And he prefers that you *are* there.

Separation anxiety is actually a positive sign of healthy development. It shows that your baby is emotionally attached to you. But it can be hard on both you and your baby. Anytime you leave the room, he will cry. If your baby is in day care, he's likely to cry whenever you drop him off.

While separation anxiety is at its peak, your baby has a very real fear of abandonment. He does not *know* that you are coming back—even if you just walked into the other room. To him you are gone, and you may be gone forever. You are his lifeline, his source of food, comfort, shelter, and safety. Simply put, without you, he will die. So when you are away from him, he is terrified. **The best way to manage the situation is to minimize the time you spend away from your baby as much as you can. By the time your baby is two years old, this phase will pass, and he will understand that you always come back.** In the meantime, anytime you have to leave him, remind him in a calm, warm voice: "I'll be back later. I always come back. Mommy and Daddy always come back."

Picking Up Clues to Your Child's Personality

Your baby's developing motor skills will shed some light on his developing personality. How does he approach a new task? When he wants a toy that is just out of reach, how does he solve the problem? He might be an experimenter, trying several different options, such as rolling over and scooting or sitting up and leaning forward. He might be an observer, preferring to think carefully before proceeding.

How does your child learn to climb? Experimenters rush in and push and pull with their arms and legs. They often fall, but they keep on trying until they succeed. Observers are more methodical. They might break climbing up onto a chair into several steps. First they pull up and stand, then they reach out to grab with their arms, then they lift a knee up, and so on. They fall less often because they reach a position of safety before moving forward.

6-9
months

Maybe your child has a different way of doing things. Your child is unique, and you can learn so much about him simply by watching him. He will have a preferred style of interacting with the world, and the more you understand his preferences, the better you can create a supportive and safe environment for him.

Let's say you have a child who gets easily frustrated. You might intervene earlier if he can't reach a toy rather than let him keep trying until he melts down. Or you might deliberately set up tasks in smaller steps so that he has smaller, more frequent successes. If you have a child who is more of a deep thinker, you might allow him more time to figure out how to reach the toy on his own.

Some children experience their emotions as big feelings. They are full of joy when the world goes their way and dissolve into tears when something goes wrong. They need you as a stabilizing force in their lives, ready to laugh with them in joy, and comfort them when they cry. Other children are more mellow, more able to modulate their feelings.

How does your child interact with other people? Some children are very social. They thrive on interaction with other people, eagerly smiling and waving at strangers. They like to play peek-a-boo and pat-a-cake, and they get bored when they're alone. They need as much interpersonal time as you can provide. Other children are introverts, requiring quiet time with just you to recharge their batteries. Learning about your child and his way of interacting with people will help you help him succeed in the world.

Activities to Enhance Your Child's Emotional and Social Development

- Have fun with your baby. Play with him! Thoroughly enjoy his presence and make him feel like the most loved person in the world.

- Loving your baby unconditionally is one of the greatest gifts you can give him. If he feels loved just for being who he is, he will develop a sense that he matters, that he is valued.

- Wear your baby in a sling or backpack. Hold him as much as you want to! He loves being touched and held close to your body.

- Always respond to your baby with love when he cries. He needs your help to fix whatever is wrong. And sometimes, he just needs you!

- Touch your baby. Kiss him, hug him, snuggle him. Massage his body. Do baby yoga together.

- Read bright colorful picture books to your baby. He'll love snuggling with you and listening to your loving voice.

- Talk to your baby as you go about your day. Tell him what you are doing, what you see. Point things out to him.

- Make eye contact with your baby. Look right into his eyes when you are feeding him, changing his diaper, and bathing him. He'll look right back. It's a great time to bond with your child.

- Observe your baby, try to understand his social preferences, and then play to his strengths. Give the social baby as much time in groups as possible, arranging for playdates or time spent with an energetic babysitter. Give the quieter, more introverted baby downtime before and after exposing him to crowds.

- Respect your baby's feelings. Be with him when he is happy and when he is crying. Try to be present and fully engaged in the moment with your child, instead of thinking about your next project or what to cook for dinner.

- Be silly with your baby. Make funny faces, wear pants on your head, and pretend to eat his toes. It's fun for you, and it makes your baby laugh. Babies this age have the most delicious laughs. A baby's laugh is the happiest sound on Earth.

- Join a playgroup to expose your baby to other people on a regular basis.

- Let people hold your baby only when he's happy and willing. If he gets upset, take him back and comfort him. You are his greatest source of comfort.

- Stay close to your baby when a new person is around. Keep him in your arms or a sling. (This extends to grandparents and other visiting relatives he hasn't seen for a while.) Ask that the person approach your baby slowly and not get too close until he feels comfortable with them.

- Explore the world with your baby; go on walks, visit a museum, or meet friends at the zoo.

6–9
months

There is no sweeter sound that that of your baby laughing. She loves to laugh and feels so connected with you when you're being silly and playful with her.

POSITIVELY PARENTING

Expose Your Baby to a Wide Variety of Foods

Your baby is now at the appropriate age for starting solid foods. As mentioned in chapter 2, there are several clues that your baby is ready for solids. He should be very interested in the food you are eating, he should have lost his primitive tongue thrust reflex, and he should have excellent hand-to-mouth coordination along with fairly good sitting skills. Remember that there is no magic to starting solids at six months. If your baby is not interested, try again in a few weeks.

There is a lot of information and advice about which foods to start with and what order to follow. We have even heard about introducing one new food a week! In our opinion, most of these rules are unnecessary. **You obviously want to avoid any food that your baby might choke on. And you want to delay foods that are potential allergens until after he is nine to twelve months old.** That is why many parents hold off starting dairy, wheat, and certain kinds of nuts and fish. But that still leaves you with a wide variety of foods to choose from.

It is best to start with single-ingredient foods. Then, if your baby has a reaction, you have a better sense of which food might have caused it. Note, though, that that doesn't mean each new food must be introduced in isolation. If your baby is already eating avocados, peas, and sweet potatoes, and you want to start him on cooked carrots, add them into the mix. Note that if your baby has a reaction, you shouldn't automatically blame the food,

because babies get rashes and upset stomachs from lots of different exposures. Instead, don't feed your baby the food for a few weeks. Try it again, and if your baby has the same reaction, take it off your list and mention it to the doctor at your baby's next visit.

We also encourage you to move beyond the bland staples and try a variety of flavors and spices. The goal of starting solids is to broaden your baby's palate. Children in other cultures eat curry and hot peppers, so there's no reason your baby can't do the same. Remember to be patient! It can take a number of exposures—fifteen or more—before a child will accept a new food.

> **RED FLAG !**
> If your baby does not want to eat solids or has difficulty eating them by the time he is nine months old, mention it to your physician at the nine-month well-child checkup. It may be a normal variation or there could be oral motor delays, which will require additional evaluation.

As your baby becomes more skilled at feeding herself, remember to give her a wide variety of colorful, healthy foods to expand her palate. Teach her body to love nutritious whole foods instead of prepackaged processed foods. That will set her up for a lifetime of healthy eating.

Respect Your Child's Stranger and Separation Anxiety

Stranger anxiety is the discomfort your baby feels when faced with a person who is not a familiar presence. It can start as early as six months but usually appears when a baby is eight to nine months old. It is a normal developmental stage and occurs because he has developed the ability to discern between the familiar and the unfamiliar.

Only *very* familiar people—people your baby sees on a daily basis—should be allowed to hold him or be close to him if you're not there. That means grandparents and other loved family members and friends can cause the anxiety. In some extreme cases, even a father can cause stranger anxiety if he is not around the baby every day.

Your baby's grip on your legs should remind you of how important you are to him. When unfamiliar people are around he's likely to want to be up in your arms to feel safe. Respect his request. He has very real fears and needs your safe arms to feel comfortable.

TIP · Introduce Your Baby to His Caregivers Early

If you plan to leave your baby in someone else's care (which would invoke both stranger anxiety and separation anxiety), introduce that person early on in your baby's life so he learns to feel safe with that person. This might be a relative, a babysitter, or a day care provider. As long as your baby is given time to feel safe with that person, his anxieties will be minimized.

If possible, don't force your baby into uncomfortable situations. If he won't go to Grandpa willingly, don't force the issue today. Instead, keep him in your arms, close to you, and remind Grandpa that he will have many, many more opportunities to play with his grandson.

Well-Child Checkups and Vaccines

Your baby's next well-child checkup is at nine months of age. Your baby's physician will review your baby's growth curves and development and answer any questions you may have. One benefit of this visit is that there are no scheduled vaccines. However, if this checkup falls during flu season, your physician may recommend the flu vaccine for your baby followed by a booster one month later (unless he already received it at his six-month checkup). Check out the Resources and Recommended Reading section on page 296 for information on finding the current list of recommended vaccines for children.

Your baby's physician will normally recommend testing your baby's lead level at one and possibly two years of age. But if there is any risk that your baby is being exposed to lead dust, you may want to ask that it be checked at the six- or nine-month well-child checkup. There is a higher risk of lead exposure if your baby lives in or regularly visits a house built before 1978 (especially if it is being remodeled); has siblings, playmates, or neighbors who have high lead levels; is cared for by an adult whose job or hobby exposes him or her to lead (construction, pottery, welding, or collecting lead figurines); or lives in a location with a high lead exposure (near highways or a battery recycling plant, or certain overseas locations). As always, if you have any concerns, discuss them with your baby's physician.

Health and Safety Tips

Some children are not exposed to **fluoride in their drinking water,** either because they are not on municipal water or, more rarely, because their municipality doesn't put fluoride in the water. **Several well-respected national organizations recommend fluoride supplementation for children ages six months to sixteen years old as a method of preventing dental cavities.** The data on fluoride supplementation appears to be sound, and we think fluoride supplements are a good idea and worth

considering. If your child's teeth are just starting to come in, see the section on teething and the order in which teeth arrive on page 50 in chapter 2.

We want to emphasize the importance of having protection on stairs and window guards. Stairs should have some sort of protection at both the top and the bottom. You don't want your baby crawling over the edge of the top stair and falling down an entire flight of stairs. And because your little explorer is getting better and better at climbing, he will climb the stairs from the bottom at his first opportunity. What fun to climb! And so easy to get halfway up and then all the way to the top. The 12-inch (30.5 cm) height of the steps is perfect for infants learning to climb. Climbing while being supervised by an adult is a wonderful activity—something your baby will want to do over and over again—but having secure gates at the bottom and top of the stairs is your assurance that he doesn't do it alone and end up falling.

As for window guards, screen windows are not designed to hold a 15-pound (6.8 kg) baby inside. So if your baby somehow manages to reach the window and leans against the screen, he could easily fall out. Make sure your windows are safe, either by keeping them closed or by installing window guards.

As mentioned previously, **limit your baby's sun exposure** because sunburns received during childhood are a leading cause of adult skin cancer. The three key steps to moderate sun exposure are avoiding the sun during the middle of the day, wearing sun-protective hats and clothing, and using sunscreen when you must be out in the sun.

6–9
months

4

INFANTS

9–12 Months

First Steps, First Words

Life is a whirlwind of new skills for your baby from nine to twelve months of age, and **you may see two of her very big "firsts" in these three months.** She is so mobile! She crawls with lightning speed and may even start walking on her own during this time. **Her first step!** She will turn sounds into words and may begin to talk. **Her first word!** And she will become more independent, readily expressing her likes and dislikes. By her first birthday, she will have changed from a helpless newborn to a walking, talking person.

As you read through this chapter on the general development of nine- to twelve-month-olds, remember that every child is unique. Her development happens at her own pace, and though you can certainly create environments and opportunities to enhance her development, you cannot speed it up. Your baby will do things when she's ready to do them. Your child may be right on target with the information we present here, or she may be ahead of or behind it. If you have concerns about your child's development, please speak with your family physician or pediatrician about them. But remember that children will develop in their own time. Relax and enjoy your child's journey through childhood!

DEVELOPING BODY

Help Her Walk Using Your Fingers as Support

By nine months, your baby should be sitting solidly and crawling all over the place. (Remember when you put her down, and she'd stay in one place? And you thought life with a baby was busy before!) Now your baby is interested in imitating others and wants to be upright. She is pulling herself up on furniture or on your legs and standing with support. Once she's comfortable standing with support, she'll try standing alone. She may even do it without realizing she's doing it. All the standing, supported and alone, will put her in the right position for dancing. And dance she will!

Once your baby has mastered the skill of standing, she'll follow that with cruising, which is moving along an object while in a standing position. She will hold on to the railing of her crib or the side of the couch for balance and move her feet sideways. She's walking along the furniture! **She can now reach objects that were previously beyond her reach, so it's time for additional babyproofing.** Your baby might pull the runner off the coffee table, and with it, the magazines, plants, and coffee will tumble to the floor.

A crib's walls are the right height for learning how to pull up to a standing position. When he has achieved that skill, your baby will happily start to cruise along the railings.

Once your baby has cruising down, she will want to walk while holding your hands. It is great fun for both of you, and she'll want to do it *all the time* because she likes to practice something obsessively until she has it mastered. But it can take a toll on your back if you are constantly bending over to hold her hands. Do your best to stand as straight as you can to protect your back from injury. You can expect your child to continue walking with support for weeks until she's ready to walk solo.

As soon as your baby can, she will walk on her own. It will probably start as a step between the couch and the coffee table. Next thing you know, she will stand up on her own and walk right into your arms. She will be so thrilled with herself!

Your Baby Is Always on the Go!

Your baby has so much energy and is always on the move. She can crawl forward and backward, climb out of her crib, and climb the stairs on her hands and knees. Even though she may start to walk, if she wants to get someplace fast, she'll get down and crawl. It will be her quickest mode of travel until she becomes sure and steady on her feet.

As your baby learns to stand, she's going to enjoy getting dressed and undressed from a standing position. She's already holding out her arms and legs to make it easier for you to get her clothes on and off. She's a wiz at pulling off her socks, hat, and shoes (much to your dismay at times).

First Steps

Although some babies walk on their own before their first birthdays, the average child doesn't walk independently until after twelve months, so don't worry if your baby is not walking by her first birthday.

Older siblings love to help a baby who is learning to walk. And it saves some strain on your back to let someone else practice with him for a while.

9–12
months

Babies will pull up to standing absolutely anywhere they can. They are committed to practicing each new skill until is it mastered.

Your baby will clap her hands when she's happy or celebrating an accomplishment, and she will happily wave good-bye to almost anyone. She likes to put objects into containers, and she will continue to put everything into her mouth. (That tendency will go away. Really. Give it a few more months.) She will point to things that she wants and will learn to do signs if you are teaching her sign language.

Although your baby is headed straight toward toddlerhood, she is still a baby in so many ways. She still loves (and needs) to be hugged, cuddled, and held in your arms. Her favorite place is wherever you are. She's firmly attached (as are you!). She needs comfort when she's sad, hurt, angry, or frustrated. She depends on you to be there whenever she needs you to be. Continue to respond to her when she cries to build her confidence in you and herself.

Your baby loves to stack blocks, although knocking them down is probably her preferred activity! Who knew that could be so much fun? She will turn the pages of a book, and when you're reading to her, she will often take the book right out of your hands. That's okay; you can either continue reading as she looks at it or chews on it (you've read it enough times that you can recite the text from memory, right?), or you can pick up another and read that. (Until she takes that one out of your hands, too.)

Encourage Fine Motor Skills Using a Variety of Food

Your baby's hand dexterity increases and will continue to improve, giving her greater fine motor control. She can open cabinets and toy chests now and remove the tops from plastic containers. She has a well-developed two-finger pincer grasp, using her thumb and index finger to pick up small items. She is able to pick up small food particles off her high chair (as well as dirt and pebbles off the ground). Even though your baby has the dexterity to hold a spoon, it doesn't mean she will successfully get the food into her mouth. Eating is still a messy affair, but she's working toward total mastery (and neatness) over the next few years.

At this age, food is food, but it's also another toy. Your baby should know by now that certain foods taste good and make her hunger go away. However, she will also enjoy the tactile experience of food such as its texture and how it feels running through her fingers. Mashed potatoes feel different than applesauce or crackers—both in her mouth and in her hands. One of the best ways to encourage your baby's fine motor skills (and a broad diet) is to introduce her to a variety of foods.

Now's the perfect time for those classic baby-covered-from-head-to-toe-with-food pictures. Think of it—unforgettable holiday cards and baby pictures to show at her wedding!

9–12
months

There is no such thing as a neat eater at this age. Babies who are learning to feed themselves are messy. Try not to stress over the mess, and give your baby the practice she needs to master this important skill.

When your baby is happy she will clap and laugh. She is so full of joy at this age and so much fun. Enjoy her every moment!

Learning to use a sippy cup can be a little tricky. If your baby isn't interested, then put away the cup for a while and get it out again in a month or so to try again.

A Menu of Options

You can't force your baby to eat, nor should you. What you can do is offer her a wide variety of healthy foods, from several food groups, and let her decide how much she wants to eat. Different babies have widely different appetites at this age, ranging from mostly breastfeeding with only a few crackers or smashed bananas to eating more than their older siblings! Your baby will not starve herself; she'll eat as much as she needs. And she will let her preferences be known. If the blended liver and onions ends up on the floor, take that as a clue that it's not her favorite food.

At this age your baby has the ability to start drinking from a cup. Most babies are interested in cups because they see you drinking from them, and they want to be like you. Sippy cups are most convenient because once your baby has learned how to suck the liquid out of the cup, she won't require constant supervision when the cup is in her hands. With a regular cup, you have to be next to her all the time because she'll develop a flair for spilling the cup's contents—accidentally at first and then purposefully as she discovers the joy of gravity. (And there's that pesky cause-and-effect thing she's learned that comes into play when she tips over her cup.)

Most sippy cups have an insert that prevents them from leaking. However, learning to suck liquid past the insert is a skill that takes time to master. If your baby can't seem to get anything out of the cup, try using a sippy cup without the insert. That way, she will learn that by turning the cup upside down, she gets something to drink. Once she has mastered that skill and learned to suck a little liquid from the cup, you can replace the insert to save yourself from having to clean up the inevitable drips and spills.

Mealtimes are inevitably followed by bath time, for once her hands are covered with food you know she's going to rub her hands on her face and in her hair. Instead of stressing over the mess, laugh with your baby.

Activities to Enhance Your Child's Physical Development

• Touch your baby. Give her hugs and kisses and tickle her tummy. It strengthens the connection between the two of you.

• Give your baby a massage by gently rubbing her back, belly, arms, and legs.

• Play with your baby down on the floor. Talk about the toys, colors, and shapes you are playing with. Roll a ball to her and encourage her to roll it back to you.

• Lie on the floor and watch as your baby crawls over you. (She'll do this without any encourage-ment, and she'll do it for many years!). Using you as a support, she'll pull herself up to standing.

• Do yoga with your baby. There are several baby yoga books available that have suggested exer-cises you can do with your infant.

• Give your baby lots of love and attention; make eye contact and smile at her. You can never give her too much!.

• Make time to hold your baby. Wear her in a sling, carrier, or backpack while you read, do house-work, or talk on the phone.

• Find support toys that help your baby learn to balance. Some ride-on toys convert to a walking support, or you might find a child-size shopping cart that she can lean on but also move around the room. **Do not use baby walkers. They have been banned in Canada for safety reasons. If a child walks to the edge of the stairs in a walker, she can fall down a flight of stairs. And walkers do not actually help your child learn to walk.**

• Make an obstacle course for your baby to move through. She will love climbing through a tunnel made out of boxes and under the chair or behind the couch.

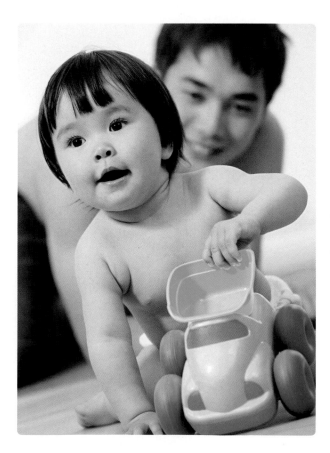

Get down on the floor and play with your baby. She'll love the time you spend with her and will feel more and more connected to you. Children learn and build relationships through play.

Some of the best-loved toys are the boxes toys (or other items) come in. Babies love to crawl into and out of boxes, peeking out of any holes you may have cut in the sides.

- Have toys with openings that your baby can put smaller items into, such as a shape sorter. (At this age, she will need your help getting the right shapes into the holes.) Your can also make your own from an empty wipes container and clean frozen juice lids. She can slip the lids into the wipes container and open it up to dump them out. That'll give her hours of fun and development!

- Have colorful toys that are easy for your baby to hold and can be washed in the dishwasher, or give her regular household items such as plastic containers, wooden bowls, and measuring spoons.

9–12 months

- Dance with your baby! Put on your favorite music and have fun dancing together.

- Get a muffin tin and some golf balls or tennis balls and let her play with putting the balls in and out of the indentations. If the weather is warm, you can let her play outside and pour water in and out of the muffin cups.

- Play with rolling toys such as balls and cars. Your baby will have the stability to sit and push these back and forth, either by herself or with you.

- Play peek-a-boo with your baby, using your hands, towels, or blankets.

- Play pat-a-cake with your baby, alternately clapping your hands and then patting her hands.

- Create games of searching for hidden objects. Put toys under small blankets or scarves and ask your baby where they are. She'll love finding them.

Who says you need to buy the latest and greatest toys? For a happy baby, just open the kitchen cupboard where the pots and pans are stored, and place a wooden spoon in her hand. Then insert your earplugs!

You are your baby's favorite toy and playmate. Make time every day to play, laugh, and connect with him. His greatest desire is to be with you.

- Make your living space a fun place to explore. Create adventure! Put interesting objects in various safe places so your baby will want to crawl over to them. Place them at different heights as well so that she will see objects when crawling, sitting, or pulling up to stand. Keep in mind that you don't need expensive toys. Just make sure the objects are big enough not to be a choking hazard.

- Give your baby items to make noise with such as pots, pans, and wooden spoons. They're fun, and banging them to make noise is an easy lesson about cause and effect.

- Your baby should have lots of freedom to move around because she needs to move to develop.

- Offer your baby a variety of foods that she can use to practice picking up and feeding herself. This helps her hand dexterity and hand-eye coordination.

DEVELOPING MIND

Your Baby Is Learning to Problem Solve

Your baby is so curious, learning more and more about her world. She is also learning to solve problems. **Curiosity and problem solving go hand in hand.** Your baby will see an object that she wants to touch, but it is just out of reach. What should she do? Well, she might try yanking on the string of the pull toy to drag it closer to her. Or she might find a box to stand on so she can reach the plant on the table. Or she might grab your hand and point, asking you to bring her the blocks from the shelf. She likes to solve simple problems, such as finding a hidden toy. She loves to look at picture books and will thoroughly enjoy the time you spend reading to her.

Your baby is becoming a more skilled imitator. She might pretend to talk on the phone, just like you, or she'll try to comb her hair. She likes to show that she knows how to use the things she sees you using, such as a spoon, cup, or ball. She will pay attention to conversations because she understands more and more words.

Your baby knows the parts of her body, if you've been teaching them to her. You can ask her where her mouth is and she'll point to it. It's a great game to play during diaper changes to keep her entertained and distracted from the fact that she doesn't want to lie there to have her diaper changed anymore.

Your baby is starting to assert her likes and dislikes. She'll say "no" verbally, or by shaking her head from side to side, or by pushing away what she doesn't want.

She might become attached to a lovey around this age. A lovey is a beloved stuffed animal, toy, or blanket that becomes her most treasured possession. It's something that she will want when she falls asleep or when she's upset or hurt. It's not a substitute for Mom or Dad, but having it is instantly comforting.

Another major concept your baby is learning is object permanence. Separation anxiety is related to object permanence. Your baby knows you exist even when she can't see you, but she still gets anxious when you are not visible. Playing games such as simple hide-and-seek and peek-a-boo is an excellent way of reinforcing the idea that Mommy and Daddy always come back.

One of your baby's goals at this stage in life is to explore interesting experiences and to make them continue. Let's say that your baby hits a toy, and it lights up and plays a short song. If she thinks the lights and song are fun, she will bat at it again. And again. And again. Much to your annoyance. But for her, it is a novelty; she has never seen this before, and it will take longer for her to get bored with it.

9–12
months

In addition, your baby is experimenting. She is testing to see whether a soft touch will turn on the toy or whether it requires a firm thwack. And does it sound different if the toy is upside down or right side up? This type of exploration will be repeated with each new experience. You will see her experimenting with water in the bath or using her mouth and hands to explore the sticks and grass and dirt in the park.

Your baby is learning so much everyday that he is exhausted by the day's end. Establish a regular bedtime based on when he is naturally tired every evening to help his body recharge and be ready for all he will learn and do tomorrow.

Activities to Enhance Your Child's Cognitive Development

- Read to your baby for at least twenty minutes every day. Show her picture books with bright colors and simple illustrations. Ask her questions when you look at books together: "Where is the horse?"

- Talk to your baby. Look at her, smile at her, and engage her in conversation. Pause to give her time to speak, and then respond to her. When you know what she said, repeat the words clearly so she can hear their proper pronunciation.

- Ask your baby questions that she can answer by pointing, such as, "Where is your nose? Where is Daddy?"

- Introduce simple puzzles that have small handles on each puzzle piece. Although your baby may not be able to put the pieces back into the board right away, she will enjoy the colors and manipulating the pieces. She will eventually learn how they fit together.

- Have nesting toys such as cups or boxes that fit into each other. Show your baby how to stack them and nest them.

- Find a toy with lots of moveable parts such as buttons, slides, and doors. Your baby will learn the concepts of up and down, open and shut, and in and out as she plays with the various parts.

- Place an unbreakable mirror next to the changing table so your baby can see her face and movements. Hang a large mirror low on the wall for her to see herself when she is crawling around on the floor.

- Hand your baby different objects that have different sounds, like a bell, harmonica, xylophone, or drum.

- Fill a box with various items made from metal, plastic, and wood. Let your baby have fun dumping out the box and hitting the containers with a wooden spoon, listening to the different sounds they make.

- Play cause-and-effect games, such as filling containers with blocks, water, or sand, and then dumping them out, or building a tower with blocks and knocking it down. (These seem to have limitless entertainment value!)

- Play find the toy. Let your baby watch you put a large toy beneath a blanket. When you ask her to find it, she will notice that the blanket isn't flat and remember that you put the toy under the blanket. She will pull the blanket off to find the toy. Next, you can hide the toy in front of her, but cover it up with one of two blankets that are next to each other. Finally, use the two blankets but hide the toy without her watching you and see if she can figure out where it is hidden.

- Give your baby a pile of clothes and linens made from various materials. Let her explore the difference between smooth cotton sheets and textured cotton towels, between leather and cloth belts, and between rubber sandals and canvas sneakers.

- Play music. You needn't listen only to kids' music simply because you have a baby. Your child will love whatever music you play for her, so choose something you enjoy and want to share with her.

- Check out new environments with your baby so that she has new things to see and watch. Go hiking so you can point to trees, plants, and birds. Visit the mall to show her lots of people. Find a pond or lake where she can see ducks, geese, and turtles.

- Engage your baby's sense of smell with various scents, such as flowers, lemons, oranges, vanilla, cinnamon, grass, dirt, and tomato plants.

- Save empty, plastic spice jars that still carry the scent of the spices and let your baby play with them.

9–12
months

DEVELOPING LANGUAGE

Listen to Your Baby to Decrease Her Frustration

Your baby is going to say her first word! What will it be? You never know. That's the thing about words at this age; it's a whole other language that you will learn. A word is loosely defined as a consistent sound used for a consistent noun or verb. So if your baby says "buh" every time she points to a ball or a bird, then "buh" is a word. It's also quite likely that your baby has been saying "buh" for *bird* for a while before you make the connection and recognize it as a word.

TIP   Listen Up

Try to slow yourself down so that you are really listening to your baby. Repeat what she says back to her as a way of confirming that you understand her words. If you cannot understand what she is saying, ask her to point to what she wants or to take you to the room where it is located. If she knows that you are listening to her, she will feel heard and understood.

Most children say either "Mama" or "Dada" plus one other word by the time they're twelve months old. However, some children talk as early as nine months, and others are delayed until after fifteen months.

Most of your baby's first sounds will sound like nonsense. The "ooos" and "eees" that you hear are her attempts to imitate the words she hears. It takes a great deal of skill to control the muscles in her lips and tongue so that they make specific sounds. We tend to overlook the rather exquisite fine motor control that's required by the oral muscles to produce speech.

Although your child isn't talking much yet, her comprehension is better than you realize. Her understanding of your words far outstrips her ability to communicate verbally. She knows dozens of nouns and verbs and may turn to listen when she hears familiar words in conversation. She will listen attentively to conversations you have with her and others. She loves to have you talk to her. She can even answer questions by pointing. ("Where is Mommy?")

Because your baby understands so much but cannot express herself clearly, she can get easily frustrated. She has so much to say but can't get the words out. This is the perfect time to teach her some simple sign language. If she can tell you what she wants or needs and be understood, she will not get frustrated. For more on teaching your baby sign language, see the section on page 83 in chapter 3.

RED FLAG!
If your baby is not making a number of sounds or nonsense syllables at this age, discuss it with her physician at her next well-child visit.

Activities to Enhance Your Child's Language Development

- Respond to your baby's nonsense syllables. Participate in conversations with her, allowing her time to talk before you respond to what she said. Talk to her just like you would talk to a dear friend. Tell her about your day, show her photographs in a magazine, and ask her questions.

- Sing your favorite songs to your baby. She may even dance while you sing.

- Read to your baby! Set aside twenty minutes or more per day for quiet time with your baby and books. Read certain books over and over so that she learns the words and knows what to expect on the next page. Read new books to see what captures her interest.

- Point out pictures in books and magazines and describe them. "That's a blue bird" or "This is a cow." Ask your baby questions you think she knows how to answer: "Where is the yellow duck?"

9–12
months

Reading to your baby is very important for his language development. As you read, point out objects that you see on the page and ask him to point out things as well.

TIP

Avoid the TV

Children under two years old should not be watching any television at all. Staring at a television is neither a social nor an interactive activity, and your baby needs both to improve her language.

- Describe what you are buying when you go shopping. "This is a red apple, and we will eat it for lunch." These sentences make a connection between the object and words, and they also make a connection between different parts of her life (store versus home).

- Name the parts of your baby's body when you are changing her diaper, bathing her, or simply snuggling. Ask her to point to the parts you've named. "Where is your tummy?"

- Name objects in your baby's environment, like people (Mama, Daddy, Uncle Max), animals (dog, cat, pigeon), and objects (chair, book, car).

- Make up stories for your baby. They don't have to be complicated, but as long as you are the storyteller, they will hold her interest.

DEVELOPING PERSON

Being Close to You Makes Baby Feel Safe and Secure

Your baby still loves to be held as much as possible. She loves to snuggle with you, read books, and crawl all over you when you lie on the floor. **She wants to be with you constantly, a desire made stronger by her sense of separation anxiety and her very strong emotional attachment to you.** Keep her with you to give her the security she needs.

Your baby will play by herself at this age, as long as you are nearby within her sight. Definitely give her time to play alone. Although it's tempting to spend every minute engaged with her because you are so in love with this little person, it's better to **give her time to play by herself when she's happy to do so**. That way, she learns to entertain herself. Otherwise, she will depend on you to entertain her for years to come, an exhausting and unhealthy arrangement.

Your baby loves to make you smile and revels in being the center of your attention. In fact, you may find her reaching up to put her hands on either side of your face and turning it so you look at her when she wants your attention. She might offer you a toy when you are playing with her, but she'll actually expect you to give it right back. It may look like she's starting to share, but that skill won't show up for another year or so.

Your baby continues to have stranger anxiety, so remember to keep her close when new people are around. If you're having friends over, scoop her up before they come in the door to avoid a meltdown.

Activities to Enhance Your Child's Emotional and Social Development

- Play with your baby! Have fun! Delight in her presence and make her feel loved every day.

- Love your baby. Unconditional love is a price-less gift. If she feels truly loved and appreciated just for being who she is, she will feel secure and develop self-esteem.

- Keep your baby close by carrying her in a sling or backpack. Hold her as much as you'd like because she loves to be close to your body.

- Consistently respond to your baby whenever she cries, and do it with love and tenderness. She still needs your help to right whatever is wrong in her world. Sometimes she just needs your presence to make things better.

Get outside to see the world with your baby. He will love to go wherever you are going and will marvel at seemingly ordinary items like flowers. You'll see the world with fresh eyes when you're out with him.

No Hitting

Establish a family rule that applies to *everyone*: "No biting, pushing, or hit-ting." If you abide by the rule, it means no spanking. If it is inappropriate for your child to hit or hurt other people, it is inap-propriate for you to hit or hurt your child. Spanking is hitting. And deliberately hurt-ing your child teaches her that the people who love her will hurt her. That's not a healthy lesson to learn.

- Give your baby kisses, hugs, and snuggles. Touch your baby. Massage her.

- Cuddle with your baby and read books. She'll love looking at the colorful illustrations and listening to your soothing voice.

- Talk to your baby. Tell her what you are doing over the course of the day and what you are think-ing about.

- Observe your baby and try to understand her social preferences. Then play to her strengths. Give your social baby lots of time in groups, arranging for playdates or time spent with an energetic babysitter. Give your quieter, more introverted baby downtime before and after being around others.

9–12
months

- Respect your baby's feelings. Be with her when she is happy and when she is upset. Try to be fully present in the moment with your child, instead of thinking about your next project or what you need to do when you get home.

- Act silly with your baby. Make funny noises, wear pants on your head, and pretend to gobble up her fingers. It'll make your baby laugh, and it's fun to do! Babies this age have absolutely irresistible laughs. It's the happiest sound on Earth!

- Join a playgroup. Set up playdates with other families. Even though your baby won't interact much with the other children, she will interact with other adults. It will also give you an opportunity to connect with other parents.

- Keep your baby near you—in your arms or a sling—when a new person is around. (That includes grandparents if she hasn't seen them for a while.) Ask the new person to approach slowly and not to get too close until your baby has time to know she's safe.

- Take your baby out to see the world—on walks and errands, or to meet up with a friend. Head outside with your baby by your side or in your arms.

POSITIVELY PARENTING

Practice Conscious Parenting When Your Child Misbehaves

As your baby approaches her first birthday, she will start learning how to get your attention—positive or negative. She will study how her older brothers or sisters act and what elicits attention from her parents. **Make sure that you are giving plenty of positive attention to your child for "right" actions and not just negative attention for poor behavior.** One way to do this is to practice conscious parenting.

Let's say that your child wants to pull on the cat's tail. Why in the world would she want to do that? You just told her not to bother the cat. Well, she might not remember the rule. She clearly heard it when you said something a few minutes ago, but a long time has passed. She may have forgotten. (It takes consistent repetition for a rule to sink into her consciousness. *A lot* of repetition.) Plus, she has poor impulse control. Her curiosity might be stronger than her worry over your disapproval.

She is also testing boundaries. She will move toward a forbidden object and then look over her shoulder to see what you will do. Sometimes she will have mischief in her eyes, and sometimes she is asking whether what she's planning is safe or allowed.

So what are your options in this situation? You might gently say "No" and see whether that suffices. That might work if she is asking permission, but not if she is planning mischief. You could yell "No!" in frustration. After all, you just told her to stay away from the cat. But this will either scare her and make

9–12
months

Your little scientist is born to explore the world. This includes finding out what is inside every box and basket in the house, discovering what dirt tastes like, and playing with cause and effect for years to come.

her cry, or make her smile because she's made you pay attention. Or you might distract her with a joke or a tickle and make her forget about playing with the cat.

The thing to realize is that while your baby explores the world, she is also exploring the world of relationships. Instead of wondering how the ball bounces or what kind of noise the rattle makes, she is now wondering how *you* bounce and what kind of noise *you* make when she does a certain action. Her endless curiosity makes her want to discover the world around her.

We suggest you look at these situations as science experiments, as if your child is testing a hypothesis. She is unconsciously thinking, "If I pull the cat's tail, what will Mama do?" **She is not deliberately trying to make you mad or push your buttons in a malicious manner. She is merely exploring her world, and you happen to be part of it.**

So, if your baby is conducting a science experiment, then you should respond to the situation as if you are the science teacher. Ask yourself what do you want your baby to learn from the experiment and then base your response on that goal.

First consider whether you even want her to conduct the experiment in the first place. If the answer is no, you might move the cat or distract your baby so that she won't pull his tail anymore. By consciously planning in advance, you are avoiding unpleasant situations. Bringing conscious parenting to bear on situations like this may, therefore, prevent undesirable behaviors from even starting.

But if you can't avoid the experience, consciously think about how you want to react. Select your words carefully and describe the action you want, not the action you *don't* want. In this situation, many parents would say, "No! Don't pull the cat's tail!" Their tone of voice and the "No" would clearly tell the baby to stop but wouldn't tell her what to do instead. She needs an action she *can* do. Show her and tell her what you'd like her to do. "Touch the cat gently." And guide her hand as she gently strokes the cat.

So much of our lives are lived by merely reacting to situations. **When we practice conscious parenting, we think more about how we want to react and what our goals are in a given situation. We become proactive rather than reactive.** It requires more energy, but the payoff is more lasting and therefore much more valuable.

When your baby makes a mess, take a deep breath and think about whether it really is a big deal and worth getting upset over. Remember to revel in her joy of exploration that is a natural part of your baby's development at this stage of life.

Show Your Baby the Emotions and Actions You Want Her to Imitate

Your child is a great mimic, and the person she will mimic the most will be you. *You* are the primary role model for your baby. And over the next several years, you are going to see what a great influence you are on her developing person. Think about these questions for a moment: What kind of person would you like your child to become? How do you hope she will approach life? Are you a good model for her by approaching your life in that same way?

Life is not always easy. But though we can't control the rest of life, we can control how we react to it. We choose our reactions. We can choose to get upset, or we can choose to take pictures when our child proudly pours pancake mix all over the living room floor. "Mama, look! I'm making pancakes!"

TIP Don't Treat Minor Mistakes as Major Mishaps

Try not to take every mistake or misbe-havior too seriously. Save that for the truly *serious* and dangerous missteps. It will make those teaching moments much more powerful. For all the rest, approach them with a positive attitude. Look for the silver lining while you gently teach your child how she can do better the next time.

Our philosophy is to take the pictures! Do you want your child pouring baking mixes around the house? Of course not. And you should talk with her about why you don't want her doing it. But by snapping a few photos and not overreacting with a yelling fit, you are celebrating your child's creativity, keeping her self-esteem intact, and enjoying the surprises of childhood. Just think of the joy and laughter those photos will bring in years to come! Think of the great story you have to tell! *Everyone* wins. Everyone feels good. You can still get the message across that you don't want her making such a mess again, but if you rant and rave, you've only succeeded in getting upset and unhappy, and making your child feel the same way. What good does that do? None.

Just as we suggest making your home a "yes" environment, we suggest making your interaction with your baby full of positive "yes" statements. Then when you have to say "No," or have to be serious, she will pay more attention because it happens so rarely.

If this doesn't come naturally to you (and it doesn't for many parents), don't give up. Just prac-tice. And practice again. Then practice some more. We become skilled in any tasks we practice regu-larly. So if we practice looking on the bright side of events, it will become easier for us. You can learn how to laugh instead of rage or cry.

Start by reframing your thinking and rethink-ing your actions. Pause before you react. Breathe. Look at the situation with new eyes. Look at it from your child's point of view. Imagine what the outcome will be if you explode. Do you want that? Imagine what the outcome will be if you laugh, take pictures, and applaud your child's ingenuity while teaching her that there are more appropriate venues for it.

You have the ability to change how you look at the world and your child's behavior. If you con-sciously decide to have a brighter outlook, your life and your child's life will be brighter. But more important, you will pass that skill on to your child as well. She is imitating you, copying your every action, expression, and mood. If you can give her the gift of learning how to live a happier life, doesn't she deserve that?

9–12
months

Make Sure All Caretakers Are Consistent in Their Discipline

A child may have several adults involved in her care on a daily basis. Many children are in day care, and some families share a home with another family or have a relative such as a grandparent living with them. **When several adults participate in the care of a child, it is critical to have consistent rules, schedules, and discipline.**

The most important thing to remember is that *you* are the parent. She is your child. Only you and your spouse or partner make the rules when it comes to your child and how she will be disciplined. If you do not hit your child (and that includes spanking), then no one may hit your child. It doesn't matter whether Grandma or Grandpa think it's appropriate, effective, or deserved. They do not have the authority to make those decisions or to go against your conscious parenting choices. It doesn't matter whether you are living in their house. She is *your* child. *You* make the rules. The more predictable you make your child's world, the better she will know what to expect in a given situation and how to behave appropriately.

Discuss with your partner how you want to handle certain situations and discipline. Then be clear about the decisions you've made with all the adults who share in your baby's care. If you do not believe in letting your baby cry by herself, then no one caring for her should allow it to happen. She needs consistent care and consistent discipline to feel safe and to learn the rules. If everybody knows what tone of voice and what phrase to use when

Thoughtful Rule Making at Night

Setting rules and schedules requires thoughtful consideration. You should therefore avoid making snap decisions, without the benefit of having time to discuss and reflect upon them. And some decisions—such as teaching your child to sleep through the night or to get herself back to sleep—should not be made hastily in the middle of the night. Many children are excellent sleepers at this age, but some still wake up frequently, much to the despair of their parents. It is beyond the scope of this book to discuss the various methods to help your child sleep through the night. We do feel strongly, though, that it is better to make a decision in advance (preferably during the day) than in a sleep-deprived state at 3:00 a.m. However you decide to manage this stressful situation, it is always better to follow a well-thought-out plan that you have discussed with your partner in advance than to make a spur of the moment decision.

your baby hits the cat, she will get the message more quickly.

This is not to say that your house rules will apply at other people's houses. They don't. You may feel it's okay to let your kids run around in your house, but Grandma may not want them running in her house. When you're at Grandma's, you abide by her house rules. But that's a different matter from the care and discipline the parenting of your child. Those rules do not change no matter where she is—and under whose care.

Well-Child Checks and Vaccines

Congratulations! You are off the hook in this chapter with regard to well-child checks. We discussed the nine-month well-child check in chapter 3. There are no scheduled vaccines at this time. If your baby is turning nine months old during the flu season, she might need a flu booster a month after her nine-month well-child checkup. Or if you are vaccinating on a delayed schedule (meaning that you are not following the recommended schedule and are spreading out the vaccines so your child does not receive so many at once), your child might receive vaccines during these three months. Turn to Resources and Recommended Reading on page 296 for more information on where to find an up-to-date list of recommended vaccines.

Health and Safety Tips

Some children surpass 20 pounds (9.1 kg) during these three months. Remember, however, that **children are supposed to be in rear-facing car seats**

until they weigh more than 20 pounds (9.1 kg) *and* are at least twelve months old. If your baby is larger than average, you may need to exchange your infant carrier car seat for a convertible, rear-facing car seat that accommodates larger children. The convertible seat can be turned around to be forward facing when your child meets the requirements. If your baby is petite, she will need to remain rear facing until she reaches the 20 pounds (9.1 kg) mark, regardless of her age.

As your baby becomes more mobile, you need to be more aware of standing water. This includes baths, toilets, wading pools, buckets, and big puddles in the driveway. **Babies can drown in only a few inches of water.**

Keep the poison control phone number posted near every phone in your home and on your cell phone. Find the poison control phone number for your area in the Resources and Recommended Reading section starting on page 296.

If you are using a crib, lower the mattress so that when your baby pulls up to stand, her neck is either at or below the top of the railing. If the mattress is too high and her chest is at the level of the railing, she could lean forward and fall out of the crib.

Childhood sunburns are a leading cause of adult skin cancer so it's essential that you protect your child from excessive sun exposure. Be sure to avoid the sun during the hottest part of the day, dress your child in sun-protective hats and clothing, and make sure she's wearing sunscreen if you must be out in the sun.

9–12
months

5

She's Walking!... and Falling

Happy birthday, Baby! A year has already gone by, and though it was perhaps the busiest year of your life, you are probably wondering, "How did that happen so quickly?" Your baby is now a full-fledged toddler, walking and soon to be running everywhere. She's at an age when you can never leave her alone. She's too curious and too good at climbing and getting into things. She needs to be supervised constantly. Her language will expand from two to twenty or more words. And her independent streak will blaze forth in full glory. You've got a blossoming *person* on your hands!

As you read through this chapter on the general development of twelve- to eighteen-month-olds, remember that each child is unique. His development happens at his own pace, and though you can certainly create environments and opportunities to enhance his development, you cannot speed it up. He'll do things when he's ready. Your child may be right on target with the information we present here, or he may be ahead of or behind it. If you have concerns about your child's development, please raise them with your family physician or pediatrician. But remember that children will develop in their own time. Relax and enjoy your child's journey through childhood!

DEVELOPING BODY

Toddlers Walk and Toddlers Fall

Your child should already be pulling himself up to standing and is probably cruising around the furniture. He might even be walking while holding on to your fingers. The next step is for him to walk by himself. His first steps! It is so exciting whether this is your first child or your fifth. He will be so proud of himself and will bask in your delight over his new skill.

Walking requires a great deal of balance. He has to put all his weight on one foot, balance for a moment, and move his other foot forward. You may have noticed that your baby doesn't have a whole lot of balance at this age. So he's going to fall. Most of the time, he'll fall backward onto his bottom. (Diapers are great cushions!) However, sometimes he will fall forward or sideways. With his new mobility, he'll also be falling from heights such as the couch or stairs and will very likely hit his head. Your child is really at an age where he must be constantly supervised simply to keep him safe.

Your toddler will be thrilled when he learns to walk on his own. Try to make sure his environment is as safe as possible for his inevitable falls.

When Should You Worry about a Head Injury?

Most of the time, when your baby hits his head, he will cry immediately or within a few seconds. He may hold his breath for three to five seconds, and then let out a huge wail. In rare cases, you won't hear any noise for many seconds after the fall. If he has been knocked out and lost consciousness, he should be taken to the emergency room.

Watch his behavior. If he is not acting normally, you should call your doctor. For instance, if he's walking strangely or unable to do things he could do before the fall, such as feed himself, he should be seen immediately. Children may vomit after a fall, and some doctors recommend they be seen if they vomit more than once in the twenty-four hours following their fall. Also, if your child's pupils are unequal, if there is a lot of bleeding, or if you think he might need stitches, then take him to the emergency room right away.

That said, **children fall and hit their heads all the time, and it is rarely serious.** Most often, your toddler will cry immediately after the fall and continue crying for five to ten minutes. He will allow himself to be comforted and will resume normal play within another fifteen minutes. If that happens with your child, it is okay to let him fall asleep, and you do not need to check on him throughout the night. He may have a bruise in the morning, but otherwise he will be fine.

If you have any concerns, however, or would like to be reassured because it looked like he hit his head really hard, call your doctor's office, even after hours or on the weekend. That's what they are there for.

12–18
months

Your child is also standing on his own and can even sit down from a standing position. He likes to push and pull toys around when he's walking, and he will nearly always be holding something in his hands when he's walking around. When he wants to get somewhere in a hurry, he'll still crawl there, even if he can walk on his own now. Crawling is much faster than walking at this point. He'll sit on the floor and roll a ball back and forth with you or an older sibling. He loves to close doors as he wanders through the house, and he will flush the toilet as often as he can escape to the bathroom once he discovers that particular joy.

Your child will love to fill things with sand, rocks, wood chips, water ... whatever he can find. Then he'll dump it out and do it again—and again, and again. A sandbox is years of entertainment and development.

Your baby loves to fill containers and dump them out, whether it's toys, sand, or water. He'll build short towers with blocks and gleefully knock them over. He enjoys turning the pages of books to look at the pictures when he's not chewing on them. He excels at pulling off his socks, shoes, hat, and mittens. In fact, those mittens may be off before you even get him out the door to play in the snow.

I Can Climb Higher Than You Think!

Not only is your baby pulling himself up to standing, but he is also starting to climb. No place is too high! He will want to get on top of the couch or the chair. Once he climbs onto a dining room chair, he'll keep right on going and climb onto the table. Trouble starts when he can combine cruising and climbing skills. His cruising ability allows him to push a chair around the room and his climbing skills get him on top of the chair. Then onto the kitchen counter, and perhaps even on top of the refrigerator! (Seriously. Some toddlers do that!)

TIP

Create a Climbing Zone

If your child seems especially gifted at and dedicated to climbing, consider creating a safe place for him to climb in your home or yard. That way, whenever he wants to climb, he has a safe place to do it and won't feel thwarted every time he wants to flex his climbing muscles. Give him a place where he is free to climb while teaching him where he can't.

You can never leave him alone. And you need to be more aware of potential dangers: the knife you left on the cutting board or the pan of boiling water on the stove. And the cupboards that you never dreamed he'd get into are now a treasure trove. He will be able to stand on the counter and open the cupboard doors and have everything at his fingertips. Can you imagine his joy at such a coup?

Your baby's desire to climb means he can also climb out of his crib. If you have been using a crib, you may want to take it down and place his mattress on the floor so he cannot tumble out and hurt himself. Toddlers can break bones or get stuck in the slats when trying to climb out of their cribs. Your child may also try to climb up bookshelves, which is very dangerous because he can pull them over on top of himself. The same goes for dressers. He may try to use the drawers as steps to reach the top. When more than one drawer is pulled out, it destabilizes the dresser and makes it easier to topple over. It's worth investing in safety mechanisms that will securely attach bookshelves and dressers to the wall so they cannot be pulled over.

12–18 months

Toddlers not only love to walk but also to climb— anything and everything. Nothing is off-limits to a toddler when it comes to climbing. If you can, create a safe place for him to climb either in your home or yard.

Let Your Toddler Feed Himself with a Spoon

Your toddler is feeding himself now, and he actually won't tolerate you feeding him anymore. He wants to do it himself. (You're going to notice that as a consistent theme over the next several years.) He's still not terribly good at getting the food into his mouth, but he's quite adept at getting it everywhere else. The only way he'll learn to get better at it is to practice. Let him. You may need to change his clothes after every meal (or let him eat in only a diaper and bib), but he really needs to do this on his own to master the skill.

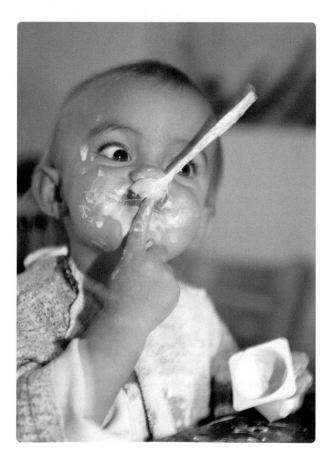

He's not only wielding a spoon, but also a crayon. He will take pen, pencil, or crayon to paper (or floor or wall). Become well acquainted with the mantra, "Draw only on paper." (You will say this thousands of times over the next two years.) He will need a reminder every time he wants to draw, and for as long as he's armed with a writing implement. Scribbling is the forerunner of drawing and writing.

TIP   **Get Out the Paint**

Help increase the dexterity and strength of your child's hands and fingers by letting him paint with his fingers. You can easily find nontoxic (and washable) paints at local craft stores or online. Or try using shaving cream on a flat table. It is easy to clean up and is loads of fun to play with.

Your child needs to practice feeding herself to learn how to do it. So even though she gets food everywhere when she eats—and needs a bath rather than a napkin afterwards—it's really important that you let her make the mess as she learns. She really will get better at it!

Activities to Enhance Your Child's Physical Development

Activities for Large Motor Skills Development

- Play with your child! Get down on the floor with him. Tell him about the toys, colors, and shapes you are playing with. Roll a ball to him, and ask him to roll it back to you.

- Visit playgrounds to help your child develop large motor skills such as balancing, running, climbing, and jumping. Encourage your child to go up and down the slides.

- Show your toddler how to throw and kick a ball. Play with small and large balls.

- Find a small stepping stool for your child to use to reach the bathroom sink so he can wash his hands. The step is also great for practicing going up and down stairs.

- Save large boxes for your child to play with and in. Cut holes in the sides for windows and doors. He'll love crawling in and out of the boxes, and it's a great hiding place.

- Provide your child with push or pull toys. He's at the right age for pulling something along with him as he walks, and he'll also love pushing around large cars and trucks, other push toys, and even some of your furniture.

- Have ride-on toys for your child to play with: little cars that are powered the Fred Flintstone way (with feet on the ground), tricycles, or rocking horses.

Ride-on toys are great for large motor skill development, plus they get your child outside in the fresh air. Go outside to play as often as you can. It's good for you, too!

12–18
months

- Offer support toys that can help your toddler learn to balance. Some ride-on toys will convert to a walking support that can be pushed or you might find a child-size shopping cart that he can move around the room. **Do not use baby walkers. Canada banned the sale of them for safety reasons. If a child walks to the edge of the stairs in a walker, he can fall down the stairs. And they do not actually help your child learn to walk.**

- Watch your child climb all over you if you lie on the floor (no need to encourage him, he'll naturally do it now and for years to come). He'll also lean on you as a support when he is standing.

- Set up an obstacle course for your toddler to practice walking. Put boxes and chairs a few feet apart so that he can move around the room easily but needs to take only a few steps at a time.

- Create an obstacle course for your child to practice crawling. Use tunnels made of boxes or blankets draped over chairs.

- Teach your toddler to safely climb up and down the stairs, and give him plenty of opportunities to practice. Remember that the safest way to climb down stairs is going down feet first on his tummy.

- Dance with your child. Put on some music you love to dance to and boogie!

- Turn your home into a space for exploration. Position enticing objects in various safe locations for your child to discover. Put them at various heights so he will see different objects when crawling, sitting, standing, or walking. These objects don't have to be fancy or exotic, just big enough for him to notice—and not choke on.

Activities for Fine Motor Skills Development

- Play with nesting blocks or cups that stack.

- Assemble simple puzzles. The best are shapes with handles that fit into recesses on a board.

- Provide a small table and chairs, if possible, for your child to use for playing, drawing, and eating. Have play dishes for him to pretend with.

- Sing and do the hand motions to "Itsy Bitsy Spider," "Wheels on the Bus," and "Head, Shoulders, Knees, and Toes."

- Show your child how to blow bubbles.

- Play clapping and hand games such as peek-a-boo and pat-a-cake.

- Create games that involve searching for hidden objects. Put toys under small blankets or scarves and ask your child where they are. He'll love finding them.

- Give your toddler blocks to stack and knock down. The one-inch wooden blocks you remember from childhood are too small for him at this age and fall over too easily. Look for blocks or boxes that measure four to six inches on each side because they are easier to stack.

12–18
months

Nesting cups that also stack are a wonderful toy for encouraging fine motor skills development. She will love putting the smaller cups into the larger ones, and will delight in knocking them over when they are (momentarily) stacked into a tower.

Kids this age (and beyond) love to play in water. Find bath toys that let your child pour water into and out of containers.

- Pour sand or water from container to container. Playing with water can be done outside or in the bath. Provide several small containers for your child to use.

- Have a shape sorter toy for your child to put shapes in and take them out, though he'll need help getting the right shapes into the holes at this age. Or make a homemade one from an empty wipes container and clean frozen juice lids. He can drop the lids into the wipes container and open it up to dump them back out.

- Give your toddler colorful toys that are easy to hold and can be washed in the dishwasher, or normal household items such as wooden spoons, measuring cups, and plastic glasses.

- Let your toddler make noise with things like pots, pans, and wooden spoons. Encourage him to bang to his heart's delight because making noise is fun, and he enjoys cause and effect.

- Draw with your child. Encourage scribbling. Buy large crayons that are easy to grasp and give your toddler a few colors to choose from. Tape paper onto the surface of a table or on the floor, making it easier for him to draw. For outside drawing, use brightly colored sidewalk chalk.

- Make mashed potatoes or mix together flour and water and let him play with it. Or make or buy play dough. (You can find recipes online.) The consistency is fun for him to play with and also encourages fine motor development.

- Collect 12- to 18-inch (30.5 to 45.7 cm) cardboard boxes for practicing dump and fill. Shoes boxes also work well for this. Children love to pour objects out of a box and then put them back in.

- Stock a variety of healthy foods for your child to use while practicing to feed himself. This exercise improves his manual dexterity and hand-eye coordination.

DEVELOPING MIND

Your Curious Toddler's New Mobility Means He Can Explore and Learn So Much More

Your toddler's thinking is becoming more complex. Where he used to recognize broad categories, he is now breaking them into smaller groups. Animals are broken into cats and dogs and cows (or at least their respective sounds). Trucks are different from cars, which are different from airplanes. And people fall into different categories too. At first, "Dada" might mean all adult men, but over time your toddler will distinguish between his father and everyone else.

Your toddler has learned how to ask for what he wants by pointing or using words, if he has the necessary vocabulary. You can encourage this skill by rephrasing his desires into full sentences. His face will glow when he realizes that you understand and are listening to him.

Your toddler is learning how to manipulate the world around him. When he wants you to read him a book, he will bring it to you. If he is hungry, he will pull you to the refrigerator and point, telling you that he wants something. If he knows the appropriate word or sign, he will use it, but because his spoken vocabulary is limited, pointing is usually how he expresses what he wants.

Your toddler's curiosity is still limitless, but with his new skill of walking he has more opportunities to interact with his environment. Simply by being able to stand, he can touch and taste more things. He can find things on shelves and in drawers that he didn't notice while crawling. He is an explorer by nature, and now the world he can explore is much larger.

Of course your child cannot be left unsupervised because his innate curiosity will get him into trouble. Think about what will attract his attention. Is it color? Will he want to get the jar of vitamins because they are colorful? Will he want to touch the pretty goldfish and end up pulling the bowl onto the floor? Or is he attracted by motion? He might want to touch the fan because its constant movement mesmerizes him.

He understands and will follow one-step directions at this age. "Please put your shirt in the dirty clothes hamper." He can identify objects in a book, and he will happily point out whatever you ask him to find. He'll love to look for things you hide under blankets, and he will eagerly play peek-a-boo with you. He's also starting to take things apart, even if he can't get them back to together yet.

12–18
months

Activities to Enhance Cognitive Development

- Read to your child! He is soaking up so much information at this age. If possible, aim for at least twenty minutes of reading per day. While looking at a book, ask him questions such as: "Where is the teddy bear?"

- Recite nursery rhymes.

- Sing songs with your child. Listen to music in the house and in the car, and choose music that you won't mind listening to again and again (and again). He'll start to sing along, and you may even recognize what he's singing from time to time!

TIP   Read for Fun!

Reading to a child this age is so much fun. He's much more focused on the illustrations, especially when you ask him questions about what he sees. He will love to point to things on the page and will happily look at one page for quite a while until all the objects have been named and pointed out. Besides pointing, ask him what sounds various animals make that appear on the book pages. He'll gain a repertoire of animal sounds that way.

- Talk to your child. Engage him in conversation, make eye contact, and smile. Give him time to speak and respond to him. When you've understood what he has said, repeat it so he can clearly hear the words being properly pronounced.

- Ask your child questions that he can answer by pointing, like "Where is your hand? Where is the duck?"

- Help your child identify familiar noises: airplane, vacuum cleaner, barking dog, and garbage truck.

- Introduce simple inset puzzles with handles on the puzzle pieces.

- Talk about shapes, colors, and numbers all day long. "That's a round, red ball." "We have only one banana left." "Let's find your green T-shirt."

- Give your toddler nesting toys, such as cups or boxes that fit into each other. Help him stack and nest them.

- Play a simple version of hide-and-seek. Put a blanket over his head and ask, "Where's Baby?" He'll pull the blanket off, and you can exclaim, "There he is!" Put the blanket over your head and ask, "Where's Mama?" He'll pull the blanket off with great delight. "You found me!"

- Find an interactive toy with plenty of moveable parts such as slides, buttons, and doors. Your child will learn the concepts of up and down, open and shut, and in and out as he plays with it.

- Hang a large mirror low on the wall for your child to see himself when he is playing on the floor or walking around.

- Teach your toddler the names of his body parts and then ask him to point to his nose, eyes, ears, etc. Ask him to point to your nose, eyes, and ears.

- Play games with instructions. Your child is increasingly able to follow simple directions and will be so proud of himself when he can do what you ask. This might include closing the door or bringing you the purple ball.

- Fill a box with objects made of various materials such as metal, plastic, and wood. Let your child dump out the box and hit the objects with a wooden spoon, learning about the different sounds they make.

- Play cause-and-effect games such as filling a container with water or sand, and then dumping it out or building a tower with blocks and knocking it down. (This game will be a particular favorite for years!)

- Play a more complicated version of find the toy. Hide the toy in simple locations, such as behind a pillow on the couch or in a box without a lid. As he walks around the room, he will notice the doll in the box and learn that a box can be a hiding place.

- Explore new places with your toddler so he has new things to see and learn about. Go to the shore to look at shells, seaweed, and gulls. Go to a restaurant to show him lots of people. Visit a pet store where he can see hamsters, rabbits, and parakeets.

- Once you finish plastic jars of herbs or spices, let your child play with them, exercising his sense of smell.

12–18
months

Your child can identify objects in a book and will happily point out whatever you ask him to find on the page. Keep reading to your child every day and encourage him to look at books on his own as well.

DEVELOPING LANGUAGE

Repeat and Articulate to Help Your Child Learn Language

Your toddler's language will slowly expand from twelve to eighteen months, and he will pick up new words regularly. A typical twelve-month-old speaks two or three words and will learn more than thirty new words by the time he's eighteen months old. His words won't be perfect or recognizable to most people, and you will need to translate for others. Once he learns them, he will say "Hi" and "Bye" clearly, however.

Make sure that you are articulating words clearly when you speak to your toddler because he is learning to say words the way you say them. When he says a word, repeat it back to him, talking as if he pronounced it perfectly. And add

details to help him learn more words. If he points to a bird out the window and says, "bir," you might respond by saying, "Bird. Yes, that's a bird. It's a little yellow bird. That's a goldfinch." He'll amaze you one day by saying "go-fish" for goldfinch.

You can encourage his language development by naming objects that appear in daily life: "That is a yellow banana. The boat is in the water." You can also help by describing actions to him, either his own actions or someone else's: "We are putting on our coats to go outside now. The dog is barking good-bye."

Some of his words will still be a sort of sign language, like "Bye-bye" and "Up." Almost every baby learns to wave good-bye before he learns to say the word. And the child with two arms raised over his head is a universal sign for "pick me up." Whenever he asks to be picked up with this sign, say "Up!" as you're lifting him into your arms so he'll learn the word.

Your toddler is an amazing mimic. He will repeat words back to you all day long. And he remembers the word you said three days ago and uses it appropriately. If you point out a fire station and say that the fire truck goes "ding-ding," he will surprise you with the same "ding-ding" the next time you drive past the station or the next time he sees a fire truck.

Your baby is starting to talk, which is such an exciting moment in his development—whether he is your first child or your third. Language development varies so much from child to child that it's always fascinating to watch how it blooms.

Activities to Enhance Your Child's Language Development

- Read, read, read, and then read some more! Talk about the illustrations when you're looking at books together. Ask him to point out specific objects on the page. Read alphabet books to lay the foundation for learning the ABCs.

- Encourage your toddler to turn the pages of a book and describe the story to you. He will tell a simple story. He might say "moo" or use his hands to show you how the chicken is eating food, but it gets him involved in the storytelling process. The more stories he tells, the better his language skills will develop.

- Throughout the day, describe what you are doing as you are doing it.

- Talk with your child like he's an intelligent person. (He is!) Consciously hold a conversation with him. Ask his opinions, likes, and dislikes. Listen intently when he talks to you. Respond in a manner that shows you understand what he's saying. Repeat what he says back to him, not only to model appropriate articulation but also to model good listening skills.

- Use proper grammar when you speak to model it for your child. He'll learn to speak (and write) the way you speak.

- Help expand your child's language abilities by speaking to him in complete sentences. If he asks, "More?" and points to the crackers, say to him, "You want to have more crackers." Model for him correct word order and clear pronunciation.

Your child will love to sing songs with you. You may find that singing with your child calms and soothes him if he is upset or melting down. It can instantly lift his mood, bringing him back to his normal, happy self.

12–18 months

- Play with a toy telephone. Soon your child will be picking up the phone and saying, "Hello." (pause) "Good." (pause) "Bye-bye!"

- Tell your child stories. You can talk about your experiences or make up stories from scratch. Make up stories that feature your child as the leading character.

- Sing songs with your child. Listen to music. Soon he'll be singing along! Listen to local musicians. Find a children's musician and start listening to her music at home. Attend a concert with your toddler. He will be excited to realize that he already knows the words!

- Read rhymes out loud. Find books that have rhyming text or poetry for children.

- Point out pictures in books and magazines and describe them: "That's a chickadee," or "This is a raindrop." Ask your child questions you think he knows the answer to: "Where is the blue hat?"

- Talk about what you are buying as you shop: "These are grapes, and we will eat them with our lunch." These sentences make a connection between words and objects and also make a connection between different parts of his life (home versus store).

- Name the different parts of your toddler's body when you are changing his diaper, bathing him, or simply snuggling. Ask him to point to parts you name: "Where is your hair?"

- Name items in your baby's home environment. This includes people (Daddy, Grandma, Sis), animals (cat, cow, horse, goose), and objects (towel, table, bicycle).

Put Away the Television

Sure, the TV can be a handy babysitter, especially when you really need a break. But do your child a favor and save TV viewing for when he's older. Children under age two should not be watching any television at all. Staring at a screen is neither social nor interactive, and your child needs both kinds of activity to improve his language.

DEVELOPING PERSON

Separation Anxiety Is Still Real for Your Child

Your child is so very attached to you by now that he will continue to get upset whenever you leave the room or leave him with someone else. If possible, try to avoid separations as much as possible. If you are working and your child is in day care, there's not much you can do about it other than to remind him lovingly that you'll be back later to pick him up. Keep in mind that **separation anxiety is a very real fear** of his. He's not trying to manipulate you or control you. He's not that devious, and he doesn't have the cognitive complexities for such things at this age. His world centers around you, and he does not want to be without you for even a moment. That's how strong his love and attachment are for you. He will get over this phase by the time he is two, but until then do your best to be with him as much as you can to lessen his fears.

Your child is playing by himself more and more, exploring toys and checking out what's under the bed and on top of the coffee table. He'll play happily when you are near and within sight, but if you get up to answer the phone or get a glass of water from the kitchen, he'll want to come with you. When he's playing with you, he'll want to hand things to you. He'll also like you to hand things to him.

RED FLAG!

Many parents worry about the possibility of their child developing autism. This stage, twelve to eighteen months, is when parents are most likely to sense that something is not quite right. If you have a feeling that your child isn't developing normally, or if you answer "No" to one or more of questions 1 through 6 or "Yes" to question 7, make an appointment with your doctor to discuss your concerns.

1. Does your child respond to his name when called by a parent?

2. Does your child point with an index finger?

3. Does your child wave hi or bye?

4. Does your child share attention with others? Does he look at something with the other person, indicating that the airplane is flying in the sky and wanting the other person to look, too? Does he follow another person's gaze to see what is interesting to that person?

5. Does your child seem to react emotionally to others? Does he appear concerned when other people are crying?

6. Does your child maintain eye contact in conversations? Can he carry on a conversation with an adult, including the give-and-take between people?

7. Does your child perform certain repetitive movements such as rocking or hand flapping? Does he have certain rituals or patterns, and does he become extremely upset if something disturbs the pattern?

12–18
months

Your toddler now recognizes himself in the mirror and in photographs. He actually realizes that the person he's looking at is him. He will love looking at himself in the mirror. If you have a full-length mirror or a mirror you can hang low on a wall, he will be contented to watch himself periodically throughout the day. If you can, get a small photo album for him that holds pictures of him, his parents, the family pet, grandparents, friends, and any loved person. He'll enjoy looking at the familiar faces, and it'll make the people who live farther away more recognizable when he sees them in person.

He loves to be held, snuggled, and read to. Really, he just loves being with you and being close! He likes to have you watch what he does and will thoroughly appreciate applause for his accomplishments. He's imitating you, copying the sounds you make such as sneezes and coughs. And he's getting very good at the animal sounds you've been teaching him. He'll have a whole repertoire of animal sounds soon enough. It'll be like having the entire animal kingdom living in your house!

Activities to Enhance Your Child's Emotional and Social Development

- Go out! Take your child to restaurants, museums, stores. Run errands. Do everyday life stuff that involves interacting with people to model how to do it, and give your child opportunities to practice it himself if he wants to. He will start to interact with people of all ages when he's ready.

- Make playdates and attend playgroups. Give your child plenty of chances to learn the art of cooperative play. Remember that it is a learning process.

- Play with children of various ages (one of the benefits of a playgroup). Offer your child the opportunity to engage with adults of various ages as well. Give him the chance to become comfortable interacting with anyone of any age.

- Play games with your child such as rolling a ball back and forth. Games help your child learn to take turns.

- Have fun with your child. Enjoy being with him and make him feel special and cherished.

- Show your child unconditional love, one of the greatest gifts a parent can offer. If he feels loved and appreciated just for being him, he will develop a sense of self-value, a sense that he matters.

- Always respond to your child with kindness and love when he cries. He needs your help to fix what's wrong and make things right.

- Touch your child. Give him kisses, hugs, and snuggles.

- Read to your child. He'll love the one-on-one time with you, looking at colorful images, and listening to your calming voice.

- Talk to your child throughout the day. Tell him what you're up to and what's on your mind. Point things out to him for him to see and notice.

- Help your child identify his emotions by naming them. He might be overwhelmed by anger, fear, or sadness. Giving him names for his feelings makes them less scary.

- Celebrate your child for being good. If he wants attention and gets more of it when he is mischievous than when he is behaving well, he will tend toward being more mischievous in the future.

- Try to understand your child's social preferences by observing how he interacts with the world. Then play to his strengths. Give the social child plenty of time in groups, arranging for playdates or time with an energetic babysitter. Give the quieter, more introverted child downtime before and after playing with others.

- Respect your toddler's feelings. Be with him when he is happy or when he is crying. Try to be present, fully involved with your child, instead of thinking about your to-do list.

- Feel free to act silly with your child. Make funny faces, do a crazy dance, and wear pants on your head. Doing silly things is liberating and it makes your child laugh. It's great for everyone!

- Keep close to your child when you're in the company of a new person. (That includes grandparents who come to visit when he hasn't seen them for a while.) Ask that the unfamiliar person approach gradually and not get too close until your child has time to feel comfortable.

12–18
months

Explore the world with your toddler. Expose her to other people by taking her with you on your daily errands, such as the grocery store, the bank, or filling your car with gasoline. But be sure to leave time for special events like picnics in the park or feeding the ducks.

POSITIVELY PARENTING

Make Your Life Easier by Picking Your Battles

Your little baby is turning into an autonomous toddler. Not only does he want to learn about the world, but he also wants to do it in his own way. He is on a quest for independence! He wants to feed himself and dress himself, and he is very clear that he doesn't want his hair washed. **To have a happy and peaceful household, do your best to respect his autonomy while setting appropriate boundaries.** But how do you do that?

Be clear on what is negotiable and what is nonnegotiable. Nonnegotiable rules are usually limited to safety issues. He has to be buckled into his car seat, he can't run into the road, he must hold your hand in the parking lot, and he may not hurt another person or animal. Keep the nonnegotiables to a bare minimum. If you have come up with a long list of nonnegotiable rules, you are setting yourself up for lots of conflict. The more unbreakable rules you have, the more conflicts you have. And the goal is to minimize conflict.

Other nonnegotiables vary from house to house. For some parents, making a mess with paint or staying up past bedtime falls into this category. For other families, these kinds of issues are not important but healthy eating is critical. What is important is that non-negotiables are rules that you will never bend or break. So think hard about what is genuinely nonnegotiable. Once you've decided on the nonnegotiable rules of your house, make sure all the adults living in the house are aware of them and able to enforce them.

So that leaves everything else up for negotiation. Remember that you are not negotiating with another adult. It is a lovely dream to think that you are going to teach your child the give and take of negotiating, of compromise. It ain't gonna happen. Not for a long time. Children view the world in black and white with no shades of gray. You have to supply the black and white structure for the negotiation.

When you are offering a choice, give only two options. Banana or cracker. Red socks or blue socks. Offer options whenever possible because it gives your toddler a measure of control. That's important to him. And to his development. And if you really don't care, be willing to accept an option your child comes up with. So if you offer the blue shirt and the green shirt and he pulls the yellow shirt out of his drawer, say, "Yes!" His happy cooperation is what's important.

It comes down to the simple, though not always convenient, idea that if you can say "yes," then say it. Only say "no" when you absolutely must. Your child is going to hear so many no's, he doesn't need or want any more. He needs to be told "yes" more often.

Bear in mind we're not recommending that you simply give in to your child's every whim. We're not suggesting you be a pushover. When you have rules, you have to uphold them consistently. However, we believe that so much of a child's life is beyond his control (because adults make the rules) that when you can give your child some control, you should.

12–18
months

Use laughter to defuse a tense situation. If your toddler doesn't want to go to bed or to fall asleep by himself, telling him a story about a bear hibernating for winter might be enough to change his attitude. In the end though, a consistent routine is the best way to ensure a peaceful bedtime.

Another way to keep the peace at home is to rely on routines in your daily life. **Children thrive on consistency.** Your toddler wants to know what is going to happen next. He wants predictability; he wants to know he can count on things happening in a certain order or at a certain time of day. This predictability also gives him a sense of control over his life in that he knows what's going to happen next. If he knows that you always brush teeth and then lie down to read a book and fall asleep, that helps him relax into his nighttime routine. There are no surprises, no variables; he can trust in what's going to happen. There's a lot of comfort in that.

Another advantage to consistency is that once your toddler gets used to doing things a certain way,

he's likely to be very cooperative throughout the routine. If there is no routine, he may have something else in mind and will balk when you want to do things differently than he imagines they should be done. So try to have the same patterns for waking up, meals, and naps. It makes the day more predictable for him and smoother for all of you.

Develop Healthy Eating Habits for a Healthy Child

You may be worried about whether your child is eating well and will make healthy choices as he grows. By following these simple rules, you can **establish a healthy diet for your child.**

Fill the house with healthy, whole foods. Stock your fridge, pantry, and kitchen with healthy foods. Whole foods are unprocessed foods in their natural state: fresh fruits and vegetables, meats, milk, grains such as rice and oatmeal, beans (dried or canned), etc. They make the best ingredients for meals and snacks. Processed foods are less healthy because vitamins, nutrients, and fiber are lost during processing, and they contain excess sugar, fat, and salt as well as additives.

Your child will eat what you have in the house. He may not eat everything as he develops his own likes and dislikes, but he will eat most of what you stock in the cupboards and refrigerator, so make sure you have only healthy foods to help his body grow.

Limit sugar. This is so important, and it's so easy to do. You can influence your child's sweet tooth by what you give him when he is young. True, your child is going to eat sugary foods at some point. However, you do not need to get him hooked on sugar from an early age. Delay introducing sugary treats for as long as you can. There is no reason to give candy to a twelve-month-old. (Or an eighteen-month-old, a two-year-old, etc.) Give your child other sweets instead. Help him develop a taste for natural sweets such as fresh and dried fruits.

For liquids, only give your child water, milk or 100 percent fruit juice—no fruit-flavored drinks, chocolate milk, or soda. Stay away from pastries (give him bagels!) and most packaged cookies (to avoid their high sugar content as well as the partially hydrogenated oils they contain). If you like to bake and want to treat your child to a cookie here and there, give your cookies some nutritional value by using whole wheat flour in place of some of the white flour. Add wheat germ and ground flaxseeds. There's nothing wrong with enjoying a treat now and again, but how much better to make them slightly healthier!

Choose healthy fats. Your child needs fat to grow, so make sure the fat he is getting is good for him. Buy whole milk and whole milk yogurt for him. Give him avocadoes or make guacamole. (Kids love dip!) Use peanut and other nut butters.

Most important, avoid partially hydrogenated oils, also called trans fats. These oils have been altered in such a way that our bodies don't process them well, and they raise bad cholesterol levels while lowering the level of good cholesterol. Read the ingredients lists on the foods you buy to make sure you are not buying products with partially hydrogenated oils in them. (Don't just trust the food label if it says there are 0 grams of trans fats; there can still be partially hydrogenated oils in the product, so you really must scan the ingredients list.)

Always have healthy snacks available. Toddlers are grazers. They need to eat every couple of hours, not just three meals a day. So always have healthy snacks ready for your child to eat when he gets hungry. Offer a few choices from different food

12–18
months

Offer an array of healthy foods to your child to establish good eating habits from the start. Your child won't be missing anything if you skip the junk, and you'll be helping his body grow used to healthy choices rather than craving unhealthy ones.

groups for him to choose from to make sure he's getting a good variety. Try to offer a protein, a grain, and a fruit or vegetable. Some great healthy snacks include: cheese, crackers (plain or with peanut butter spread on them), raw veggies (carrot sticks, cucumber circles, sweet pepper strips), healthy dips (guacamole and hummus), fresh fruit (apple slices, orange sections, banana slices, melon pieces), dried fruits (raisins, apricots, mango, banana chips), and pretzels.

Listen when your child says he's full. Babies and children naturally stop eating when their bodies feel full. If they are encouraged to keep eating, disregarding their body's signals, then they lose that skill and will overeat. This can happen to bottle-fed babies who are pushed to finish their bottles even though they clearly indicate they are done, or to children who are forced to finish their plates before they can have dessert or even get down from the table. These are unhealthy practices because you're teaching your child to override his body's natural cues, and you're setting him up for a lifetime of overeating.

Instead, listen to your child when he shows you that he is done, that he is full. Plates do not need to be finished. Let him decide how much he wants or needs to eat, because he's the best judge of what he's feeling inside. Honor his body, and give him the tools to continue paying attention to how his body feels and when he wants to eat more—and when he should stop eating.

Don't make food a battleground. You cannot force a child to eat. If your child does not like a particular food, don't try to force him to eat it. Battles over food at mealtimes make the meal an unpleasant, stressful event for the whole family. Do you really want your mealtimes to be so contentious? Or would you prefer a family that looks forward to sitting down together to talk, relax, and share a meal?

Keep in mind that your child is a person, like you, and there are foods that are going to taste good to him and foods that are going to taste terrible. There are going to be textures he likes and doesn't like. Your tastes are not his tastes. If you recognize that there are foods you do not like, then you must accept that the same is possible and true for your child.

If you expose your child to a wide variety of foods as he grows and stock your house with healthy choices, then he's going to get the nutrition he needs. By encouraging him to try new dishes, he's also going to develop a palate for a variety of foods. He may get picky and stop trying new things, in which case you should continue to offer the food

Be Flexible When It Comes to Mealtimes

You may want to adjust your family schedule around your toddler for more pleasant mealtimes. Most people eat dinner when Mom or Dad comes home from work, which is often after 6:00 p.m. However, your toddler might be hungry at 4:00 p.m. Consider serving a dinner meal at 4:00 p.m. for your child(ren). Then when the working parent arrives home, the child(ren) can sit down and have a snack while the parents eat a full meal. Being flexible means no hungry, grumpy kids while you're making dinner, and no meltdowns at the table. It can make a big difference and keep mealtimes enjoyable for everyone.

and eventually he will come around and try it. And give him the freedom to not like something. "Try one bite. If you like it, you can have more, but if you don't like it, you don't have to eat it." He may be more likely to take one taste if he knows he's not going to be forced to eat a large amount of something he suspects is yucky.

Go for quality, not quantity. An important thing to realize about food is that children's weight gain slows once they pass their first birthdays. That means that your child, who might have gained 2 pounds (0.9 kg) per month as a baby, now gains only half a pound (0.5 kg) per month. This is perfectly normal. If you look at the growth curves, you will see that the weight curve climbs steeply over the first six to nine months and then flattens out after a year.

So don't worry about the *quantity* of food your child eats, just make sure you put high-*quality* food in front of him. Some parents worry so much about the quantity, convinced that their baby is not eating enough, that they substitute less healthy but tastier choices just to make sure he is eating something. Reassure yourself that your child is growing well by following his growth curves at the well-child check-ups and noticing how healthy he looks to you. Offer him a range of quality foods and let him choose what and how much to eat.

Gentle Discipline Teaches Your Child to be Gentle

At some point, your child is going to hit, push, bite, or kick you or his siblings or friends. All children go through this phase, and how you handle it will teach your child how to treat other people. Treating someone gently teaches him to be gentle. Hitting someone to teach him not to hit simply doesn't make sense. Imagine this scene: Your child hits his sibling. You say, "No hitting!" and hit your child. What message are you sending? What do your actions tell him? (Children actually pay more atten-

tion to your actions than they do to your words.) If you hit him while telling him not to hit, he's learning that the bigger person gets to hit. He's not learning that hitting is unacceptable. He's learning that it's okay for Mom or Dad to do it. When he grows up he's likely to hit his kids, too.

Hitting a child is *never* okay. Never. Hitting includes slapping, smacking, and spanking. (Yes, spanking is hitting. It is not a reasonable teaching method; it is hitting.) They are all unacceptable forms of disciplining a child. If you're not entirely convinced, think about it this way: In what way is it okay for a 180-pound (82 kg) adult to hit a 25-pound (11 kg) child? It isn't. Ever. There is no circumstance in which it would be okay.

So let's talk about what you can do in terms of discipline. (Also read the section about the difference between discipline and punishment on page 204 in chapter 7.) For a child this age, the most effective approach is to redirect your child away from the undesirable behavior to avoid the situation altogether. If you see him raise his hand to hit someone, catch his hand before he can hit, remind him in a soothing voice to touch people gently, and get him interested in something else. Let him know what he can do, and phrase it in the positive ("Touch gently. Be gentle with people") while gently stroking his cheek to model the behavior.

12–18
months

Make sure your home is a "yes" environment so he's not getting into trouble with things you don't want him to touch. If he's not allowed to touch it, remove it. If he keeps climbing onto the chairs and then onto the table, remove the chairs so he can't climb up there. Or put up a gate so he can't get into the room and climb on the table or countertops. And remember to phrase things in the positive. Keep telling him what he *can* do, rather than what he can't. Give him images of the acceptable behaviors so he can imagine them: "You want to climb? Let's go outside and climb on your playground."

Time-outs are a popular discipline tool these days, and we have mixed feelings about them. They are not that effective, and they don't really teach the child how he can do better next time. (Let us also point out that at this time your child is much too young for a time-out. It just wouldn't work at all.) But sometimes it is appropriate to remove your child from play, especially if he's hurting other people. But consider using a *time-in* instead. That's where you and your child move to another place and sit *together*, calm down, and talk about a better way to handle the situation next time. A time-in is approaching your child's mistakes as teaching moments, telling him what was not okay about what he did and teaching him how to handle it appropriately in the future.

Make dental hygiene a family affair with everyone brushing and flossing at the same time. Your child is more likely to want to brush his teeth if he sees Mom and Dad taking care of their teeth at the same time.

Create a Daily Brushing and Flossing Routine for Your Child

A significant part of your child's development depends on a healthy body, and a crucial aspect of good health is dental hygiene. Your child will have teeth by his first birthday. So let's talk about how to take care of those teeth.

Most important, you want to make sure that no food or sugary liquid sits next to his teeth for a prolonged period of time. This is likely to happen if he's falling asleep at night with a bottle in his mouth. The liquid—formula, breast milk, or juice—pools next to his teeth and can cause tooth decay. So it's not a good idea to let your baby fall asleep with a bottle. If he must have a bottle in order to fall asleep, fill it with water only.

TIP Avoid Giving Your Child Too Much Fluoride

When you are picking a toothpaste for your child, we suggest using one that does *not* contain fluoride. Young children tend to swallow toothpaste instead of spitting it out. If there is fluoride in your tap water or if your child is taking fluoride supplements and ends up swallowing fluoridated toothpaste, he might get too much fluoride in his diet. Excess fluoride can stain a child's teeth permanently. In general, if your child is getting fluoride in the tap water or from supplements, there is no need to use fluoridated toothpaste.

As soon as your child's first teeth appear, you should begin cleaning them on a daily basis. You can either use a baby toothbrush or just wipe his teeth with a piece of cloth or gauze. However, do not use toothpaste yet. It's best to delay using toothpaste because sometimes a child doesn't like the taste of it. If he has yet to get used to having his teeth brushed, he might reject the whole process if the toothpaste tastes terrible to him. If he has become accustomed to brushing and then rejects the toothpaste, you can try a different brand or flavor of toothpaste or just go back to brushing without it.

Brush your baby's teeth once or twice a day. It's easiest to brush your teeth at the same time you are brushing his. It becomes a family project if you do it together, and it might make him more cooperative because he likes to imitate you so much.

After several months of brushing with a toothbrush and toothpaste, it's a good time to introduce dental floss. Your child may not need floss if his teeth are widely spaced, but if you introduce floss now, it will become part of his dental habit. Over time, your child will always associate brushing his teeth with flossing. That's a very healthy habit to encourage!

Some experts recommend visiting the dentist after the arrival of your baby's first tooth or by twelve months of age. However, many practicing dentists prefer to wait until children are three or four years old. Ask your dentist when she recommends scheduling an initial visit for your child.

Well-Child Checks and Vaccines

There are three well-child checks at this stage of life: at twelve months, fifteen months, and eighteen months. At each visit your child will be weighed and measured, and your doctor will go over the growth curves with you. Then your doctor will discuss your child's development and make sure it is on track. She will answer all your questions and conduct a physical exam. Your child may also receive several vaccinations if you are following the recommended schedule. In the Resources and Recommended Reading section on page 296 you can find out where to go to get the most up-to-date list of recommended vaccines.

Health and Safety Tips

Once your child turns twelve months old *and* weighs 20 pounds (9.1 kg), it is safe to turn his car seat around to face forward. However, many experts feel it is safer to have children facing backward in the car for as long as possible. As long as your baby does not exceed the weight requirements for facing backward, he may continue to ride facing backward. (Check your owner's manual for your car seat's requirements.)

The middle seat in the back of the car is considered the safest position for children in car seats. If your baby weighs less than 20 pounds (9.1 kg), he must continue to face backward—no matter how excited you are to have him facing forward! Some children are not big enough to face forward until they reach fifteen or eighteen months old.

Keep the national poison control center phone number readily available just in case your little scientist eats something he shouldn't. Post it on your phones and your refrigerator, put it in your purse or wallet, and program it into your cell phone and portable electronic devices. Check the Resources and Recommended Reading section on page 296 to find the poison control phone number in your area.

Sleep is still critical for your baby (and for you!). He should be sleeping twelve to fourteen hours a day. This will be divided between his nighttime sleep plus one or two naps during the day. Children usually transition from two shorter naps to one longer nap sometime in their second year of life.

Don't forget to check your smoke detector batteries twice a year and replace them when necessary. A convenient time to remember to check is when the clocks change in the spring and the fall due to daylight savings. In addition, check all smoke detectors, battery operated and hardwired, and write down the expiration date on the outside

Although you can turn your child's car seat to face forward once she is 20 lbs. (9.1 kg) and a year old, many safety experts feel it is safest for your child to remain in the rear-facing position until she exceeds the rear-facing weight limits for your particular carseat.

of your smoke detector. Some smoke detectors are meant to be replaced every ten years.

If you keep guns in your house, please keep them locked away—separate from the ammunition, which should also be locked up.

If you smoke, try to quit, and if you can't, smoke outside. Make your home and your car smoke-free zones for the sake of your child's health.

As your child grows, he will be able to manipulate faucets in sinks and bathtubs. Keep your hot water heater no higher than 120°F (49°C) to avoid accidental scalding.

Remember to protect your child from excessive sun exposure. Childhood sunburns are one of the leading causes of skin cancer in adults. Stay out of the sun during the middle of the day, put sun-protective hats and clothing on your child, and slather sunscreen on his skin when you need to be out in the sun.

Nurture Yourself to Better Nurture Your Baby

Remember that your baby's first birthday is more of a celebration for you as a parent than for him. He won't remember the occasion at all, but you have survived one of the hardest years of parenthood.

Take a few moments to appreciate all the changes that have occurred in your life this past year. You have learned so much—how to calm a crying baby, how to change a diaper, how to survive on a few hours of sleep at night. You have been present at a number of firsts in your baby's life—his first smile, his first sounds, his first foods, his first steps. You have matured as a parent. Try to savor that concept. All too often we are busy putting out fires in our daily lives. Make sure you step back to see the forest instead of the trees and appreciate how you and your baby have evolved.

And while you are savoring the changes, reflect on how you want to reintroduce balance into your life. Some parents find that their life during their first year as parents has been focused exclusively on the baby, to the detriment of themselves and their relationship with their partner. Now is the time to sing in the choir, to resume an exercise regimen, and to plan and keep those dates with your partner.

We know a couple who are raising two children while running a business together. From early on in their lives as parents, they hired babysitters two nights a week. One evening was spent discussing work and business matters. The other was devoted to them as a couple. They feel that those two nights a week are one of the best investments they have ever made in their marriage.

12–18
months

6

TODDLERS

18–24 Months

The Independent One-and-a-Halfs

The time from eighteen to twenty-four months is a roller coaster ride of delights and challenges. The eighteen-month-old child is into everything! Your little natural scientist will experiment with anything she can get her hands on. She will walk, run, and climb. She will explore her surroundings over and over again and practice going up and down the stairs (and up and down . . . and up and down . . .). She will climb onto the table 200 times. No, make that 2,000 times. She will learn more words—sometimes several a day— and even combine them into short sentences. She will collapse into a puddle of frustrated tears if she is thwarted. She will interact more with other people. She will try your patience and wear you out, but she does so with the purest of intentions: to learn about her world.

As you read through this chapter on the general development of eighteen- to twenty-four-month-olds, remember that each child is unique. Her development happens at her own pace, and while you can certainly create environments and opportunities to enhance her development, you cannot actually speed it up. She'll do things when she's ready to do them. Your child may be right on target with the information we present here, or she may be ahead of or behind it. If you have concerns about your child's development, please speak with your family physician or pediatrician. But remember that children will develop in their own time, so relax and enjoy your child's journey through childhood!

RED FLAG!

If your child is not taking a few steps independently by the time she is eighteen months old, discuss this missing skill with her doctor at her eighteen-month well-child visit.

DEVELOPING BODY

Your Toddler Will Run Faster Than You Think!

By eighteen months, your toddler should be walking comfortably even if she does not have the skill perfected yet. She might still be bowlegged and walk with her belly protruding. That's okay. Over the next six months, you'll notice increased confidence and stability in her walking. Your child will be able to bend over and pick an object off the floor without falling over. She will be able to climb up and down the stairs. She may learn to kick a ball around before she turns two. And she will run. Sometimes quite fast!

As children discover the joy of running, some of them become excellent escape artists —with no thought to safety. They love the sensation of running—running fast—and want to explore everything! Keep your child safe by carrying her in the parking lot or requiring her to hold your hand if she insists on walking to the car. Or, when leaving the car, you might want to place her directly into a grocery cart or stroller.

18–24
months

Close to twenty-four months, learning to play catch is great fun for you and your child. Using large balls or balloons increases her chances of a successful catch. She'll be delighted with the game, regardless of whether she catches the ball.

Reasons *Not* to Play "I'm Going to Get You" with Your Child

The natural parent-child game of chase is so much fun, especially to a child of this age! You'll have her squealing and giggling— even hiccupping with joy every time you play. However, before you start playing the game too often, take a moment to think about what you're teaching your child: You're teaching her to run away from you as a game. As a result, you may find yourself with a little person who suddenly dashes away in the parking lot because she wants to play the chasing game.

It's a terrible conundrum, and it's hard to know precisely what to do. When she is older, she will learn that there are times and places to play—and *not* to play—the chasing game. But she won't be able to discern this at her age. You need to decide what you want to do. Realize that she may think she's playing a game with you when she goes running for the street. When this happens, you need to react appropriately. Spanking is never okay and neither is scooping her up with a smile and a laugh when it's a genuinely dangerous situation. Pick her up, talk to her in a serious, slightly scared voice. Your tone will grab her attention and get the message across. She'll do it again, but if you repeat the safety rules and the emotional tone, she'll learn pretty quickly.

It is so much fun to play chase with your child—for you and for him. But it can set a bad precedent, if he decides to play in an unsafe situation like a parking lot.

Toddlers Interact with Their Environment through Touch

Your child is feeding herself more skillfully now, and using utensils quite well. She'll still make a mess when she eats, but she's getting better at using spoons and forks at every meal. She loves to make towers of two, three, or more stacking blocks. She's scribbling with a crayon or marker and may be able to draw a reasonably straight line by the time she's two. As all parents learn, a child's artistic talents are not limited to paper. Tabletops and walls are fair game. The best you can do is to keep reminding her to "draw only on the paper" and remind yourself to keep a close watch while she's armed (and dangerous) with a crayon.

TIP

Keep Your Toddler Safe by Clearing Counters and Removing Chemicals

Your toddler's new skills require another safety check of the household. She will figure out that by pushing the chair up to the kitchen counter, she can explore the countertop. You therefore cannot leave the cheese knife or cleaning chemicals on the counter and assume that they are out of her reach. Some children are even adventurous enough to climb onto counters and explore the cupboards. If that sounds like your child, you need to move dangerous and fragile objects even higher. How high is high enough? We've heard of toddlers who climb all the way to the top of the refrigerator!

18-24
months

The activities you do to enhance your child's development should be fun. Children learn through play, so make sure your child is having fun and enjoying your play and development time.

Right- or Left-Handed?

You may see your child showing a preference for one hand over the other when it comes to certain actions. More than 85 percent of children are right-handed; the rest are left-handed (with a few rare exceptions who are ambidextrous).

There are so many skills that crop up at this age. Your child will love to put smaller toys into a bigger container and then dump them out. (Please make sure the small toys are not choking hazards.) She will enjoy playing with push and pull toys. She will also learn to throw. She won't have great aim (though she will manage miraculously to get a ball into your morning coffee at least once), but she will love to see objects flying through the air. And as she gains more confidence in both her fine and gross motor abilities, you will see her carrying several objects in her hands at once while walking or playing.

Activities to Enhance Your Child's Physical Development

Keep activities fun for everyone. Don't push your child to do something she doesn't want to do simply because you think it's good for her physical development. If she's enjoying herself, if it feels like play, then she'll want to do it. If it's not fun, or if she doesn't like a particular activity, don't force it, and don't worry about it. It doesn't mean she won't gain whatever developmental skills are involved. It just means she'll learn them another way. That's okay. There are plenty of different things you can do with your child to help enhance her development.

Activities for Large Motor Skills Development

• Make sure your child gets at least an hour of physical activity most days.

• Spend time at playgrounds to help your child develop large motor skills such as balancing, running, climbing, and jumping. Encourage your child to go up and down the slides.

• Teach your child how to throw and kick a ball. Play with different size balls.

• Play soccer! Kick balls around your yard or a local park or playground to enhance your toddler's coordination.

• Position a small stepping stool in the bathroom for your child to use to reach the sink and wash her hands. The step is also safe and handy for practicing going up and down steps.

• Keep large boxes for your child to play with and in. Make holes in the sides for windows and doors. Let her decorate them with markers or crayons. She'll love crawling in and out of them, and they're great hiding places.

• Let your child play with push or pull toys. She's at the perfect age for pulling something along with her as she walks, and she'll also love pushing around large cars and trucks and other push toys. She may even rearrange some of your furniture.

• Find ride-on toys for your child to play with: little cars that are powered with feet on the ground, tricycles, or rocking horses.

• Have a wagon available for your child to pull around the yard, to put items in and to take them out. A wagon is also a great way for your child to help clean up the yard at the end of the day. You and she can gather things in the wagon and she can pull it to put the items away.

• Enlist your child's help with simple household tasks such as vacuuming, picking up toys, and putting clothes into the washing machine or laundry basket.

18–24
months

Toddlers make a fantastic mess with markers, drawing on themselves purposely and accidentally. Protect your table by taping newspaper to it, and then tape down your child's drawing paper so it won't move when she draws on it.

- Give your child access to wooden spoons, mixing bowls, and pots and pans. They are great for imitating Mom and Dad in the kitchen (or just for making lots of noise).

- Find child-size tools (gardening tools, snow shovel, broom, etc.) so she can help you sweep, shovel, etc., while learning how to use tools that are appropriate for her size.

Your child will love to help you in the garden. She can help dig, plant seeds, and pull weeds. And she'll especially love watering the plants, happy to fill her watering can and pour it out over and over.

Activities for Fine Motor Skills Development

- Play together with nesting blocks or cups that stack.

- Do simple puzzles with your child. The best for this age range are simple shapes attached to handles that fit into indents on a board.

- Set up a small table and chairs for your child to use for playing, drawing, and eating. Have play dishes for her pretend play.

- Sing and teach your child the hand motions to the "Itsy Bitsy Spider," "Wheels on the Bus," and "Head, Shoulders, Knees, and Toes."

- Improve hand-eye coordination by building with blocks, stringing large beads, using blunt scissors, and drawing.

- Help your child develop strength, control, and dexterity by squeezing water out of a washcloth, squeezing a ball or a soft bath toy, and drawing with large crayons.

- Pour sand or water from several small containers. Playing with water can be done outside or in the bath.

- Using large blocks, build with your child, but also give her the time to build on her own.

- Draw with your child.

Learning to blow bubbles is immediately gratifying as your child gets to delight in watching the bubbles float away or chase after them to catch them. She'll also love to pour the bubble solution out on the ground!

18-24
months

- Show your child how to blow bubbles.

- Supply your child with paper, markers, stickers, and large crayons. Keep them on a shelf that is within her reach, if possible, so she can get what she needs without asking for help. She'll also enjoy using her hands with play dough, clay, and paints (finger paints or washable watercolors and acrylics with paint brushes).

- Thread large beads or buttons onto a string or shoelace.

DEVELOPING MIND

Read to Your Child to Develop Her Mind

At this age, books have moved beyond the realm of chew toys to become cherished objects that communicate information. Your child doesn't eat them anymore; instead, she holds them and turns the pages correctly. If you give your child a book upside down, she will turn it right side up because she knows that people and animals are not supposed to be standing on their heads.

Your child loves to look at books! Keep her engaged with plenty of large, bright picture books with few words and heavy pages that she can turn on her own. Make a point of visiting your local library on a regular basis to expose her to all sorts of wonderful books without stressing your household budget. **Do your best to read to her for *at least* twenty minutes every day, and you'll help instill in her a love of books and reading.**

Reading to your child is not only good for his development, but it's also a great way for you to connect with him. Make time to read during the day and include reading in your bedtime routine to help him settle down for sleep.

"Where's the Apple? Where's the Horse?"

Did you know that your child can identify objects on the page already? She may also know certain books well enough that she will spontaneously act out the activities they depict or describe, such as brushing her hair or waving good-bye. For a book that beautifully and simply explains the advantages of reading to your child, we recommend *Read to Your Bunny* by Rosemary Wells.

Your Child Can Look in a Mirror and Tell You What She Sees

Your toddler loves to look at herself in the mirror. Younger children treat their reflections in the mirror as if it is another child and reach out to the mirror to touch the "other" baby. However, by this stage, your child realizes that the reflection she sees is her! So, if she notices some food on her face while looking in a mirror, she will pat her own face to wipe it off, instead of trying to wipe it off the baby in the mirror. If possible, hang a mirror low on a wall so your child can watch herself when she's playing or just moving around the room.

Pointing out body parts may be your child's favorite activity right now. She may walk over to you at any time and say "Nose," while touching your nose. If you ask, "Where's your nose?" she'll touch her own nose and say "Nose." You can also use a mirror as another way to teach the parts of the body. When you ask, "Where is my nose?" she can look at you and see your nose while she touches it. However, she needs a mirror to be able to both see and touch her own nose. The mirror also allows her to compare her ears, eyes, and teeth to those of her mother, father, sibling, etc.

Your Child Can Do Simple Math and Recognize Patterns

Your little one is beginning to understand the simple mathematical concepts of one, two, and more. She begins to comprehend that *one* means a single object and *two* means another object alongside it. *More* simply means a larger group of things. She may also be able to count, in a sense, or at least know when she has all the pieces she wants. We knew a child this age who had to have all five of her pacifiers with her at bedtime. If she was missing any, she recognized that she didn't have them all and would ask "All?" Although a rare few can "count" from one to ten at this age, what they are doing is not true counting but rather memorization, like memorizing the words to a song.

Your toddler can recognize patterns, such as the routines of her day. Mom leaves for work after breakfast and comes home before dinner. Bedtime is preceded by brushing teeth, getting into pajamas, and reading books. Other patterns she'll notice include color, size, and shape. For instance, *these* blocks belong together because they are all square or all brown. Pattern recognition allows us to make sense of and find order in our world.

Your child may start developing a sense of humor at this age. **As she grows to recognize patterns, she also starts to understand when something doesn't fit into a pattern.** She will laugh at silly behaviors like trying to brush her hair with a toothbrush. You can use this as a helpful distraction in certain situations. Changing diapers can be much funnier and less stressful if you wear your toddler's pants on your head!

Activities to Enhance Your Child's Cognitive Development

- Do simple puzzles with your child, and let her do them without you.

- Play together with shape sorters. Talk about the shapes, and name the shapes and colors of the pieces every time you play.

- Ask your child to identify noises she hears: a knock at the door, the dishwasher, a barking dog, a fire truck, etc.

Your child will love to help pick out items at the grocery store, and it's the perfect time to practice counting and colors with him. "How many yellow bananas are in this bunch?"

- Give your child the chance to select between two choices as often as you can: "Would you like apple or orange juice?" "Do you want to wear your red shirt or your yellow one?" "Shall we read *Goodnight Moon* or *But Not the Hippopotamus*?"

- Sing the alphabet song, and read books that highlight the ABCs.

- Count everything! Count how many apples you buy at the grocery store. Count the number of books on a shelf. Count the number of butterflies on a page in a book.

- Talk about shapes, colors, and numbers all day long. "That's a square, blue napkin." "We have only one banana left." "Let's find your pink PJs."

- Read to your child. Read stories or nonfiction books on her favorite subjects. Go to the library together to pick out books she might enjoy. She will start to memorize text as you read books over and over again. Talk about the pictures and ask her to point to the green ball or the sheep's black nose. She is taking in an incredible amount of information at this age.

- Recite nursery rhymes with your child.

- Sing songs together. Listen to music in the house and when driving in the car. Select music that you like well enough to play over and over again. She'll start to sing along as she recognizes the songs, and you may even recognize what she's singing from time to time!

DEVELOPING LANGUAGE

Talk to Your Child to Improve Her Language Skills

At eighteen months, your child may be able to speak more than fifty words and understand more than 200 words. Her articulation will improve over the next six months, and she will become much more understandable to you as well as to others, making it less necessary for you to "translate" what she's saying.

> ## RED FLAG!
>
> If you can't easily understand what your child is saying by eighteen months, if she has fewer than fifteen spoken words, or if you have other concerns about her language ability, make sure you discuss this matter with her doctor at the eighteen-month well-child visit.

From eighteen to twenty-four months, your child's language development will explode. She will learn new words at an astounding rate, sometimes several a day. **Most two-year-olds have a vocabulary of more than 200 words and are able to put simple two- or three-word sentences together.** She is also better able to understand what you say to her.

Your toddler is likely to become less frustrated with this burst of language. The more she can communicate, and the better able she is to make herself understood, the less frustration she will experience in her day-to-day interactions. If you've been using sign language to communicate with her, keep it up. Giving her multiple ways to communicate means that she will still be able to express herself when she's too tired or grumpy to get the words out just right.

At this age, your child is able to follow simple requests. "Would you go put your shoes away, please?" "Can you take this over to Dad?" She recognizes names of familiar toys, people, and places, and she will even start to ask you what something is called. She may point to something and say "That?" Name everything for her! When she says a new word, repeat it again after she says it as if she pronounced it perfectly. "Tree. That's right. That's a tree." By doing so, you are modeling correct pronunciation while boosting your child's confidence in her speaking abilities.

18–24
months

Understand That Your Toddler's "No" Doesn't Always Mean "No"

One of the most frequently used words in a toddler's vocabulary is *no*. When spoken by an adult, the word is easy to comprehend: It is a negative, plain and simple. Your toddler's "no," however, is more nuanced. Her "no" is a word of independence, of control, and not always used as a negative. Remember that, just like you, she wants to control her world, wants her environment to follow her rules and her expectations. **When she says "No," she may not be saying "I don't want" as much as "I want to do it my way."**

TIP **Don't Take Offense When Your Child Says "No" to You**

Think of her "no" as a request for independence and control, which is a normal developmental stage. Replace "no" in your mind with other words. Almost everyone responds poorly to a flat "No," bristling at the negativity in the word. If you translate her "no" into other words such as "Mine," "I do," or "No, thank you, I'd rather do it myself" (we can dream, can't we?), then you'll understand her better and know that she's working toward independence, just like she's supposed to.

Let's say you ask your eighteen-month-old whether she wants more pasta, and she says "No." However, when you start to put the pasta away, she bursts into tears. Her "no" didn't mean that she didn't want more pasta. It meant that she wanted to make the decision in some way that you didn't understand. Maybe she didn't want the pasta now, but she wanted it left out so she could have some later. Or maybe she wanted to fill her own bowl and said "no" to tell you not to fill it for her.

Activities to Enhance Your Child's Language Development

- Read to your child every day, several times a day. Discuss the illustrations when you're looking at books together. Ask your child to tell you what she sees. Ask her to point out specific items on the page. Read alphabet books to lay the groundwork for learning the ABCs.

- As you go about your daily routine, describe what you are doing as you are doing it.

- Treat your child like she's an intelligent person. (She is!) Consciously hold conversations with her. Ask for her opinions, likes, and dislikes. Listen attentively when she talks to you, and respond in a way that shows you understand what she's saying. Repeat what she says back to her to model appropriate pronunciation as well as good listening skills.

- Add details to what your child says. "Yes, that's a bus. It's a blue and white city bus. It's really big!"

Have conversations with your child. Laugh with him! Delight in what he finds interesting and funny. You're not just helping to build his language skills; you're continuing to build your relationship, too.

- Use proper grammar when you speak to model it for your child. She learns to speak (and write) from you.

- Help expand your toddler's abilities by speaking to her in complete sentences. If she asks for "More banana?" say to her, "You want to have more banana." Model correct word order and clear pronunciation.

- Play with a toy telephone. Soon your child will have entire conversations on the phone, complete with "Hello." (pause) "Good." (pause) "Bye-bye!"

- Tell your child stories. You can recount an experience you had or make up stories that feature your child(ren) as the leading character(s).

- Sing songs and listen to music together. Your toddler will be singing along soon!

- Read books that have rhyming text or poetry for children.

- Provide your toddler with puppets, dolls, stuffed animals, and make-believe play materials such as scarves, hats, old clothes, shoes, recyclables for making costumes and props, blankets for building forts, etc. Make hand puppets out of paper bags decorated with markers, paper, and glue, or out of socks decorated with buttons, yarn, and thread. Show her how the puppets can have a conversation with each other or with you or her. Put on a puppet show.

DEVELOPING PERSON

Enjoy Your Toddler's Expanding Personality

Your eighteen- to twenty-four-month-old child is becoming more and more who she is. You may find yourself thinking that she's turning into this little *person*. She is! She is showing you more of her wants and needs. She is communicating much more clearly and is not shy about telling you when she doesn't like something. She has her own likes and dislikes, and they may differ from yours.

Your toddler still needs constant supervision because she is busy exploring her world, getting into anything and everything she can. She's not doing it to upset you or to go against the rules; she's doing it because that's what she's programmed to do. She's supposed to explore, figure out, test, and learn through trial and error. She's learning! She's growing! Help support this aspect of her growth by providing her with an environment that she can explore safely. Say "yes" as often as you can, keeping "no" to a bare minimum.

Speaking of rules, she really doesn't remember them at this age. It is important for you to remind her of the rules: "Draw only on the paper." But keep in mind that you'll be repeating the rules for months (and months) to come. She's not deliberately going against the rules; she just isn't capable of retaining them yet. That'll come—not soon enough for your preference perhaps, but all in good time.

 Do Your Best to Phrase Rules in the Positive Rather Than the Negative

When you tell your child what she *can* do ("The chair is for sitting"), that is the image she will hold in her head. That's what she will do. If you tell her what she *can't* do ("No standing on the chair"), then that is the image that develops in her head. She's likely to stand on the chair because that's what she's thinking about. (Imagine standing in a group of kids and saying, "Don't chase me!" What would they immediately think of doing?)

Even as your child is growing and developing into a little person, she still needs a lot of your attention. She needs your focus and your time. She needs your arms to hold her, help her, and hug her. She needs to know that you are there for her whenever she needs you—day or night. Always answer your child's cries with your loving presence and support. She'll grow up to be a confident, independent kid if she knows she has a reliable base to lean on whenever she needs it.

Your child is working toward independence every day. She'll want to do things herself, like getting dressed or pulling up her diaper or wiping her bottom during a diaper change. She won't willingly give up the bottle of salad dressing she snagged off the table, but she'll put it back on the table without a fight when asked because she wants to do everything herself. "Me," "mine," and "I do" may be her favorite words. Or she may just point to herself to tell you that she wants to do it.

When your child doesn't want to do something or you interrupt her plans, boy will she let you know it loud and clear. (Do you remember how easy it used to be to just pick her up and go when she was twelve months old and younger? Not anymore.) This is a part of her growing sense of self. She knows what she wants or doesn't want, and she tells you in no uncertain terms. That's good! It may be frustrating for you at times, but it's essential for her developing person.

It's up to you to figure out a way to get your toddler to do what needs to be done while keeping her dignity intact. So if she balks at getting into her car seat, wiggling and crying, you need to find out what will help her do it willingly. Can you entice her into her seat? "Let's get you into your seat and you can have your water bottle." Or "I'll give you some raisins as soon as you get into your seat." Or even, "Will you help me buckle your seatbelt?" Can you make a game out of getting her into the car seat? We know a father who would whisper,

"Let's trick Mom!" and quickly buckle his daughter into her car seat. Then he would loudly say, "Mom, Shannon is being so uncooperative and won't get buckled." His wife would come out in mock distress because they had to leave and Shannon was making them late. When she found Shannon all buckled, she would exclaim, "You tricked me!" sending Shannon into delighted giggles.

The more often you get your child into her seat without a struggle, the more likely she'll learn to do it without a struggle. This way you both win, and everyone is happy. If you have to force her into the seat every time, then she always loses. And nobody likes to lose every time. She'll put up a fight for a lot longer if that's her experience.

Your toddler loves to make you happy and wants to be just like you. She'll love to feed you just as you have been feeding her, and will giggle with happiness every time you eat whatever she tries to feed you.

18-24
months

You will begin to recognize yourself in your child's actions around this age. She's a great imitator. She tries on every action she sees, every word she hears, every tone of voice. You may find yourself noticing how some of the things you say or do around her are not so nice when they're coming out of her mouth or through her actions. You'll realize that you need to adjust what you say or do to teach her more appropriate ways of relating to others. Everyone goes through this, even the most conscientious parents. Remember to model the behavior you want her to have. Model the words and tone of voice you want her to use. Those are your best teaching tools for every age.

The Toddler's Creed

If I want it, it's mine.
If I give it to you and change my mind later,
    it's mine.
If I can take it away from you, it's mine.
If I had it a little while ago, it's mine.
If it's mine, it will never belong to anybody
    else, no matter what.
If we are building something together,
    all the pieces are mine.
If it looks just like mine, it is mine.

—Author Unknown

An eighteen- to twenty-four-month-old child is so delightful! She is quick and easy to laugh, and she finds the silliest things funny. Her laughter sounds like pure happiness. Sing silly songs, jump around, dance with her in your arms, make funny faces and encourage her to laugh and play. She will love to feed you, laughing as she places a pretzel in your mouth. She will still giggle at peek-a-boo games at this age. She will find her older siblings, friends, or cousins hysterical.

Your child may start to empathize with others by the time she's two. She may show concern when someone is crying. She may bring you a tissue when you're upset or feeling sad. She may hug you and pat your back just like you do when she's upset. She'll also start to show her affection for you with kisses and hugs.

At this age, most of your toddler's playing will be alongside other children rather than with them. This is called *parallel play*. You may notice some interaction here and there, but mostly she'll play on her own right next to other kids. She will start to play pretend, perhaps by imitating you talking on the phone. (Anything and everything can be a phone—a calculator, wooden spoon, car, stuffed animal, even her foot!)

TIP	**Loveys Are Off-Limits for Discipline**

If your child has a lovey, it should be respected as sacred. It should never be taken away or used as part of a threat or as a bargaining chip. On a smaller scale, that would be akin to using a parent as part of a bargain—imagine someone manipulating your child by saying, "If you don't do as I say, then your mama won't come back to pick you up today." In addition, using a lovey as part of a threat or negotiation is likely to cause more harm than good. The impact on your child will be to make her extremely upset, making it impossible to reason with her or get her to calm down. That doesn't do you or her any good.

Your child will be very possessive with the toys she has in her hands, and she will cry with intensity if someone takes them from her. However, she may also start to share some of the time. She may be willing to hand a toy to her sibling or friend. Sharing is based on the idea that if you let someone play with something now, you will get to play with it later. But because she doesn't comprehend yet that the future is certain, that the sharing really will take place, she understandably doesn't want to give up her toy now. If you say, "Thank you! That makes Sasha so happy that you shared with her," it will encourage her to do it again. Give her ownership for the action, and let her know how her actions affect others.

This is also the age when your child may become attached to a lovey—a special toy or blanket. Not all children do, but if your child develops an attachment to a particular object, be sure to take it with you when you travel. Be aware that if your child has a lovey, it is not a replacement for Mom or Dad's attention when she is crying, upset, or unhappy. Although the lovey will comfort your child, there is no substitute for a parent's support and love. She will learn to self-soothe when she is ready, but when she's telling you through her actions that she needs *you*, please believe her and go to her. You do her more good by comforting her when she needs you than by trying to get her to comfort herself before she is developmentally ready to do so.

When your child gets angry, she will cry intensely. **Her feelings are sometimes overwhelming, and she doesn't know how to handle them. Frustration can very easily lead to meltdowns or tantrums.** These are highly emotional states. Your child is experiencing an overload of emotion, and she's lost control. It can be very scary for her, and embarrassing for you if you're out and about.

Your child needs your understanding and support when he's overwhelmed with emotions and melting down or tantruming. Stay with him. Stay calm. Be a safe presence he can bring himself back to as he starts to regain control.

The best thing you can do for your child is be there for her, supporting her through her emotional turmoil. Look at her with your heart, not through the eyes of strangers passing by. Try not to worry about what other people are thinking of you and your parenting skills. They do not know your child or what she's going through. Only you do. We know it's hard to ignore the pressure you feel from strangers when your child has a meltdown in public, but you can help by reminding yourself that your child is far more important than what strangers think of you. It is more important that your child feel loved, supported, and understood. (And you may be surprised when someone congratulates you on handling the situation so calmly!) It is about what is best for your child.

At this age, your child will be likely to say "hi" and "bye" to people on the street or in stores. Although she may be experimenting with her extroverted side, she can still act shy with strangers when they approach. She will hold on to you more tightly at first, but her inquisitive nature will have her exploring new people as soon as she feels secure in doing so. Allow her to venture out in her own time.

Activities to Enhance Your Child's Emotional and Social Development

- Get out of the house! Take your child to bookstores and museums. Run errands. Do normal everyday stuff that involves interacting with people to model for your child how it's done and to give her the opportunity to try it herself if she wants to in her own time. She will start to interact with people of all ages when she's ready.

- Make playdates and be part of a playgroup. Give your child lots of chances to learn cooperative play. Remember, though, that it's a learning process that takes time.

TIP

Support Your Child with Your Loving Presence

Stay in physical contact when your child is having a meltdown or tantrum, if she will let you. If she doesn't want to be held or touched, don't force it, and don't take offense. Just stay close so she knows you are there and that you love her. You don't have to talk (she may not hear you anyway). You can simply offer your quiet love and attention to help guide her back to emotional equilibrium.

- Arrange to play with children of a wide range of ages (which is one of the many benefits of a playgroup). Offer your child opportunities to interact with adults of various ages as well. The idea is to teach her to feel comfortable around people of any age.

- Play games such as kicking or rolling a ball back and forth. Games help your child learn about taking turns.

- Help your child recognize her emotions by naming them. She can easily be overwhelmed by anger, fear, or sadness. Giving her names for her feelings makes them less scary.

- Give your toddler dolls, stuffed animals, toy telephones, and make-believe play materials such as scarves and hats, old clothes and shoes for fashioning costumes and props, and blankets for building forts. Make homemade puppets out of paper bags decorated with markers, paper, and glue, or out of socks decorated with buttons, yarn, and thread. Have the puppets hold a conversation with each other or with you or her. Put on a puppet show.

- Create an alone spot for your child, where she can hide when she wants to, such as a large cardboard box or a closet with pillows on the floor. (This is *not* a time-out spot.)

18–24 months

POSITIVELY PARENTING

Say "Yes!" for a Happier Household

When a child wants to do something that's potentially messy or inconvenient, parents frequently respond with an automatic "No." "No, you can't put on your own boots, we are in a hurry." "No, you can't play in the sink, you'll get water everywhere."

Can you imagine how frustrating that must be for a child to be told "no" over and over again? Can you imagine how it's possible that she feels as if she never gets to do anything she wants to? Can you imagine how you would feel if someone said "no" every time you wanted to do something?

Think about it for a minute. Do you really care whether your child wears blue socks instead of white socks to church? Does it really matter that much? How messy is a nest made of pillows or blankets? How disastrous is it if you are five minutes late because she is deeply involved in playing with her dolls?

We are big believers in the power of "Yes!" **Saying "yes" as often as you can (and that probably means a lot more often than you're doing right now) benefits both you and your child.** Yes, you'll have to wipe up the water in the bathroom when she's done playing in the sink, but that's better than wiping your child's tears after the meltdown when she is told "no" for the hundredth time today. And, hey, she'll actually love helping you wipe up the

water, so hand her a towel, too! She'll also learn a valuable lesson that when you've made a mess, you clean it up. We'd be willing to bet it won't be long before she's grabbing the towel to wipe up spilled water before you even realize she's done playing. In fact, it will become a part of her play.

If you can say "Yes," do it. When your child wants to do something and you feel that immediate "no" bubbling up, pause, count to three, and think about whether it really matters. Will it hurt anyone or damage anything? Is it dangerous or might it set a bad precedent? If the answer is no, then say "Yes!" If what she wants to do will cause a mess, can you say "yes" but make it less of a hassle for you? For example, if she wants to paint, can she do it outside? If she wants to play in the sink, can you take a big bowl of water into the bathtub with some wooden spoons, cups, and bowls for her to play with? If she wants to jump on the couch, but you really don't want her to (setting a bad precedent), is there somewhere else that she *can* jump? Perhaps on a mattress on the floor? Be creative when you try to meet her wants and needs.

Making sure your child is well fed with plenty of healthy foods also makes for a happier child who won't grump, tantrum, or melt down due to hunger. Whenever your child seems particularly prone to meltdowns consider whether she might be hungry.

How to Say "No" Effectively and with Empathy

When your child wants something and you feel you must say "no," you can soften the blow by empathizing with your child and offering an alternative. If she wants grape juice, but you don't have any in the house, simply saying "Nope, we don't have any" will not bring the asking to an end, and it may even result in a meltdown or tantrum. One approach that can help children through a disappointment without melting down is to say, "Oh, I wish we had grape juice because I know you *really* want some. We'll get some when we go to the store next time. Would you like some apple juice?"

Empathizing helps the child feel heard, and it gives her the sense that you understand her want or need and wish you could fulfill it but can't at that moment. "I wish we could go to Joshua's house, but he's not home right now. Why don't we call later to make a playdate?" "I wish we could go to the playground, but we don't have time today. Let's go to the playground tomorrow."

Of course, there will be times when your convenience comes first. If you're throwing a party, you're not going to want your child to make a fort in the living room that you just finished straightening, now that every pillow and piece of furniture is in place. But if she hears "yes" most of the time, when you need to say "no" and explain why, she'll be okay with it. If there's a safety issue involved, then absolutely say "no," explain why, and don't budge. Safety is always critical and nonnegotiable. She has to be buckled into her car seat, she has to hold your hand in the parking lot, and she may not hurt another person. You might give safety rules their own name—maybe they're known as Big Rules—and your child will learn that they're nonnegotiable because there are never any exceptions.

Saying "yes" as much as you can has many important benefits. You are encouraging your child's development by letting her explore and be independent. That's an incredible gift. Also, because she is hearing "no" less frequently and will feel frustrated less often, there will be fewer tantrums. (That's a gift for both of you!) And you will be setting clear boundaries. When your "no" is thoughtful and truly means no, your child will learn that it is futile to argue. Children can sense when we are firm with our decisions and when we are wishy-washy. The clearer you are on the reasons behind each decision, the less resistance you will run into from your toddler.

Encourage Independence, Even If It Drives You Crazy!

Most parents have heard the unfortunate term the "Terrible Twos," an age that some experts claim is a time of negativity and temper tantrums, resulting in friction between children and parents. In our opinion, the Terrible Twos are misnamed. Toddlers are not terrible! They are incredibly cute and fun; they can also frustrate the heck out of you occasionally, but they are not terrible. **It would be far more appropriate and accurate to call this developmental stage the Independent One-and-a-Halfs.**

Your child wants to do so many things by herself—including things she may not have the skill for yet. Allow her the opportunity to try things on her own while staying close by to keep her safe, and help her when she asks for your help.

This age is about a child's growing independence, not her quest to frustrate you. Your toddler is not waking up in the morning thinking of ways to try your patience. She is merely going through an appropriate developmental stage. Her new physical and cognitive skills allow her to explore her surroundings more. She is learning about the world and trying to figure out how she fits in. She was doing this before, but her explorations were limited. She couldn't reach the books on the bookshelf, so she contented herself with playing with her toes. At the most basic level, your child is trying to find the patterns of daily life so she knows what to expect. Children crave consistency, and this exploration stage allows them to learn the rules that govern their lives.

This desire for independence can be incredibly trying for parents. It takes extra time and slows down the rhythm of the day. At the very least, you can help yourself by scheduling an extra fifteen minutes into everything you do with your child. Try not to live by the clock. If you're late, you're late. Other people who have children will understand.

Allow for a ridiculous amount of time in the morning for you and your child to get ready. If it takes you two hours to get her up, dressed, fed, teeth brushed, and out the door—but it's an enjoyable two hours of calmly getting ready—then go with that. It's much better than trying to cram all of that into sixty minutes of nagging, yelling, whining, and crying. (Not to mention that it's stressful for both of you and a really unpleasant way to start the day.)

18–24
months

Second, and more important, you can change how you view your child's actions. Put a positive spin on it. She's learning! It takes time to learn new skills. No one learned to play the piano in a week (or even a month!). And yet we sometimes expect children to "get it" more quickly than they can. The way for your child to learn new skills is to practice them over and over again, doing it her way in her own time.

Remember that independence waxes and wanes, sometimes over the course of hours or even minutes. The child who wants you to leave her alone while stacking blocks might be pulling on your arm minutes later, demanding that you play with her. Some days she will firmly tell you, "Bye-bye now, Daddy!" when you drop her off at day care, but other days she is clinging to your leg as you try to leave.

This phenomenon is called *rapprochement*, which is French for "a bringing together or reconciliation." **Developmentally, children need to explore and try new things. They need to test their independence. At the same time, they need a safe home base to come back to in order to recharge their batteries.** You'll see this in action when your child wanders over to a new situation but looks over her shoulder back at you before diving in. A few minutes later, she might come back to you for a hug or to sit in your lap for a few seconds before returning to play again.

For Fewer Tantrums Figure Out Which Triggers Set Off Your Toddler

Temper tantrums can be very challenging for both you and your child. They can be caused by her inability to clearly communicate what she wants or needs, or the fact that waiting is really hard for her at this age. She may want to show you the butterfly outside the window and doesn't understand why you keep cooking dinner at such an important and urgent moment. She doesn't know that you will come over and look at the butterfly in five minutes. That's such a long time away! She cannot see into the future and know—as you can—that you will look at the butterfly very soon.

Don't Make Your Child Share at This Age

Your child does not understand that when she shares a toy, she will eventually get it back. Consequently, it's unfair to force her to share right now. You can encourage sharing by modeling it and giving specific praise on those rare occasions when she willingly shares a toy. (Instead of "Good sharing!" or "Good job!" say something like "Thank you! You've made your sister so happy by sharing your toy with her. You can have it back when she's done.") Read the section on specific praise in chapter 7's Positively Parenting on page 202.

18-24
months

Wait until your child is calm again before talking to her about inappropriate behavior. She's more likely to hear and understand you if she's over her own emotional turmoil. Tell her specifically what she can do next time to do better.

Tantrums can happen when your child is overwhelmed by her feelings. She might be angry that her toy was taken away and frightened by your tone of voice when you insisted that she share. **Or tantrums can occur simply because your toddler is hungry, tired, or overstimulated.**

If your child hurts someone during her tantrum, wait until she is calm again before gently explaining to her that it's never okay to do that. Validate her feelings. **Look at your own actions to see whether perhaps something you did, how you treated your child, may have pushed her into a tantrum.** When we treat our children unfairly, when we overreact to something, or simply react poorly, they take their cues from us. How you treat your child directly relates to how she will respond to you. If your reaction is inappropriate, she'll respond in a way that matches your reaction. Study your interactions with her, and you'll see what a great impact your behavior has on her behavior.

Handle Hitting, Pushing, and Biting in a Calm and Gentle Manner

The best way to put a stop to hitting, pushing, and biting, and related acts of aggression, is to handle them calmly and gently. If you give a big, loud reaction, you are unintentionally reinforcing the behavior, encouraging your child to do it again and again. What you focus on is what you will get from your child. So if you gently say to her, "Touch gently. We don't hit," while gently stroking her cheek or touching her victim gently to model how to do it, she'll touch him gently as well. She'll learn in that instant that the way to touch someone is gently. **Focus on what she *can* do; focus on the behavior you want.** She's sure to slip up and hit, push, or bite again when she's overwhelmed and upset, but she'll learn.

Remember that gentleness begets gentleness. Model the behavior you want to see in your little one. Hitting (including spanking) a child is never okay, and it models the wrong behavior—aggression—for her.

When it comes to tantrums, the best defense is a great offense. In other words, do your best to prevent them. Pay attention to what triggers your child's tantrums. Do they happen most often when she's tired or hungry? Then make a concerted effort to give her plenty of rest at night and during the day. Make sure she snacks often to keep her body feeling good. Pay attention to her cues and replenish her batteries frequently. Are there certain places where she tends to melt down? A particular time of day? Does it happen when she plays with a certain friend? Are you saying "yes" to her enough? Are you saying "no" too robotically and too often? Is she feeling frustrated, as if she has no control over any aspect of her world?

When your child is tantruming, stay with her and try your best to be a calm, supportive presence. She needs you. She may feel scared or out of control. Her whole system has become overrun with intense emotions. Hold her, if she'll let you; if not, simply stay nearby. Your acceptance of her feelings and loving support will help her through it. Comfort her when she's calm again. Make sure that she knows you love her no matter what.

Well-Child Checks and Vaccines

An easy way to remember to schedule your child's annual well-child checkup is to do it each year around her birthday. She will continue to be weighed and measured, with those numbers plotted on her growth curves. Your doctor will go over her growth and development, examine her physically, and answer any questions you may have. If you've been following the recommended schedule, there are no vaccines at the two-year-old checkup, but your physician will recommend that your child receive the flu vaccine every year at the start of winter's flu season. You can find out where to go to find the current list of recommended vaccines by turning to the Resources and Recommended Reading section on page 296.

Tantrums are no fun for your child, just as they are no fun for you. But your child is genuinely upset and emotionally overwhelmed when in a tantrum—which can be scary for him. Treat him with kindness. Comfort him as you would an upset friend.

Health and Safety Tips

If your water supply lacks fluoride, your doctor or dentist can give you a prescription for fluoride supplements in either drop or pill form.

Keep your child out of the sun as much as possible. Sunburns suffered during childhood are a leading cause of skin cancer in adults. If you are going to be in the sun, remember to dress your child in sun-protective hats and clothing, put sunscreen on any exposed skin, and limit your exposure to times when the sun isn't at its hottest (the middle of the day).

Your child still needs to be in a car seat with five-point restraints until she weighs at least 40 pounds (18 kg), probably around age four.

Remember to review the basic ongoing safety precautions. Keep medications and unsafe home and garden products out of your child's reach. Check smoke detectors' batteries twice a year when the clocks change in the spring and the fall. Change your smoke detectors when they expire, usually every ten years. Install a carbon monoxide detector if you have a woodstove or fireplace. Keep the poison control phone number prominently posted near every phone in your house and programmed into your cell phones and handheld electronic gadgets. (Your local poison control number is listed in the Resources and Recommended Reading section on page 296.) Don't store guns in your home; if you must store them, keep them locked up, with the ammunition locked in a separate location.

18–24
months

7

Learning (and Moving) at Lightning Speed

Your child is dashing into full-fledged kid-dom from the ages of two to three. He's a little kid, now! He may have lost his essence of babyhood, but he is still very dependent on you for most things. And he still needs your arms to comfort him just like he always has. He's learning (and moving) at lightning speed—saying every word he hears, trying it out in his mouth. He's climbing, exploring, and running even faster than before. (Is that even possible?) He's into everything and needs your constant supervision to keep him safe. He plays hard and crashes even harder at the end of the day. He's your own little wonderful whirlwind!

As you read through this chapter on the general development of two- to three-year-olds, remember that each child is unique. His development happens at his own pace, and though you can certainly create environments and opportunities to enhance his development, you cannot actually speed it up. He'll do things when he's ready to do them. Your child may be right on target with the information we present here, or he may be ahead of or behind it. If you are concerned about your child's development, please speak with your family physician or pediatrician. But remember that children will develop in their own time. Relax and enjoy your child's journey through childhood!

DEVELOPING BODY

Your Baby Is a Little Kid!

By age two, your baby no longer looks like a baby; he now looks like a little kid. He's also acting like a little kid; he's starting to dress and undress himself. He can wipe his nose with a tissue, he'll wash and dry his own hands without help, and he may even show interest in learning to use a toilet this year. (Don't fret if it doesn't happen until next year; many, many children learn after age three. For more on toilet learning, see Positively Parenting on page 232 in chapter 8.)

Your child has a full set of teeth by now, or he will be getting those last molars in very soon. This is a good time to schedule your child's first visit with a family dentist. Most dentists will get a child this age in the chair, count his teeth, take a quick look, and send you all happily on your way. It's a quick introduction and a great way to transition into getting regular dental checkups. Good dental health is important for whole body health, and getting your child into a routine of taking good care of his teeth from an early age is very beneficial. It may save him from unpleasant dental visits down the road.

Your baby really looks like a little kid now. She's longer and leaner, walking steadily, and running every chance she gets. She's learning to do so much for herself, working toward independence.

Your Child's Physical Development Grows with a Variety of Play

Your child is now walking on his own very steadily. He may even be experimenting with walking backward! He loves to pull something along behind him or carry something in his hands when he's walking around. He can walk up and down the stairs while holding on to a railing or someone's hand. He can also stand on tiptoe (and may do so to reach some desired, forbidden item on the kitchen counter), and he can bend over to pick something up without toppling onto his head. That's a pretty nifty skill.

This is a child who needs lots of opportunities for large motor play inside and out. He loves to roll, crawl, walk, jump, run, and climb. You'll start to see him crawl around pretending to be a dog or cat or some other animal, as he growls, barks, or meows. At two, he may fall often when he runs, but that will stop as the year progresses and he becomes more and more sure on his feet.

Your child will climb anything and everything; he can get on and off the furniture completely on his own. He can also get himself stuck with his penchant for climbing. Don't be surprised to find him on a perch from which he can't get down with arms outstretched, saying, "Mama, get!" Give him plenty of safe climbing opportunities—in the backyard or at a playground. It may help to keep his feet on the ground at home.

Your child likes to push and pull things, fill things up, and dump them out. He can catch a rolled ball, but he probably can't catch a thrown ball yet. He can, however, kick, throw, and roll balls himself. In fact, he will love to play with balls any chance he can. It's great for hand-eye coordination and large motor development overall.

Children this age love to climb! Take your child to the playground or get outside if you have a play structure in your yard to give her lots of time to climb at least several times a week, if not daily.

2–3
years

Your child will dance whenever he hears music, especially familiar tunes, and may even sing along! He will love to imitate the dance moves of others. Play music and dance with your child on a daily basis. It will encourage his physical coordination while instilling a love of music. Don't be limited to kids' music; instead, play music that you like, whether that's the B-52s, Frank Sinatra, Mozart, or all three!

Did we mention how much children this age love to climb? If your child is still in a crib and regularly climbing out of it, that's a sign that it's time for a big kid bed—for his safety and your peace of mind.

Your Child Loves to Use His Hands

You may see your child "reading" by now, looking through a book by himself and turning the pages one by one. If he's been read to frequently, he already loves books; keep reading to him every day to ensure that his love grows as he does. Choose books with bright illustrations, rhyming text, and a sentence or two on each page. Use the public library as a resource for finding an assortment of books. Look for titles that focus on an area of interest your child is developing. If he's fascinated with birds, horses, or tractors, for example, collect books on those subjects.

Your child is starting to scribble with pencils, crayons, markers—whatever he can get his hands on. (He still needs a reminder to "only draw on the paper.") He may show a preference for one hand in his scribbling, as well as in feeding himself and in his play, using one hand more often than the other. He is feeding himself with a spoon or fork, a skill he's still working to master. Yes, he's a messy eater, but keep in mind that he's neater than he used to be! And he'll be a pro by the end of this year.

Your child is a very tactile person; he explores things by smelling, touching, and tasting them. (Yup, he's still putting things in his mouth, but it will go away this year. Really.) He loves to shake maracas, bang on drums (or anything he can find to bang on), and basically make a lot of noise! He's enthralled by the different sounds he can make using anything from musical instruments to ordinary household items. He likes finger play songs such as the "Itsy Bitsy Spider," "Wheels on the Bus," or "Head, Shoulders, Knees, and Toes."

Making noise—especially banging on things—is a child's greatest delight some days. (Okay, most days.) For a happy child, find things he can bang on whether it be real drums, an empty popcorn tin, or an oatmeal container.

Much to your chagrin, your child loves to pour out the contents of any container, be it his water cup or his bowl of crackers. It doesn't happen *every time* he has a drink or snack, but some days it feels like it does. This maddening tendency to spill whatever is in his hands won't last forever, and it does have educational value. He's learning cause and effect and refining his knowledge of gravity. He'll grow out of it, so try to take it in stride. Don't make a big deal over it, or he might prolong his experiments, noting the cause and effect value it has with you as well. (Wow, when I pour my drink on the floor, Mom gets really red in the face and yells. I wonder if she'll do that again. Let's find out! Wow! She did it again! Cool! What about if I do it one more time?) Do remind him that his cup of milk/water/juice is for drinking, not for spilling on the floor. The same goes for his bowl of snacks. He'll learn. Eventually.

Besides pouring his drinks and snacks on the floor, he can also turn handles to open doors, open cabinets and drawers, and screw and unscrew lids in a single bound. So let's talk about safety for a moment. If your child can open doors, he could potentially let himself outside without your knowledge. (But he can't maneuver the locks on doors yet, right? Maybe not, but he will soon. Harry Houdini had nothing on a two-year-old who wants to find out what is on the other side of the door.) **You will need to be more aware of his location in the house at all times, and you may want to consider adding another lock to your outside doors that is placed out of his reach.** Read more about this at the end of this chapter in Positively Parenting on page 201.

When your child is not letting himself out the door, he may be found building towers with blocks. He can stack at least four blocks now. He'll still delight in knocking them over; that may be the only *real* reason to build a tower at this age. He loves to play with clay or play dough, too, rolling it out and pounding, pulling, and squeezing it. It's great for his hand dexterity and strength.

2-3
years

Activities to Enhance Your Child's Physical Development

Keep activities enjoyable for everyone. If your child doesn't want to do something, don't push him simply because you think it will benefit his physical development. If he's having fun, if it feels like play, then he'll want to do it. If it's not fun, or if he just doesn't like a particular activity, drop it, and don't worry. He will still gain whatever developmental skills are involved—just in another way. There are so many different things you can do with your child to help enhance his development.

If your child is especially talented at unlocking and opening doors, consider placing a lock out of reach at the top of any door leading outside to keep him safe.

Activities for Large Motor Skills Development

- Ensure that your child gets at least an hour of physical activity most days.

- Go to playgrounds, where your child can develop large motor skills such as running, jumping, climbing, and balancing. Challenge your child to go up and down the slides.

- Throw and kick balls together. Teach your child how to catch a ball and play catch with small and large balls.

- Show your child how to hop, jump, and walk on tiptoe.

- Help your child learn to pedal a tricycle by showing him how to press down with his feet one at a time on the pedals.

- Place a small stepping stool in the bathroom for your child to step on to reach the sink so he can wash his hands.

- Save large boxes for your child to use. Cut out windows and doors. He'll get a kick out of crawling into and out of the boxes and turning them into hiding places.

- Give your child push or pull toys. He'll love pushing around large cars and trucks and other push toys. He'll also redecorate for you by moving some of your furniture around.

Playgrounds are the best places to go for lots of large motor skill practice. Kids this age need to be outside climbing, running, jumping, and sliding. Try to make outside play a part of your daily routine.

- Have ride-on toys for your child to use, such as little cars that are child-powered with feet on the ground, tricycles, or rocking horses.

- Have a wagon for your child to pull around the yard so he can put items in and take them out. He can even help clean up the yard at the end of the day! Load up the wagon with what needs to be put away, and he can pull it to where things will go for the night.

- Play soccer! Kick balls back and forth in your yard, the park, or a playground to enhance your child's coordination.

- Enlist your child's help with doing simple housework like vacuuming, picking up toys, and putting clothes into the washing machine or laundry baskets.

- Find child-size tools (gardening trowel, snow shovel, broom, etc.) so he can help you while learning how to use tools that are appropriate for his size.

- Hammer golf tees into Styrofoam. Collect big blocks of Styrofoam when you buy large appliances or computers and buy a box of golf tees. Find some soft mallets and let your child hammer the tees into the Styrofoam. It's fun and safe, though you should supervise him during this activity to be sure he doesn't put a golf tee in his mouth.

2–3
years

Activities for Fine Motor Skills Development

- Encourage your child to play with nesting blocks or cups that stack.

- Have an array of simple puzzles to work with.

- Set up a small table and chairs that can serve as your child's headquarters for eating, playing, and drawing. Include play dishes and pots for him to pretend with.

- Sing and do hand movements to the "Itsy Bitsy Spider," "Wheels on the Bus," and "Head, Shoulders, Knees, and Toes."

- Improve your child's hand-eye coordination by building with blocks, stringing beads, doing puzzles, using scissors, drawing, spreading butter or jam on bread, and pouring from a small pitcher into cups.

- Blow bubbles with your child.

- Develop strength, control, and dexterity by using scissors, squeezing water out of a washcloth or squeezing balls or soft bath toys, and drawing with large crayons.

- Have blunt scissors, paper, markers, stickers, and large crayons available for your child. Keep them on a shelf that is close enough so he can reach whatever art supplies he needs without asking for help. He'll also like to use his hands to work with play dough, clay, and paints (finger paints or washable watercolors and acrylics with brushes).

- Thread large beads or buttons onto shoelaces.

- Pour sand or water from container to container. Have several small containers for your child to use. Water play can be done outside or in the bath.

- Build structures using large blocks with your child and allow him the time to build alone.

- Draw with your child.

- Ask for your child's help when putting napkins on the table, placing utensils next to the plates, or carrying a bottle of syrup or ketchup to the table.

- Give your child the opportunity to put his clean clothes into his drawers. He loves to help!

DEVELOPING MIND

Your Child Is Coming into His Own

Your two- to three-year-old is referring to himself by name, and he's using the words *me* and *mine* to express his desires. He knows what he wants at this age; he has his own very strong preferences. (You've no doubt noticed this by now.) He'll make choices based on those preferences regardless of your suggestions or what you would like him to choose. And that's as it should be. He's learning to follow his own path—a quality you will certainly value when he hits the teen years and beyond and must deal with peer pressure.

Your child's increased cognitive and physical growth means he can participate in more activities, such as climbing at the playground, looking through books, and basically getting into everything. He's trouble at this age! (But so darn cute... which definitely works to his advantage.) He is

Your child's sense of humor is beginning to sprout at this age. He'll find physical humor hysterical, as well as verbal humor, like silly mislabeling, such as asking if his name is "Dad" or telling him "a dog says quack."

2-3
years

beginning to understand rules and will know when he has broken them. He will continue to break them periodically—doing so knowingly and looking right at you—as part of his quest for independence. It's totally natural, even if it's undesirable behavior. Keep reminding him of the rules, explaining why he cannot do what he is doing and giving him an alternative that he can do.

With your child's growing sense of how things are, he may become upset when something is not as it should be. He may not like someone else wearing his hat or Daddy's hat. Along the same lines, though, he will laugh when you suggest things are something they are not. Try telling him that "a cow says meow," and he'll almost fall over laughing. (Hello, sense of humor!) Take hold of his foot and call it an elbow, and he'll laugh a "No!" at you. Silly mislabeling is a great game to play with him now and for years to come.

Your Child Loves to Learn and Problem Solve

He is better able to focus on a task now, especially an activity that he likes to do over and over again, such as reading a favorite book, rolling a ball back and forth with a parent or sibling, or stacking and knocking down blocks. This is timely because he's also at the stage where he wants to learn how to use things. He wants to do it himself, and he wants you to show him how so *he* can do it. Once he learns how to do something new, he will practice that skill many times until he has it mastered. Being his own person, he likes to be the one choosing which tasks he works on.

A new tactic in your child's problem-solving skills is trial and error. He's getting more creative in trying several different ways to solve a problem, rather than simply repeating the same approach over and over again as he used to. He now understands that things don't simply disappear, and he can find objects you've hidden under several layers of blankets. He'll keep looking until he finds them! That's his problem solving and persistence paying off.

And your child loves to solve problems just as much as he loves to explore his environment. Your child is a scientist at heart, searching for the answer, the truth. **As the year progresses, he may start to ask "why," "how," and "what" questions about the things he sees, hears, and experiences. He is filing a great amount of information into his brain, for immediate and future use.**

Your Child's Creativity Grows

By the time your child is two, he may begin to identify colors. During this year, he will also start categorizing objects, giving them labels such as big, small, soft, and hard. He will probably even begin to sort items by shape and color.

Speaking of color, your child's drawings will become more deliberate over the coming year, and he will begin to draw things that are more recognizable. He'll be drawing circles, and possibly faces, by the time he's three. His creative flair also extends to the beginnings of pretend play this year.

Make-Believe Play Helps Your Child Learn and Process Emotions

Your child is starting a journey into make-believe that is incredibly important to his development. Make-believe play encourages creative thinking and expression, problem solving, and empathy, and it helps your child conquer his fears. He can work through any strong emotions in a safe, controlled environment called make-believe. He can face scary monsters and realize they are not so scary. He can work through an injustice and heal from the hurt it caused. He can pretend to be the powerful one to balance out his feelings of powerlessness as a child in an adult world.

To illustrate just how important make-believe play is, consider the following example. A mother was trying to involve her two-year-old daughter in her new brother's care and asked if she would help by throwing a dirty diaper into the garbage can, which she did in a cooperative manner. Later in the day, the mother noticed her daughter throwing her stuffed animals, dolls, and old baby clothes into the garbage can. She couldn't articulate to her mother that she was scared that her baby brother was going to replace her and that she wished that the baby could be thrown out of the family, but her actions spoke louder than any words she could have used.

Make-believe play is not always so psychologically revealing. Most of the time it is just good fun: turning chairs into a train or a couch into a boat. The pillows on the floor may become islands of safety as your child walks through a field of hot lava. And the big box that held the new refrigerator can become a tree house, an ice cream shop, or a cave.

Some children engage in a special kind of make-believe play that involves having an invisible friend. Many, if not most, children develop one or more invisible friends during the first several years of their lives. Invisible friends are wonderful ways for children to test out new roles of interaction. Your quiet child who is a follower with his day care friends can be a leader with his invisible friend. The invisible friend can also be a resource for your child. When asked why he wants to stay up late, your child might say, "Anna's mom let's me stay up late when I'm sleeping over at Anna's house!" Some invisible friends may even come on vacation with your family.

2–3
years

Your child's creativity is starting to blossom now as she learns to identify colors, gets more deliberate in her drawings, and ventures into the magical world of make-believe play.

How can you encourage make-believe play? Turn off the TV and computer and put aside the battery-operated toys. Get out blankets and make a fort in the living room. Build with blocks. Draw on blank paper rather than coloring books. Go outside and explore. Pretend to be animals. Act silly. Let your child lead you into his pretend worlds.

Most important, make sure your child has plenty of unstructured time to play, to be, to create.

Every day, if you can. Your child does not need to be entertained all hours of the day. He does not need to be scheduled into activities constantly. What he does need is time to just be a child and imagine himself as something or someone other than what and who he is. Give him the freedom and space to explore his thoughts and possibilities, to face and triumph over his demons, to feel powerful, to feed his creative mind, to grow.

TIP — Let Your Child Do Nothing

Your child needs downtime just like you do—time to just *be* and let his imagination take over. A child who is continually entertained—either through a tight schedule of planned activities, by television, computer games, light-up noisy toys, or a parent or caregiver who is overzealous in his or her quest to keep the child engaged—is a child who will grow up always needing to be entertained by some external source. He will grow into an adult who will need constant stimulation and entertainment from someone or something else. There is great value in "doing nothing," in having blocks of unscheduled time in which to imagine, dream, and create.

Activities to Enhance Your Child's Cognitive Development

- Do simple puzzles together, and allow him to do them without your help.

- Play with shape sorters with your child. Name the shapes and colors of the pieces every time you play.

- Ask your child to identify noises he hears: birds, an airplane, cars honking, etc.

- Create a rhyming treasure hunt with simple clues, such as "Where do you laugh and laugh and laugh, When Daddy pours water on you? (The bath!)"

- Give your child choices as often as you can: "Would you like grape or apple juice?" "Do you want to wear your blue or green pants?" "Shall we read *Click, Clack, Moo* or *Fix-it Duck*?"

- Sing the alphabet song, and read ABC books.

- Practice numbers and counting. Read counting books. Count how many pretzels are in the bowl. Count the number of bananas in a bunch. Count the number of bugs in a picture.

- Talk about shapes, colors, and numbers all day long. "That orange box is a square." "We have only one yellow lemon left." "Let's find your blue sweater."

- Read to your child! He is learning and filing away so much information in his brain at this age. Read stories or nonfiction books about his favorite subjects, from fire engines to spiders. Go to the library together to pick out books he might enjoy. He will memorize the text of the books you read over and over again.

- Sing songs with your child and listen to music wherever you are. Choose music that you won't mind listening to repeatedly. He'll start to sing along, and you may even be able to identify what he's singing once in a while!

- Encourage make-believe play by filling your child's play space with building blocks, stuffed animals, wooden animals, and make-believe play materials such as hats, old clothes, shoes, blankets for building forts, whatever you can think of. Engage in his make-believe worlds some of the time to learn about how your child thinks and feels. Follow his lead and rules of play; don't try to change it or "fix" it.

- Have a tea party for all the stuffed animals in the house.

- Create a grocery store full of old cereal boxes, plastic fruit, and household supplies. Ask if your child wants to be the cashier or customer—and then switch roles.

DEVELOPING LANGUAGE

Your Child Understands More Words Than He Can Speak

Your two-year-old understands 500 to 700 words. By the time he is two and a half, he'll understand 800 to 900 words and can articulate approximately 570 words. At age two, he says many single words when he speaks, and he utters a few short phrases. When he wants to come with you, he'll say, "Come, too!" By the time he's three, he'll speak in grammatically correct sentences, saying, "Can I come, too?" or "I want to come, too!"

RED FLAG!

If your child does not speak at least fifty words, use two-word sentences, or follow simple instructions, or if he experiences a dramatic loss of skills he previously mastered, be sure to discuss these or any other concerns about his language ability with his doctor at the two-year well-child visit.

2-3 years

Help cultivate your child's creativity by keeping paper, pencils, markers, and crayons within her reach. She may start to write some letters by the end of this year.

Your child's pronunciation will improve throughout the year, although there may be words here and there that need to be "translated" by you and his other caregivers. By the time he's three, his speech will be generally understandable to most adults and other children.

Given the opportunity, your child can learn one to two new words per day. He learns most easily when he hears an adult name an object, and he'll repeat any and every word he overhears, mimicking the speech of adults (including their inflection and tone). When an object is named for him, he can then point to the object or a picture of it: "Where is the brown shoe?" He knows many of his body parts, and he will point to them when asked: "Where is your ear? Where is your other ear? Where is your knee?"

He understands common phrases that he hears frequently, and he recognizes the names of familiar people. Additionally, your child can follow one-step instructions, such as "Put your shoes away, please," and he can understand simple explanations.

Although your child is definitely more verbal than he used to be, he is still not at the point where he can fully express himself, especially when he's upset. He's likely to get frustrated, have meltdowns, and be unable to tell you what's wrong. Try asking him yes-or-no questions and offer names for the emotions he's expressing: "Wow, I can see that you're feeling really mad right now" or "You look so sad."

Your Child Loves to Read and May Start to Write

He is getting to the age where he likes to look at books and will closely examine the illustrations. He really enjoys stories, songs, and nursery rhymes, and he will chime in on words at the end of phrases or sentences in the books and rhymes he knows. He'll even start to sing the songs he knows all on his own. When "reading," he's very likely to point to something in the book and ask, "What's that?" He's also capable of answering that question when asked by an adult who's reading to him.

Although your child can be very talkative, he is unlikely to initiate a conversation with adults other than Mom and Dad. He's still on the shy side, sticking close to his parents, perhaps a little unsure of other adults. He will, however, answer questions more often when asked by other adults, but you may have to answer for him part of the time. Pretty soon, though, he'll be doing it all on his own. So no need to worry or push him to talk when he's not comfortable doing it. When he feels secure and comfortable—when he's ready—he'll do it.

2–3
years

By the end of this year, your child may try to write the first letter of his name. When writing, he will use his whole arm to make the letters rather than using just his hand and wrist. (He'll do the same thing when he draws.) His letters will tend to be very large, and one letter may take up most of a piece of paper. If you've been singing the alphabet song with him, he may be able to sing it solo by the end of the year, but he won't really understand that the letter names correspond to the symbols we use when reading and writing. That'll have to wait until next year.

Activities to Enhance Your Child's Language Development

- Read nonstop to your child! Talk about what you see on the page. Read alphabet books to work on the ABCs.

- Play with alphabet puzzles and magnetic refrigerator letters.

- Speak with your child like he's an intelligent person. (He is!) Find out what he likes and dislikes. Give him your full attention when he talks to you. Listen to him and then respond to show that you understood his words.

- Add details to what your child says. "You're right, that's a bicycle. It's a red and black bicycle. It's so shiny!"

- Use appropriate grammar and pronunciation when you speak to model it for your child. He'll learn to speak (and write) as you do.

- Help expand your child's language abilities by speaking to him in complete sentences. If he asks "More book?" respond by saying, "You want to read another book. Okay, let's read some more." Model correct word order and clear pronunciation.

- Play with a toy telephone. Soon your child will be talking to Grandma and Grandpa on the real phone with a clear "Hello!" and "Bye-bye!"

- Tell stories to your child. Talk about your experiences or tell imaginary stories that have your child(ren) as the character(s). He's likely to ask you to tell those stories over and over again.

- Sing songs with your child and listen to music. Very soon he'll be singing along too!

- Read rhymes and children's poetry to your child.

- Have puppets, dolls, and stuffed animals for your child to play with. Gather make-believe play materials such as old clothes, shoes, floppy hats, and recyclables for creating various costumes and props. Build hide-outs with blankets and chairs. Make hand puppets out of paper bags that your child can decorate with markers, paper, and glue, or out of socks decorated with buttons, yarn, and thread. Show him how the puppets can have a conversation with each other or with you or him. Put on a puppet show.

Building towers with blocks and subsequently knocking them over is still a favored activity for your child. He'll love to knock them over for years. The tricky thing is teaching him not to knock over other's creations.

DEVELOPING PERSON

Your Child Will Imitate Everything

Your little person seems so much more his own *person* at this age. He is really coming into his own, with well-defined likes and dislikes (which he is not shy about sharing with you), and he is much more aware that he's a separate person from you. Socially, he likes to be around other kids. He gets downright excited about it, and he's big into imitating others' behavior, especially parents and caregivers. He likes to help around the house, doing whatever you are doing, and will want to help set the table or clear his place after a meal.

Although your child gets giddy over being around other children, he's still not interacting with them when he plays. He hasn't outgrown the parallel play phase yet where he plays alongside other children without actually playing *with* them. His play may be influenced by a nearby child—he may imitate how that child is playing—so he's definitely paying attention to other kids, but he hasn't quite figured out how to play with them. He will in another year or so.

2–3
years

He likes pretend play. He can imitate everything he sees when he's pretending, and he's likely to pretend to talk on the phone, drive a car, etc. **You'll see a lot of yourself in what he pretends, which can be a wake-up call to change some aspect of how you treat your child.** If he's pretending to do something you do and it's not something you're proud of—especially hearing it come out of his mouth or seeing him doing it—then you have a chance to change what *you* do. You have been given the chance to improve your parenting. Make it better.

Your child is very possessive at this age. He may offer toys to others, but he may not actually mean to give them away. Or if he does give a toy away, he wants it back immediately. That's okay. It's a step toward genuine sharing and taking turns. He's practicing right now, and soon his offers will be authentic. You can encourage him to share by noting aloud how his generosity affects others: "Thank you for letting Sarah play with that train. You made her feel so happy by sharing with her." (Describe what you see in specifics rather than simply using generic praise like "Good sharing!" See the section on praise on page 202.)

There may not be anything more fun for your child than dressing up and pretending to be someone or something else. You can create costumes for your child with things you have around the house like scarves, hats, and old clothes.

Look at Your Child's Defiance and Persistence as Positive Signs of Independence

Your child is showing more independence in that he wants to do *everything* himself. You're going to hear "Me!" or "Me do!" and a lot of "No!" (Read the section on understanding what your toddler's "no" really means on page 162 in chapter 6.) As he grows more independent, he will be more demanding and more persistent when pursuing something he wants to do (regardless of whether you ask him not to do it), and he begins to be defiant. These are all good things. Seriously. These are necessary traits

for a person who will one day be fully independent. Think about these qualities in terms of an adult: demanding (someone who knows what he wants and asks for it), persistent (someone who keeps trying to attain a desired goal until he succeeds), and defiant (someone who knows his own mind, wants to do it his way, and won't simply bow and obey). Does that sound like someone you'd like your child to be when he is all grown up?

Demanding. Persistent. Defiant. These are all parts of becoming independent. We spend so much time and energy worrying about how to help our kids become independent. Articles appear in almost every issue of parenting magazines that discuss how to nurture your child's independence. And yet some of the healthy signs of independence can be taken as undesirable traits in our children. Your child says "No," and suddenly he's being disrespectful or defiant rather than merely exerting his wishes and reaching for independence. Experts write books and articles on how to get your child to obey and how to keep him in line, which works directly *against* our universal parental desire for our children to become independent.

If you can reframe your thinking on this issue, you can see these new traits for what they really are: your child learning to be independent. **Demanding, persistent, and defiant are precisely the traits that we as parents hope our children have when they are faced with peer pressure as teens and later in life as adults.** We want to raise confident, strong, independent people.

TIP · Help Your Child When He Asks for It

Even though your child seems to want to do things all on his own, you'll find that he occasionally asks for your help with things you know he can do himself. A child's striving for independence ebbs and flows, and sometimes he will need to reconnect with you by having your help when he doesn't actually need it. Follow his lead. Reconnect. Feed him if he asks you to, even though he's perfectly capable of feeding himself. He's simply checking in, reaffirming the strength and safety of his home base, and making sure you're still there to love and care for him. He'll go back to doing it by himself when he's ready. (You can expect him to revert back to wanting your help from time to time over the next several years.)

2-3
years

Kisses, hugs, and snuggles are given quite freely to those your child knows well and loves. She'll not only show her love with her actions, but she'll also tell you that she loves you, too, when you express your love for her.

So how do you deal with the inconvenience and (let's be honest) annoyance of having a demanding, persistent, defiant child? To begin with, use different language to describe his behavior. A demanding child is someone who is clear about what he wants. So say that he is communicating clearly. Or you might call a child who is into everything and wreaking havoc "spirited" instead of "mischievous." For more on this topic, read *Raising Your Spirited Child* by Mary Sheedy Kurcinka.

Even more important, try to work *with* your child, not against him. How can both of you get what you want or need? Be creative. Talk to him. Give him a chance to do what he wants, even if you know he can't do it. All he wants is to try. If he can't manage on his own, he'll happily let you do it, but only if you've given him the opportunity to try it first.

On some level, we all want our children to do what we say when we say it. But if you think about it, can you see how blind, unquestioning obedience is unhealthy for your child? A child who does whatever he is told will grow into a teen who does the same (think about the peer pressure to try drugs, have sex, etc.), and then into an adult who may form unhealthy relationships—at work or with friends or lovers—timidly following what another person wants him to do. So, difficult as it will be at times to deal with your child's budding independence, know at heart that it's essential and healthy for his development.

Your Child Is More Affectionate with Loved Ones

At the same time that your child is clarifying what he wants and doesn't want, he is strengthening relationships with familiar adults and children and showing a preference for them when he's around others. He's affectionate and freely doles out kisses and hugs to those he loves. He'll throw himself into your arms when you return home—even if you simply ran out to the store. He's such a little love! He will also comfort other children or adults when they are sad or hurt, patting their backs and hugging them to make them feel better.

Your child needs a lot of support to work through his emotions. He understands emotions better, and he may feel better when you name whatever emotion he's experiencing at a given time. He can also label other people's emotions. "Mama sad," he might say as he pats your back. He gets frustrated really easily and has a hard time regulating his emotions. He gets overwhelmed and may melt down or have a tantrum. Read the section on tantrums starting on page 167 in chapter 6 for ideas on how to help your child through an emotional overload.

You may witness episodes of separation anxiety at the age of two, but it will fade as the year progresses. Your child is shy around strangers and may hide behind your legs or bury his face in your shoulder at the park or grocery store when someone talks to him. In spite of his growing independence, he continues to be very dependent on you. He may look like a little kid, but he's still a baby in so many ways. He looks to you for help and comfort. He comes to you when he is upset or has some sort of conflict. You are the foundation of his world, the foundation upon which he is building his independence.

Your child is still wary of people he doesn't know and will cling to you or hide behind you when an unfamiliar person approaches. Don't force him to be more social if he is not comfortable. He'll get there in his own time.

2-3
years

Kids love to do everything that you do, including tasks as simple as pushing their own grocery cart. (Thank you to whoever came up with the idea to put child-size carts at the grocery store!) Helping you gives them great joy, so let them help whenever they offer.

Activities to Enhance Your Child's Emotional and Social Development

- Socialize with your child. Take him to restaurants and stores or to your office. Interact with people to model how it's done. Being out also gives your child opportunities to practice it himself if he wants to. He will start to interact with people of all ages when he's ready.

- Make playdates and participate in playgroups. Give your child the chance to learn the art of cooperative play on a regular basis. Keep in mind, however, that it is a learning process.

- Surround your child with children of various ages and offer him chances to engage with adults of different ages so he becomes comfortable interacting with people of all ages.

- Play games with your child such as rolling or kicking a ball back and forth, or play catch. Games help your child learn to take turns.

- Have puppets, dolls, stuffed animals, and toy telephones available for your child. Encourage make-believe play by stockpiling materials such as hats, old clothes and scarves, shoes, and recyclables for making costumes and props. Create forts or tents with blankets and furniture.

- Play with puppets, either handmade or store bought. Show your child how the puppets can talk with each other.

- Participate in noncompetitive team activities such as planting a community garden, painting a mural, or building a tree house.

- Give your child words to use when he is upset, angry, or sad. Keep reminding him to express himself with words, not with pushes, hits, or kicks.

- Create an alone spot for your child where he can hide when he wants to, such as a large cardboard box or a closet with pillows on the floor. (This is *not* a time-out spot.)

POSITIVELY PARENTING

Time to Babyproof Again

With your child's expanding abilities, it's time to take a look around your house and see how you can make it safer. Your child is taller now and can probably reach most things on the kitchen counter. He's opening drawers, cupboards, and doors. He may be able to unlock safety gates, and he certainly can lock and unlock (and open) your front door. He is climbing on anything he can and will push a chair into position to reach something on a high, previously out-of-reach shelf. He's into everything! He wants to see, touch, and explore!

How can you keep your natural scientist safe? Put all medicine and anything containing toxic chemicals in locked cabinets. Keep your kitchen counters clear of anything sharp and potentially dangerous, such as knives and scissors. Install a chain lock high (adult eye-level or higher) on the front door of your house (and any doors leading outside or into your garage—anywhere you don't want your two-year-old venturing on his own). Keep breakables safe in boxes. Continue to use plug protectors in every electrical outlet. Most important, always know where your child is; supervise him constantly. That doesn't mean you should be playing with him or entertaining him nonstop; it does mean that you should always know where he is and what he is doing. You can certainly be in different rooms; just check on him regularly.

TIP Hold on to the House Keys

If your two-year-old is able to lock and unlock doors, it's essential that you take your keys with you every time you step outside—even for a two-second excursion to bring out the garbage. He may unintentionally lock you out of the house and not understand how to unlock the door to let you back in. Being separated by a locked door can be traumatic and scary for both of you.

Your child is getting taller and may be able to reach hot pans on the stovetop now. Remind him that the stove is hot and it's not safe to reach for pans on the stove. Remember to turn pot handles in so they are not sticking out and tempting little hands to touch them.

2–3
years

Another way to keep your child safe is to make sure he gets lots of outdoor playtime. If he does all the climbing he needs and wants to do in a safe place, such as the playground or backyard, he's apt to do less of it inside your house. Continue to keep your home a "yes" environment. If you find yourself saying "No!" to certain things, remove them for now, thereby removing the temptation.

TIP   ## Switch to Natural Cleaning Products

Consider getting rid of household cleaning products that contain toxic chemicals (dispose of them properly, please!) and switching to products made from natural ingredients. Substances such as vinegar, baking soda, and borax are highly effective cleaning and disinfecting agents and won't expose your family to harmful chemicals. For information on how to clean your home naturally, there are several books on the subject as well as plenty of resources on the Internet. Making the switch makes for a safer house (no chemicals for your child to ingest accidentally) and a safer environment for your child (no exposure to chemical residue by breathing in vapors or ingesting them during exploration and play).

Too Much Praise Can Be a Bad Thing

We believe in the power of the positive in helping children grow into self-assured, independent people. As a related matter, we want to discuss the issue of praise. **Praise has a central place in parenting, but overpraise can lead to problems.** Using praise to recognize something your child has accomplished is important, but using praise in response to everything your child does makes it meaningless to your child. Let's talk about specific examples.

Praise has become such a popular tool that it's become generic, making it less authentic and diminishing its meaning for a child. Imagine saying "Good job!" when a child eats his lunch or gets up after falling over or turns the page of a book. Should he really be praised for those actions? Are they so impressive that they deserve distinction? Probably not, but many of us fall into the habit of praising virtually everything our children do.

You may be thinking, why is that bad? Isn't it good to praise our children? Aren't we encouraging their continued good and appropriate behavior by praising them? Not really. When you overpraise, you are actually undermining the power of praise and stripping it of meaning for your child. When your child gets the same "Good job!" for using a fork that he gets for building a teetering tower of seven blocks after many failed attempts, the authentic praise (for erecting the tower) is lost on him. He'll grow to disbelieve the praise if he is praised for inconsequential deeds.

And he'll also become a praise junkie, needing more and more praise and recognition for everything he does, even if that praise has become meaningless for him. He'll need more of it in the hopes that it will eventually ring true. But it will never ring true if he's been overpraised. Excessive or misplaced praise also makes him not value his own deeds; instead, he will be dependent on others' approval and praise to feel good about himself and his accomplishments. He'll not know whether his drawing is any good until you or a teacher tell him it is. Wouldn't it be better for him to be able to consider his work and actions and inherently know their value? If he depends on others for praise—and to validate his abilities—he won't develop a sense of his self-worth.

Don't panic. **You can still praise your child, but it's best to do it is by using** *specific praise.* So, if you've been responding with a near-automatic "Good job!" for a while, it'll take concerted effort to change your ways. And once you become aware of just how often you say "Good job!" you may realize how silly and unnecessary it is in many circumstances.

To shift from overpraising your child to offering specific praise, here's what you do. Praise your child when you feel genuinely excited about something he has done. Be specific to the situation and describe what you see. Mostly your child is looking for recognition, not for how valuable you think what he's done is. For example, let's say your child climbed the ladder to a slide all by himself, and he looks down at you beaming with pride and excitement. You probably feel the same as he does because you are attuned to him, so you might say something like, "Wow! You climbed the ladder all by yourself!" Don't gush, and don't tell him what an amazing feat it is, because it isn't. But it is an exciting accomplishment for him, and he wants you to acknowledge it. He doesn't need you to qualify his action as "good," he just wants recognition.

How to Be Specific in Your Praise

- Praise when you are genuinely excited for your child, or when you are authentically impressed.
- Be specific. Describe what you see without adding a judgment of how good it is: "You built a really tall tower!"
- Try not saying anything at all. Sometimes your silent, but focused, attention and a smile is all your child needs.
- Praise effort, not intelligence.
- Thanking your child is a form of praise. "Thank you for sitting in your seat so I can buckle your seat belt."

2-3
years

Here's another way to understand how using specific praise to encourage good behavior works. Let's say your child has just shared a toy. Skip the "Good job" or "Good sharing" and go straight to "Thank you for sharing that toy with Leo. Look at how happy you made him feel!" Thanking your child for doing something nice and pointing out how his actions positively affected another person encourages him to repeat the behavior or action.

Praise effort, not intelligence. Studies have shown that kids who have been praised for their intelligence ("You're so smart!"), will often not try new things or work as hard because they are afraid to fail, afraid someone might think they're not smart anymore if they don't do well on the next project or next skill. Why would they want to risk losing the title of Smart Kid? Children who are praised for their efforts ("I can see that you worked really hard to build this airplane") will keep trying new things and new skills and will keep working hard to achieve whatever is before them.

You'll find that the number of times you praise your child will dramatically decrease once you get the hang of specific praise. There are many times that you can simply watch what your child is doing to fulfill his need for acknowledgement. Sometimes you don't need to say a word. You'll find that offering genuine praise feels more meaningful, more authentic, and it will feel the same for your child.

Discipline vs. Punishment

Let's talk about the difference between discipline and punishment. **Discipline is teaching your child what is and is not appropriate behavior.** (The word comes from the Latin word *disciplina*, which means "teaching or learning." It is also rooted in the Latin word *discipulus*, which means "pupil" and from which *disciple* comes.) It is recognizing mistakes as learning moments. It is meant to encourage and help your child do better next time by offering explanations for why his current behavior is not appropriate and providing advice for how to handle the situation better in the future. It includes using natural consequences if he continues the unacceptable behavior. It teaches your child that you love him no matter what, and that when you love someone you do not hurt him. It helps your child learn the art of self-discipline.

Punishment is an applied consequence. It has no logical connection between the inappropriate behavior and the subsequent consequence. To understand the difference between a natural consequence and an applied consequence, consider the following example. Imagine that every Tuesday morning you go to the library at 11:00 to listen to story hour. On this particular Tuesday, however, your child is dawdling and despite your insistence that it is time to go, he decides to play at home for another thirty minutes. The natural consequence of

Talk to your child about how to do better next time. The only way children learn is if we teach them, and sometimes we need to teach them acceptable ways of handling a situation.

his behavior is that he misses the first half of story hour. A punishment, or an applied consequence, would be that because he dawdled and you were late to the library, he doesn't get dessert after dinner.

In this example, the punishment has no relationship to the inappropriate behavior. Missing dessert after dinner has no logical connection to dawdling on the way to the library. Even worse, the consequence occurs hours after the behavior, which diminishes the opportunity to make a connection between the two events.

Finally, if your punishment becomes emotional and based on either frustration or anger, it risks turning into retribution. Retribution consists of consequences that are applied as a means of getting even with your child. Retribution involves losing control of yourself, becoming so mad that you just want to make your child feel as unhappy as you feel. Compared with discipline, the attitude that drives retribution is completely different. The parent feels something akin to "You're making me so angry and miserable that I'm going to make you miserable, too!"

As parents, it's possible, inevitable even, to get angry with our children and punish them in the heat of the moment. You might grab your child by the arm and pull him away from the toy that he wants to buy or buckle him into his car seat roughly. And it is normal to calm down a few minutes later and wish you hadn't reacted the way you did. The trick is to calm down *before* reacting to what he's said or done. Give yourself a chance to cool off and to release the anger that might compel you to intentionally hurt your child. Once you've calmed down, go speak with him gently. Explain why you were so angry, why his behavior is unacceptable, and offer solutions for how he can handle a similar situation in the future. Give him words he can say ("I'm mad! Don't do that!") and actions he can do (hit a pillow or a bed, not a person; walk away; get a parent's help).

Consequences are an important aspect of learning and living in our world that your child needs to experience. They are an integral part of discipline that helps your child learn how to be and get along with others. When your child makes a choice or takes an action, there are consequences. Perhaps he decides to wear his favorite shirt to help Dad paint the fence even though you've warned him that he's likely to get paint on it. The next time he wants to wear the shirt to a party, he'll be very disappointed to hear that he can't because it has paint all over it.

Or maybe your child says he doesn't want to put his bike away when you ask him to at the end of the day. You might say to him that he needs to put it away because he was the one using it, he is responsible for it, and that if you have to put it away he won't be able to use it the following day. Give him some time to do it—perhaps he is very involved in playing, a book, or a game—and then warn him one last time. If he still doesn't put away his bike, do it yourself. And then stick to the consequence.

The next day when he says, "Hey, Mom, I'm going to ride my bike!" you can say sadly and matter-of-factly, "Gosh, you can't ride your bike today because you didn't put it away last night. That's too bad. You can ride it tomorrow." He's likely to be diligent about putting his bike away every night after that.

You should also realize that **consequences don't have to be big to be effective or a valuable learning experience for your child.** If your child won't stop throwing sand when he's in the sandbox—an action that could hurt someone—the consequence might be that he cannot play in the sandbox for a while. He doesn't necessarily need a time-out

Time-Outs Tend to Be Ineffective

We don't believe time-outs are an effective teaching tool. The theory is that the child is put in isolation so he can think about what he's done, but frankly, that's not what happens. When you put your child in a time-out, he is not mulling over the questionable wisdom of his misdeed; he's either angry at you or his sister because she's still out playing and he's stuck in his room. It works against the close relationship you're trying to build with your child and helps instill a strong sense of sibling rivalry as well. Not what you're shooting for.

In addition, you run the risk that your child will misinterpret the time-out. You may think you're saying that you don't want to be around him when he behaves inappropriately, but he may interpret the time-out as you not loving him. Instead of listening to your words, he may focus instead on the action and conclude that you don't want him around. Is that the message you want him to receive?

That's not to say you shouldn't remove your child from play when he does something inappropriate. You should, but don't isolate him. Pull him out of playing, then talk to him about why you're removing him and what he needs to do to be able to go back. Stay with him. Connect with him. Call it a time-in! He needs a break to get back on track and play gently, and he needs your guidance to get there.

One situation where a true time-out might be useful is when an explosive child throws a violent temper tantrum. Although it might be ideal to stay with him until he calms down, sometimes that is just not possible. Other children might require your attention, or it might be a matter of safety for you or his siblings. In those rare situations, find a safe place for your child to calm down away from others.

2-3
years

or to go home right away. He is apt to be unhappy with the simple, and seemingly small, consequence of not being able to play where he wants to play, and he will adjust his behavior (stop throwing sand) to be able to play there again.

TIP   What to Do When You Don't Know What to Do

You will come across times when you just don't know what to do in a discipline situation. You'll have no idea what a logical consequence might be for a given action, or you just won't know how to help your child learn an appropriate response to a situation. In these instances, give it time. Take a breath. Go ahead and take two or three breaths. Talk with your child. Tell him you just don't know what to do to help him. He may give you a good idea if you involve him in the task. You never know. But keep in mind that you don't need to instantly solve every problem. You can take your time to figure out the best solution or plan of action.

Keep it simple. Remember the differences between discipline and punishment, and keep consequences logical and related to the action being discouraged. In the previous example, not being able to play in the sandbox is a more logical and therefore suitable consequence than not getting to watch TV when you get home. The TV has nothing to do with his action of throwing sand, so it has very little teaching value for the child.

Finally, when disciplining your child, think of him as your *disciple*, or pupil. He is learning from you, learning to follow your example. Model the behavior you want to see. Be gentle with your child, treat him with kindness and respect, support him when he makes a mistake, and use it as a teaching moment. Teach him how to be by being the person you want him to be.

Well-Child Checks and Vaccines

You should schedule your child's annual well-child checkup soon after his birthday every year. He will be weighed and measured, and those numbers will be plotted on his growth curves. (The three-year well-child check is the last time he will have his head circumference measured.) Your doctor will discuss his growth and development, give him a physical exam, and answer your questions. There are no scheduled vaccines at the three-year-old checkup, but your child's doctor may recommend the flu vaccine at the start of the flu season in winter. Check out the Resources and Recommended Reading section on page 296 for where to find the most up-to-date list of recommended vaccines.

Health and Safety Tips

Your child should be visiting the dentist every six months for dental checkups and cleanings. If there is no fluoride in your household water, and you want your child to take fluoride supplements, ask your doctor or dentist for a prescription for supplements in either drop or pill form.

Do what you can to avoid too much sun exposure. Adult skin cancer is often linked to childhood sunburns. The three key steps to limiting your child's exposure are to stay out of the sun during the middle of the day, dress him in sun-protective hats and clothing, and apply sunscreen to his exposed skin when you must be out in the sun.

Your child still must be in a car seat with five-point restraints until he weighs at least 40 pounds (18 kg), probably around age four.

Review the ongoing safety precautions. Keep dangerous materials (medications and unsafe home and garden products) out of your child's reach. Check the batteries in your smoke detectors twice a year (when the clocks change for daylight savings in the spring and the fall). Install new smoke detectors when your old ones expire, usually every ten years. Install a carbon monoxide detector if you have a woodstove or fireplace. Keep the poison control phone number prominently posted near every phone in the house and programmed into your cell phones and handheld electronic gadgets. (You will find the poison control number for your area listed in the Resources and Recommended Reading section on page 296.) Do not store guns in your home. If you have to, keep the guns and the ammunition in separate locations and both locked securely.

Nurture Yourself to Better Nurture Your Child

You want to be the best possible parent for your child. To do that, you need to take good care of yourself. Think about the aspects of life that cheer you up and restore your energy and include them in your regular schedule. Whether that means meeting a friend for tea, taking a solo stroll in the woods, or attending regular yoga classes, make sure you take time for what matters to you.

Don't forget to make time for you and your spouse or partner as a couple. Nurture your relationship. Go out and spend time together without your child, if your desire. Some parents are reluctant to leave their child behind. If you're not comfortable leaving your child or simply don't feel it's necessary, then don't. Plan some couple time in the evening after he has gone to sleep. Share a glass of wine and a laugh. Get romantic. Some parents are not able to afford a babysitter. In that case, ask relatives or find other couples with children and arrange a babysitting swap. You'll know you are leaving your child with a trusted caregiver, and your night out will be less expensive without the cost of a babysitter.

As part of your couple time, be sure to check in with each other. Reconnect and make a point of telling your partner how much you love and appreciate him or her. Saying these words out loud is surprisingly important because it's too easy to assume your spouse knows how you feel. We all need to hear that we are valued, that we are good at what we do, and that someone recognizes the big and little things we do. So talk to your spouse and share your feelings. Often.

2–3
years

8

PRESCHOOLERS

3–4 Years

"I Can Do It Myself!" From Getting Dressed to Using the Toilet

You will be astounded at all the ways in which your child will grow and develop this year. To begin with, she will triple her vocabulary and will become much more understandable to anyone she talks to. Your child loves physical activity! And it's no wonder; she walks, runs, jumps, and climbs with much more assurance and control. She is also recognizing letters and colors by now, and she may even learn to write her own name. A big event in both your lives may happen this year, as well, as she will probably learn to use a toilet. That's a monumental milestone!

As you read through this chapter on the general development of three- to four-year-olds, remember that each child is unique. Her development happens at her own pace, and though you can certainly create environments and opportunities to enhance her development, you cannot actually speed it up. She'll do things when she's ready to do them. Your child may be right on target with the information we present here, or she may be ahead of or behind it. If you have concerns about your child's development, please raise them with your family physician or pediatrician. But remember that children will develop in their own time. Relax and enjoy your child's journey through childhood!

TIP Go Outside!

Kids are happier and sleep better when they get plenty of physical activity. They are also calmer inside the house when they've had enough time to run and play outside. If you can, make sure your child gets time to play outside at a playground or in your yard every day. Or take daily walks or hikes to give your child the physical exercise her body needs.

DEVELOPING BODY

You Will See Changes in Your Child's Appearance and Abilities

Look for these physical changes in your child this year: Her body will lengthen, she will look taller and leaner, and she will lose the toddler potbelly. Her physical appearance becomes more balanced, more like the body symmetry of adults. She looks less top-heavy now, which means her body is catching up with the size of her head.

Your child is adept at opening doors, which means you must be aware of where she is in the house, and whether she has gone outside without telling you. She is also more physically coordinated, and she moves with increased confidence. She hops on one foot, jumps, climbs, walks, and runs with assurance, showing better balance and control in all her moves. She can even walk backward, stand on one foot, and stop suddenly without falling down.

Your child is a whirlwind on the playground with his increased physical stability and capabilities. Continue to give him lots of outside time, each day if possible.

Physical activity is at the top of your child's list of favorite things to do. Your child plays long and hard. Her increased physical coordination means she can pedal a tricycle or bicycle with training wheels (make sure she wears a bike helmet!), she can learn to pump a swing, she walks up steps with alternating feet, and she can walk in a straight line. She's getting very good at throwing, kicking, and catching balls. She can climb up and down a slide by herself, and she can even balance on one foot for a second or two, though she may be a bit unsteady. By the age of three, she will have a full set of baby teeth. She is likely sleeping ten to twelve hours at night.

Bed-Wetting

Most three-year-olds are still wearing diapers at night. And even those who have progressed to "big kid underwear" frequently have accidents and wet the bed. One way to minimize bed-wetting is to leave your child in diapers until she is dry seven nights in a row. This shows that she has good control for the most part, and accidents, if they occur, will not be frequent.

Many children will wet the bed until the age of six or seven, and a few will continue until eight or nine. The thing to remember is that if your child is wetting the bed at night, she's not doing it on purpose. It is beyond her control and something she will grow out of. Until she does, punishing, scolding, or shaming your child is inappropriate, unkind, and counterproductive to helping her stay dry at night.

The best way to help your child is not to make a big deal about the bed-wetting. Don't talk about it with other people in your child's presence to avoid embarrassing her. If she gets upset when she has an accident, comfort her, remind her that it is not her fault, that she cannot control it, and that she will grow out of it as she gets bigger. Make the cleanup as quick and low-key as possible.

Keep your child healthy and happy by giving her time to run and play outside on a daily basis. Her growing body needs the physical exercise.

Sometimes a child will wet the bed because he's such a deep sleeper that he doesn't wake up when his body signals that his bladder is full.

3-4
years

Let her hop in the shower if she wants, or simply remove her wet clothes, wipe her off with a warm, wet washcloth, and help her put on dry clothes. Change her bed quickly and quietly. Do it all matter-of-factly, with no grumbling or sighing. If it happens in the middle of the night, you'll no doubt be tired, but remember that she's tired, too. Remind yourself that it's not her fault, and that making her feel bad will not help anyone or fix the problem.

Nighttime bed-wetting is very common, and it happens for a number of reasons, including:

- Small bladder
- Deep sleeper
- Urinary tract infection
- Emotional stress caused by a big life change (new school or day care, move, new sibling, etc.)
- Food intolerances, allergies, or sensitivities
- Genetics (If Mom or Dad wet the bed as a child, their child may do the same.)

If you are concerned about your child's bed-wetting tendencies, keep a journal of the occurrences (and possible causes if you've noticed any links) and speak with your child's doctor at her next appointment.

To minimize bed-wetting, you might try rousing your child before you go to bed to allow her to use the toilet, but don't be surprised if she doesn't appreciate having her sleep disturbed. If she's not cooperating, then let her sleep. **Promising rewards for not wetting the bed will not help, nor will a sticker chart that displays the number of dry nights she's had, because the bed-wetting is beyond her control.** We also recommend that you not make a big deal when she has a dry night because the lack of celebration on the morning following a wet night will be silently felt. If your child says, "Mom! I didn't wet last night!" you can certainly share in her joy, but remember to describe rather than praise. "No, you didn't! You stayed dry all night long." She's looking for acknowledgment of her achievement. Recognition is what she needs, nothing more.

Your Child Can Do a Lot for Herself

By the age of three to four, your child is an expert at feeding herself, though she may still spill things occasionally. She can hold a cup in one hand, and she uses utensils properly. Although she can now put on her shoes, it's unlikely she can tie her laces yet. She can undress without help, but she may require a little help when getting dressed. Buttons will continue to present a challenge; to allow her the independence to dress herself, purchase easy-to-dress clothing for her. Keep in mind that she will be learning to use the toilet at this age, so don't buy clothing that is difficult for her to take off. Think elastic-waist pants or shorts, rather than buttons, zippers, and snaps. She is also able to wash and dry her hands by herself, which coincides nicely with her toilet learning.

Drawing, Writing, and Playing on a Computer Improve Dexterity and Hand-Eye Coordination

With respect to fine motor skills, your child is holding crayons or pencils well at this age, using her fingers to hold them, rather than her fist as she used to. She can fold paper, if shown how, and can build a tower of five to six blocks. She may start to write some of the letters of the alphabet, and she might be able to write her own name by the time she turns four. She's also starting to draw people. She'll start by drawing faces, and she will add more details and bodies as she progresses through the year.

This is a great age to introduce your child to computers. Her hand-eye coordination is still developing, so she may not have complete control of the keyboard and the mouse, but computer work can certainly enhance her development. There are wonderful educational computer games made for preschoolers, and you can probably find them on the computer in the kids' section of your local library. If you do not have a home computer—or one that you want your young child to use—the library is a terrific resource for exposing her to computers.

Computer use is great for enhancing hand-eye coordination. Educational games are easy to find, including free educational websites on the Internet.

Activities to Enhance Your Child's Physical Development

Activities should be fun for everyone. Don't push your child to do anything she doesn't want to simply because you believe it's important for her physical development. If it feels like play, she'll want to do it. If she's not enjoying herself, or doesn't like an activity, don't force it and don't worry about it. It doesn't mean she won't gain whatever developmental skills are involved. It just means she'll do it another way. Her way. Keep in mind that there are plenty of things you can do with your child to promote her development.

Your child loves to do things herself—like putting on her shoes even if she puts them on the wrong feet! The abundance of Velcro closure shoes makes it an easy task she can do truly all by herself.

3–4
years

Activities for Large Motor Skills Development

- Make sure your child gets an hour or more of physical activity most days.

- Go to playgrounds to help your child develop large motor skills such as climbing, running, jumping, and balancing. Going up and down the slides is great practice.

- Throw, catch, and kick balls. Use various size balls when you play.

- Play baseball with your child, allowing her to practice hitting the ball with a bat.

- Hop, jump, and walk on tiptoe.

- Show your child how to pedal a tricycle by helping her press down with one foot at a time on the pedals. (Always wear a helmet.)

- Put a small stepping stool in front of the sink in the bathroom for your child to get up on so she can wash her hands by herself.

- Have your child pull a wagon around the yard, putting items in and taking them out. It's a great way for your child to help clean up the yard at the end of the day. You and she can put things in the wagon to be put away, and she can pull it to wherever the items need to go.

- Create an obstacle course in the yard that includes balancing, running, climbing, and jumping. Make it noncompetitive; it's just for the pure fun of doing it.

- Play soccer! Run and kick balls around the yard or park to increase your child's coordination.

- Play follow the leader at home, at the playground, and through your obstacle course. Include hopping, skipping, jumping, walking slowly, running, turning in circles . . . whatever you can think of. Let your child lead you, too!

- Practice forward rolls on a mattress on the floor or gym mat, or outside on the grass.

- Play with balloons. Hit balloons with a badminton or tennis racket. Hit balloons with different parts of the body. Practice keeping the balloon in the air without letting it touch the ground for as long as possible.

- Find smaller tools that are made just for children (gardening tools, snow shovel, etc.) so your child can help you while learning how to use tools that are appropriate for her size. She'll also love to help with adult-size tools such as a broom and a vacuum. She can help carry in groceries, unpack the bags, and help put away what you've purchased.

Physical activity is so very important for your child. Get your child outside to run around. Run and play with her! Play tag, soccer, baseball, catch, or explore the fields and forests. Just get outside!

Activities for Fine Motor Skills Development

- Play together with nesting blocks or cups that stack.

- Do puzzles that offer a little challenge, but not so much so your child loses interest.

- Play matching games, such as Concentration.

- Place a small table and chairs in your dining room or play room for your child to use for playing, drawing, and eating. Give her play dishes to pretend with.

- Enhance hand-eye coordination by building towers with blocks, doing puzzles, cutting with scissors, drawing, spreading peanut butter on bread, and pouring water from a small pitcher into cups.

- Help your child develop strength, control, and dexterity by using scissors, a stapler, a hammer, or a hole punch, by squeezing water out of a washcloth or squeezing balls or soft bath toys, and by drawing.

- Cut out coupons. This is a great activity to do together as you can let her know which coupons you would like to use, and she'll feel proud when you use the ones she cut out.

- Use tools. Pound nails partially into a board and let your child pound them in the rest of the way. Start screws in a board and let your child use a screwdriver to screw them farther in. If your child has battery-operated toys, give her the screwdriver to open the door to get the batteries out.

3–4
years

- Have the following available for your child: glue, scissors, paper, markers, stickers, and crayons. Keep them on an easy-to-reach shelf so she can get what she needs without help. She'll also enjoy working with her hands with play dough, clay, and paints (finger paints or washable watercolors and acrylics with brushes).

- Draw shapes with your child. Encourage her to reproduce them on her own piece of paper.

- Encourage your child to use a computer keyboard and a mouse to enhance her dexterity and hand-eye coordination. You can find free age-appropriate educational websites online, or you can purchase games for preschoolers to load onto your computer. Your local library may have a children's computer with a number of educational games on it to use for free.

- String large beads or buttons onto a shoelace.

- Pour sand or water into and out of several small containers. Play with water outside or in the bath.

- Build with blocks. Build with your child, and allow her the time to build alone. Create complex structures, try to make shapes, build favorite items such as airplanes or boats, and spell your child's name with blocks.

- Your child can help you cook by spreading butter and jelly on toast, cutting vegetables with a child-safe knife for a salad or stir-fry, or measuring, pouring, and mixing ingredients when you're baking (all under supervision, of course). Ask her to help put plates on the table, place utensils next to the plates, stir the lemonade, or carry the salad dressing or mustard to the table.

- Your child can put away her clean clothes in her drawers.

Building with blocks is not only good for your child's fine motor skills but also his creativity. You can make limitless creations with blocks and he'll likely enjoy building things for years.

DEVELOPING MIND

Independence and Creative Play Are Central to Your Child's Cognitive Development

This is a great age for problem solving. Your child loves to learn, asks lots of questions, and enjoys a challenge such as doing a puzzle, dressing a doll, or building an airplane out of Lego-like blocks. If the challenge is not too difficult, your child will stay focused until she tackles it. She'll try different solutions, consider alternatives, and be more flexible and creative in her thinking.

Independence really starts to blossom at this age, as evidenced by your child's quest to do things on her own. She really likes to do things independently—and will tell you so by refusing your help whenever it is offered—but she will ask for help when she encounters something that proves to be too difficult. She is also much more definitive about her preferences: "I want to read this book first and then have lunch."

Your child can focus for longer amounts of time now. **She can follow simple one-step instructions, so when helping her through a task, give her only one directive at a time.** She understands the concepts of "now," "soon," and "later," and she will remember what happened yesterday. She is also more aware of her surroundings and will avoid known dangers such as a hot stove or a moving car without being warned or reminded.

Your child's pretend play is becoming more creative. She will use objects for make-believe, such as pretending a block is an airplane. She'll also take on familiar roles in her play, pretending to be the mom or dad. She will laugh at silly ideas, like putting a pot on your head or having a monkey sleep in her bed. She'll also laugh at her own silliness, and that of her siblings and friends. Physical comedy is a hit with a child this age (and for years to come!).

TIP **Keep It Short**

Because your child has an attention span of roughly three minutes at this age, it's best to keep your "lectures" simple and to the point. When explaining why she cannot do something or why some behavior was not acceptable, be brief, concise, and clear. Don't use clichés or sayings that are beyond her comprehension at this age. Keep it simple: "Hands are not for hitting because hitting hurts. We do not hurt people. When you get mad, you can say, 'I'm mad! Don't take my toy!' but you may not hit someone." Remember always to tell a child what she *can* do when you are telling her something she can't do.

3–4
years

Your Child Knows Colors and Numbers and Can Categorize Objects

Being more in tune with her environment, your child will easily recognize familiar, everyday sounds. She can identify common colors, count two to three objects, and understand the concept of "one." She knows some numbers, but she may not get them in the correct order. That will come in time. She will also start to recognize some letters of the alphabet, and she will look through books by herself.

Your child knows where things belong and is good at putting things away when asked. She's starting to understand that things can be sorted into categories, such as knowing the difference between food and nonfood items. She can match objects with a picture of each object, as well as match items that belong in the same category (such as pants and shirts). She can match circles and squares, as well as draw those shapes herself.

Activities to Enhance Your Child's Cognitive Development

- Play games with your child! Try matching games, board games, various card games, and dominoes.

- Do puzzles with your child, and let her do them on her own. Try to find ones that give her a little challenge, but are not too difficult. If they are too easy, she may lose interest quickly.

- Practice the ABCs with your preschooler. Sing the alphabet song, read books that highlight the alphabet, and regularly write it out for her to help her identify the letters as well as to see how to write them.

- Read counting books. Practice numbers and counting on a daily basis. Count everything! Count how many people you see at the park. Count the number of grapes in her bowl. Count the number of flowers on a page in a book. Write down the numbers 1 through 10 so she will learn to recognize them. Go higher in your counting as she shows proficiency.

- Encourage your child's mathematical thinking by asking her to sort, match, group, sequence, and recognize patterns in real-life situations. Ask for her help in sorting the dirty laundry into lights and darks. Have her sort out the socks and pair them in the clean laundry. When your child helps you set the table, count how many forks, spoons, knives, plates, and glasses you'll need, then help her arrange them in a place setting pattern.

- Talk about shapes, colors, and numbers whenever you can. "That's a round, green ball." "We have only one yellow banana left." "Let's find your orange and pink bathing suit."

- Read to your child! She is like a sponge soaking up information. Find fiction or nonfiction books on whatever currently interests her. Go to the library together and encourage her to find books she wants to read. She will memorize text as you read books.

- Sing songs and listen to music together in the house, in the car—and find music that you won't tire of listening to again and again (and again). Your child will quickly memorize song lyrics, and sometimes she'll even get the words right!.

- Encourage make-believe play by having these things at the ready: building blocks and make-believe play materials like scarves, hats, old clothes, shoes, recyclables for crafting costumes and props, and blankets for building forts. Occasionally, you should take part in her make-believe worlds because it provides an eye into how your child thinks and feels. But it's important to follow her lead and rules of play, and not try to change or "fix" anything.

- Have a birthday party and invite her favorite stuffed animals and dolls.

- Create a grocery store stocked with empty cereal boxes, plastic fruit, and household supplies. Your child can choose whether to be a store employee or the customer.

DEVELOPING LANGUAGE

Your Child Will Triple Her Vocabulary This Year

By the age of three, your child knows about 1,000 words, and she will learn 1,500 to 2,000 more words by the time she is four, essentially tripling her vocabulary! She can learn four to six words a day if she's exposed to words either by being read to or simply by adults talking with her. At age three, she is using three-word sentences, and by age four she will be speaking in five-word (or more) complete sentences. At this age, your child's speech is understandable most of the time to anyone she talks with. She may still stumble as she learns to pronounce more complicated words. She'll repeat almost every word and sound she hears. She uses plurals now, such as *balls* and *dolls*, and she understands the use of pronouns such as *I, you, he,* and *she* (though she may mix up gender pronouns for the next few years as she sorts out when to use *he* and when to use *she*).

3–4
years

Your Child Is Becoming a Great Conversationalist

Your child is turning into a confident conversationalist and will actually initiate conversations with other adults. He'll tell stories, ask questions, and sometimes share information you wish he hadn't.

Your budding scientist will ask many, many questions of the who, what, where, and why variety. She knows her first and last names, can name many familiar objects, and knows the names of common colors. She understands the concepts of "now," "soon," and "later." She is also better able to understand explanations when she can see concrete examples—such as watching an ice cube melt in the sun and understanding that heat melts ice, and that ice is frozen water.

Your child loves talking to people at this age, and she will even start to initiate conversations.

She will probably say "Hi!" to strangers at the store or on the street. She will start to tell personal stories, describing things that happened to her, but she'll leave out most of the details, telling only the main events. She can add the details if you prompt her to, and she'll eventually learn that the details are part of the story as well.

Play Word Games When Reading Familiar Stories with Your Child

Your child is at the age where she is better able to listen to and understand stories, conversations, and songs. She has a longer attention span, which means she will listen to short stories without rushing to turn the pages before you've finished reading them. She loves to be read to. She especially likes stories she's familiar with and will ask you to read the same book over and over again, often in the same sitting.

Your child memorizes the text of books she's heard many times, and she will recite the words when she looks through a book on her own. (By this age, she tends to look through a book from front to back, and she recognizes the covers of familiar

books.) Because she has committed the text of her favorite books to memory, she'll know when you say a word that's not on the page or when you leave words out. And she'll let you know it! She wants to hear the book with no changes in the wording and will protest if you alter them. It can make for a fun game to play: She'll giggle at the wrong words you slip into the story, tell you the right words, and laugh when you admit your folly. "Oh, you're right! I read the wrong word!"

Singing can be a favorite activity, and your child may be able to carry a tune by now. She also likes rhymes and will repeat those she's memorized from songs, poems, or stories she's heard. She may also start to identify words that rhyme, and she will make up a list of rhyming words, some of which will be nonsense and some real. "*Car* rhymes with *far, mar, dar,* and *jar.*" No need to point out which are nonsense and which are real words. She'll learn in time.

Your child may tell you that words that begin with the same letter rhyme: "*Bat* and *ball* rhyme." You can explain to her that the words start with the same sound, but they don't rhyme. Then give her examples of words that do rhyme. "*Bat* and *ball* begin with the same sound *buh, buh,* which is the sound *b* makes. *Bat* rhymes with *cat, mat,* and *sat.* *Ball* rhymes with *all, small,* and *doll.*"

With a great talent for memorization, your child is learning song lyrics very quickly these days and will love to sing along to the music you listen to or give an impromptu a capella concert.

3-4
years

Your Child Will Write Her Name

Your child is much more aware of letters in print, and she will ask you what something says. She knows that groups of letters make words, and she will sometimes write letters or arrange magnetic letters into pretend words—just a group of random letters—and ask, "What does this say?" or "What word is this?" By the end of this year, she may be able to identify most of the alphabet letters in uppercase print, though she may still confuse similar-looking letters such as *M* and *W*.

Later in the year, your child may start to write out her name on paper. The letters might be written in various places on the page (i.e. not in a line), suggesting that she wrote the letters out of order; however, the letters were most likely written in the correct order, just not spaced properly. She will write wherever she pleases on a piece of paper. That means she may start writing on the right side and move downward or upward. She may write right to left, then left to right, then right to left again. Don't worry about or try to correct this tendency. She will learn how to properly space letters to form words on her own. She'll learn that we order letters in a word from left to right, and that we read in the same direction. She will learn by watching how you write and from reading books with you.

Activities to Enhance Your Child's Language Development

- Read to your child, and then read some more! Take time to study and discuss the illustrations when you're looking at books together. Read alphabet books to help your child learn the alphabet and letter sounds.

- Practice the ABCs. Read books that highlight the alphabet, sing the alphabet song, and write it out regularly for her. This will help her identify the letters as well as to see how to write them.

- Play with alphabet puzzles, games, and magnetic letters.

- Help your child memorize her first and last names.

- Write out your child's name often. She may start writing it herself sometime this year.

- Have conversations with your child. Talk to her like she's intelligent—she is!—by asking for her opinions, likes, and dislikes on various subjects. Be an attentive listener when she talks to you. Respond in a manner that shows you understood what she meant.

- Spell words for your child whenever she asks you how something is spelled. If you are not sure how to spell a specific word, look it up in the dictionary. You'll not only guarantee a correct spelling for your child, but you'll also be modeling how to find information when you don't know the answer.

- Fill in the details on statements your child makes. "Yes, that's a dog. It's a big, brown dog. It's bigger than our dog."

- Tell your child stories about your experiences or make up stories from your imagination. If you make up stories that feature your child(ren) as the leading character(s), you'll be asked to tell them over and over again.

- Model proper grammar when you speak so your child learns correct word order and pronunciation. She'll learn to speak (and eventually write) the way you speak.

- Make jokes with your child, and she'll learn to make jokes, too. She loves a good laugh, and she will enjoy playing with language.

- Ask your child to tell you stories. Encourage her to tell you about something that happened to her or something she saw. She'll also love telling you imagined tales.

- Listen to music and sing songs together. She'll memorize song lyrics quickly.

- Read rhymes and books of children's poetry. Talk about words that rhyme. Make up rhymes with your child. "What rhymes with *tall?*" Write rhyming poems!

- Provide your child with make-believe play materials such as capes, shoes, hats, sunglasses, blankets for building a hideaway, etc. Create hand puppets out of paper bags decorated with markers, paper, and glue, or out of socks decorated with buttons, yarn, and thread. (She'll love to make puppets, and it's also great for her fine motor skills development.) Show her how the puppets can have a conversation with each other or with you or her. Perform a puppet show.

DEVELOPING PERSON

Your Child Is Showing Signs of Maturing Emotionally

Thanks to all the time you've spent discussing feelings and labeling them for your child, she is finally old enough to start talking about her feelings. She can label her feelings as well as other people's feelings. She notices facial expressions and understands the corresponding emotions. She may start to authentically comfort someone who is upset, whether it's a child or an adult.

Your child has progressed from expressing her feelings physically to being better able to do so verbally. That said, she'll still get physical quite often. Remind yourself that it's a learning *process* and a long road to consistent self-control. Look at every instance when she uses her words as a step forward, and gently remind her of the appropriate way to handle herself when she does lash out physically. It's not a step back. It's a teaching moment. Take it as a good sign that the lesson is starting to sink in, and that she is learning alternatives to aggression in conflict resolution.

3–4
years

Another Tantrum or Two

You still may see the periodic meltdown or tantrum when your child gets stressed or overwhelmed. Reread the section on tantrums starting on page 174 in chapter 6 for a reminder of how you can help your child through these tough moments. Your child is still very young, striving for independence, and getting thwarted on a regular basis as she comes up against the unrealistic expectations you or her other caregivers may have and the stresses that cause you to lose patience and snap. As your child becomes older, it's easier to expect her to behave more like an adult rather than the child she is. She doesn't have a very long attention span, so it's unrealistic to expect her to sit quietly and calmly through a wedding ceremony, for example. If your unrealistic expectations are triggering the tantrums, think of them as teaching moments for you. (Parenting is a string of teaching moment after teaching moment for the *parents*, too.)

When you help resolve conflicts with your child, she will usually accept whatever compromise you come up with. "Yheva is using the truck right now. You can use it when she is done." She may even ask for your help in resolving conflicts from time to time. She is open to suggestions at this age, and she will follow simple directions. She can make simple choices between two options, and she should be given the opportunity to do so as often as possible throughout the day. **Giving her a measure of control over her world is very important for her development. She learns the important skill of decision making, learns to weigh the pros and cons, and learns to deal with the consequences of her choices.**

Your child delights in making others laugh and loves to be silly. She really loves to hear stories about herself, and in her world everything still centers on her. She shows stronger preferences and is firmer in what she likes and doesn't like. She's more of an individual. She will go through times of showing preference for one parent, and it can change back and forth from one to the other. She still needs familiar adults around to feel secure when she plays and explores. She likes to check in, either by simply looking at you or coming over to make personal contact, for reassurance that she still has her home base.

Your child will interact more with other children in play and other social situations. She's becoming more social and beginning the process of making friends.

Your Child Loves to Imitate You and All You Do

Art imitates life in your child's pretend play. She will frequently play "house" and will assign roles: "I'm the mommy, you're the baby." She loves to imitate housework, and she is likely to beg to help you. Let her! Encourage her help. Yes, it may take you twice as long. Yes, you will have to do it anyway once she's finished. But it's important that she's learning to be a contributing member of the family. She's learning that everyone helps out, and has a responsibility to keep the household clean! And she'll even get good at it if you give her plenty of opportunities to practice.

Your Child Develops Friendships This Year

Your child likes to be near other children. She'll spend a lot of time observing other kids; she's fascinated by what they are doing. She may even copy what she sees them do. She might still like to play by herself, but she's likely to want to do it near other kids. She may play in a small group of two or three children for a while, though she's not terribly good at sharing just yet. **During this year, you will see her moving away from parallel play (playing alongside but not with another child) to more interactive play (actually engaging and playing with another child).**

3-4
years

By the end of the year, you may also see signs that your child is forming real friendships. She won't fully understand the concept at this age, but she'll definitely show a preference for some children over others. Encourage the friendships that you think are beneficial to your child, but also respect her choices in friends.

Activities to Enhance Your Child's Emotional and Social Development

- Take your child with you to restaurants, museums, and stores. Do everyday life stuff that involves interacting with people so your child sees how it's done. She will start to interact with people of all ages when you are out and about when she's ready.

- Keep going to playgroups and make playdates. Present your child with regular opportunities to learn the art of cooperative play. Remember that it is a learning process.

- Play with puppets—handmade or store bought. Have the puppets talk to each other about issues you think are important to your child.

- Allow your child alone time if she wants it.

- Provide your child with an alone spot where she can hide when she wants to. A large cardboard box or a closet with pillows on the floor may be just right. (This is *not* a time-out spot.)

- Get together with children of various ages (a huge benefit of being in a playgroup). Let your child engage with adults of various ages, as well. Give her opportunities to become comfortable interacting with anyone of any age.

- Provide your child with dolls and make-believe play materials such as scarves and hats, old clothes and shoes, recyclables for building costumes and props, blankets for making forts, etc.

- Supply your child with words she can use when she is upset, angry, or sad. She'll need to be reminded often to say it in words, not in pushes, hits, or kicks.

- Join in on noncompetitive team activities such as planting a community garden, painting a mural, or beautifying your neighborhood.

- Let your child help plan activities, playdates, and parties. Welcome her input, preferences, and help. She loves to be involved!

- Play games with your child: board games, card games, dominoes, tag, hide-and-seek, etc. Games are a fun way for your child to learn to take turns.

The beginnings of friendships appear this year, with your child showing clear preference for some children over others. Allow your child the freedom to choose her friends.

3–4
years

Encourage healthy habits like brushing teeth at least twice a day. Be sure you, or another adult, do the brushing at least once each day to make sure her teeth get really clean.

POSITIVELY PARENTING

Make Personal Hygiene a Priority for a Healthy Child

It's important to make personal hygiene a part of your child's daily routine. It helps keep her whole body healthy, and it also establishes good habits that she will carry with her throughout the rest of her life.

Your child is still of an age where you need to do much of the brushing and washing. She needs to have her teeth brushed by an adult every day; if she resists, be creative in your approach to getting it done. Offer her the chance to brush her own teeth before or after you brush them. Give her choices of different toothpaste flavors. Let her pick out a special toothbrush at the store. Ask her where she wants to sit or stand to have her teeth brushed, or even if she wants to lie down on her back. (Seriously. It's actually the best position for you as the brusher to see all her teeth and get all of them clean. Try it! Have your child lie down on the floor. Sit at her head—or with her head in your lap—and brush her teeth.) Try an electric toothbrush. It's more effective at cleaning your child's teeth, and the novelty of it may get her excited about brushing her teeth.

TIP   Use Fun to Get the Job Done

Giving your child some control over brushing her teeth can really make a difference, so let her choose which toothpaste tastes best, which position works well, etc. Also, try to "schedule" brushing before some desired activity. "Let's go brush your teeth, then we can go to the park! Come on!" Make it sound fun. Heck, go ahead and make it fun! Play music, sing a tooth-brushing song (make one up or choose a song you like to give rhythm to your brushing), dance in between brushings, be silly, let your child brush your teeth while you brush hers. Do whatever it takes to get the job done with the least amount of resistance and frustration—on your part and hers.

For baths or showers, help wash your child's body at least part of the time. Have your child wash her body while you wash it. Talk about the different parts of her body that need to get clean as you are washing them. If she wants to do the washing entirely on her own some of the time, let her. It's unlikely you need to wash her every single time she bathes, unless she tends to get pretty dirty in her daily life.

Make a habit of having your child wash her hands before snacks or meals, and always wash her hands after she uses the toilet. Put a step in front of the sink so she can reach the faucet and soap herself. If your child is resistant to washing her hands, put up a sign in the bathroom that reads: "Please wash your hands." Whenever she balks at washing her hands, point to the sign and tell her, "That's the rule, it says so on the sign right here. We must wash our hands whenever we use the toilet." This technique works well for some families.

Your child still needs help washing her body in the shower or bath. Let her do it herself sometimes, and often do it together to be sure she gets her whole body clean.

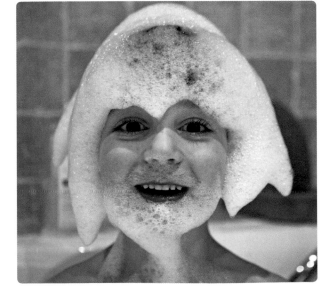

3–4
years

TIP — House Rules

If you find yourself getting into a power struggle over certain matters, try setting some "house rules." Then instead of it being *your* rule that she has to sit at the table for ten minutes to eat dinner, you can say, "In this house, everyone has to sit at the table for ten minutes while eating dinner." Or, "In this house, everyone has to hang up their coat after they walk in the door." Posting these rules around the house in the appropriate locations can work wonders.

The advantages of this are that everyone has to follow the rule, even the grown-ups, so your child won't feel as if she's being singled out. Also, this is not a parent rule, it is a house rule. This takes away the parent-child power struggle. Finally, it models the concept that there are different rules in different houses. So when she asks why her friend Virginia gets dessert every night and she doesn't, you can simply say that different houses have different rules—a valuable lesson.

Toilet Learning Takes Care and Patience

Learning to use the toilet is a big milestone for your child. It's a large leap in her development as an independent person. And it may feel to you like the quest for the holy grail. Does it really exist? Will my child ever master it? Will she stop having accidents? Is she going to be in diapers forever?!

Toilet learning takes time. The entire process, from the moment you notice that your child seems interested in using the toilet to the day she actually masters it can *feel* like a long time. In truth, the act of mastering it once she's *really* ready can take just a few days. However, it does require considerable patience. Keep it positive. Be casual about it. And most of all, don't pressure her! Applying pressure can really backfire, leading to regression in any progress she's made.

The best time to begin toilet learning is when your child shows an interest in the toilet and shows an awareness of her bowel and bladder functions. Talk about using the toilet, wearing underwear, and not wearing diapers anymore. Let your child come into the bathroom with you when you use the toilet. When she poops in her diaper, take it to the bathroom to flush the poop down the toilet, telling her that poop goes in the toilet. Get a child-size toilet seat and have it available where she plays or in the bathroom. If she shows interest in it, ask her casually if she wants to sit down on it and try to pee or poop in it. Try your best to keep it casual, and don't get your hopes up, for as soon as you start pushing because you're excited that she might be learning this new important skill, she's likely to start resisting.

Read books about learning to use a toilet. Talk about people your child knows who use a toilet. "Grandma pees in the toilet. Patrick pees in the toilet." Mention people your child loves and state it matter-of-factly.

Accidents happen. To repeat: Accidents happen. A lot. Keep in mind that your child not only needs to be aware of the urge to pee or poop, but she also has to notice it *before* it happens and stop

Children Learn to Use the Toilet When They Are Ready

Children will learn to use the toilet when they decide they want to use the toilet. Many children suddenly decide that they want to use the toilet, and within a week they've made the transition from going in their diaper to going in the toilet.

Gently offer the toilet to your child without any pressure. Parents too often ask, "Do you want to use the potty?" in a bright, enthusiastic voice that says we really want her to use the potty. Offer the toilet in the same voice you offer other things. "Do you want a banana? Do you want to use the potty? Do you want to play outside?"

Placing an extra training toilet out where your child plays, in addition to one in the bathroom, may help speed her learning and increase her successes as she will have the visual reminder and proximity of a toilet when she is struck with the urge to go.

it until she can get to the toilet. Oh, and she has to remember that she needs to run to the bathroom. She's not used to doing any of these things. It's going to take time to stop automatically going wherever she's standing or sitting at the moment she feels the urge.

So, accidents happen. We've found that the best way to respond is to state the facts without judgment or reproach. "Oops! It looks like you leaked. Let's get you to the toilet in case you still have to go, then we'll clean this up."

3–4
years

It can also be very helpful to let your child run around bare-bottomed. There are fewer accidents when there's nothing there to catch the urine or poop. Your child may be much more aware that she needs to get to the bathroom if she's not wearing underwear or a diaper. Of course, if you're in the house, you should keep watch at all times to see the signs that your child has to go and remind her to go to the bathroom to do it. If you live where your child can be outside, then you don't need to be as vigilant. Celebrate when your child makes it to the toilet or pees outside in the grass. Say, "That's great! That's where pee (or poop) goes!"

TIP Choose Boxers over Briefs

If your child does very well when she's naked and always makes it to the bathroom in time but consistently has accidents when she's wearing underwear, here's a trick to try. Put your child in boxer shorts. (Yes, they do make them that small!). It's possible that snug-fitting briefs and panties are too reminiscent of a diaper in how they fit and feel and may be sending the wrong message to your child.

When It's Time to Wait

If you find that your child is having lots of accidents, and you're getting upset about repeatedly having to clean your floor or carpet, it may be best to go back to diapers for a while and give it a try in a month or two when everyone is ready again. It does your child no good to watch you getting upset about her accidents, and in fact it can hinder her learning and development. If you and your child are happier and calmer when she wears a diaper (even though you're desperate to be done with diapers!), then do so until both of you are ready to give toilet learning another go.

Well-Child Checks and Vaccines

Your child's annual well-child checkup should be scheduled around her birthday every year. She will be weighed and measured, with that information plotted on her growth curves. Your doctor will discuss her development and give her an exam. He or she will also attempt vision and hearing tests at this time. Don't be surprised if your child can't cooperate long enough to complete these tests; many children can't. However, if there are concerns with her vision or hearing, you will be referred to a specialist for more formal testing. There are no scheduled vaccines at this checkup, but your child's physician will recommend that your child receive the flu vaccine at the start of the flu season, which occurs during the winter months every year. For where to find the most up-to-date list of recommended vaccines, turn to the Resources and Recommended Reading section on page 296.

Health and Safety Tips

Every six months, your child should go in for a dental checkup and cleaning. If your water supply lacks fluoride, your doctor or dentist can give you a prescription for supplements in either drop or pill form.

Do not expose your child to excessive sunshine. It's been shown that a leading cause of adult skin cancer is childhood sunburn. The best way to protect your child from sun damage is to avoid the sun during the middle of the day, dress her in sun-protective hats and clothing, and use sunscreen on her when you need to be out in the sun.

Your child must continue to ride in a car seat with five-point restraints until she weighs at least 40 pounds (18 kg). Make sure your child wears a helmet while biking, in-line skating, or other activities with a high risk of head injuries. It is also recommended to wear a helmet when skiing or snowboarding.

Take time to review the basic ongoing safety precautions. Dangerous substances like medications and unsafe home and garden products must be kept out of your child's reach. Check smoke detector batteries twice a year when the clocks change in the spring and the fall. Be sure to replace your smoke detectors when they expire, usually every ten years. Install a carbon monoxide detector if you use a woodstove or fireplace in your home. Keep the poison control phone number prominently posted and programmed into your cell phones and handheld electronic gadgets. (Check out the Resources and Recommended Reading section on page 296 to find the phone number of your area's poison control center.) Guns should not be stored in your home; however if you have to store guns, keep them in a locked cabinet and the ammunition locked elsewhere.

3–4
years

DECIDING WHETHER TO SEND YOUR CHILD TO PRESCHOOL

Sending a three- or four-year-old to preschool has become much more commonplace today than it would have been in the past. Where kindergarten was once considered preparation for school, preschool is now considered preparation for kindergarten. We think preschool can be a positive experience for children who are ready to separate from their parents at this early age. That said, if it's possible for one parent to stay at home with his or her child, we also feel that there are great benefits to the child to be home with a parent for as long as possible.

The choice of whether to send your child to preschool or keep her home is a personal decision based on what you feel is best for your child. Some children are not ready to let go of Mom or Dad at this age, and dropping them off at a preschool even for a few hours a day may be more traumatic than good for them. If this sounds like your child, keep in mind that there is no rush to enroll your child in preschool. You can try again next year or just wait until kindergarten. Preschool is not necessary for your child's education and won't improve her learning or give her a head start. However, preschool can be a fun place to for her to expand and practice social skills and get used to a classroom setting, *if* she's ready to go out on her own.

To see whether your child might be ready for preschool, try leaving her with a very familiar adult in a comfortable, well-known environment. Take her to play at a friend's house while you run to the store for half an hour or grab a cup of coffee at the local bakery. Try it out to see how she does without you. If she adapts easily, then she might be ready for several hours a week at preschool.

Getting Ready for Preschool

Once you have decided to have your child attend preschool, take her to visit the school and her prospective preschool teachers. Arrange playdates with future classmates so she'll recognize a few people during those early days at school. Some preschools have "summer classes," which are really playdates for incoming children that take place at the school. Your child will get to meet her teachers and hang out in her new classroom but with the safety net of her parents being in the same room.

You should also talk with your child about going to preschool. Tell her about all the fun things she will get to do, the new friends she will meet and play with, and the things she will learn. Be excited for her and make it sound like a great new adventure. Check out books from the library about going to preschool and read them together. Talk about her friends who will also be attending preschool, or those who are already in preschool.

Preschool Options

Most preschool programs are available for a fee. So you'll have to do some research into your local preschool scene to see what options are available for your child and how much they cost. Many day cares offer preschool programs, and you can find Montes-

With regular exposure to other children, your child can get plenty of social skills practice without going to preschool. However, if your child thrives on social gatherings, especially larger groups, then she may love the preschool experience.

sori, Waldorf, religious, and other private preschools as well. If you have trouble imagining your child enjoying a classroom experience, then homeschooling might be a worthwhile option to consider. Remember that if you select a preschool that's not a good fit for your child, you can always switch to another or wait a year and restart the process.

Troubleshooting Preschool

If your child has been at home with you or another caregiver (rather than in a day care setting), the transition to preschool may be difficult for her. Although she may talk a good game at home about being excited about going to school, the reality of getting dropped off at a strange place all by herself may stop her in her tracks.

If you've decided to give preschool a try and your child gets upset every school morning and doesn't want to go, give it a couple of weeks to see whether she adapts to the new experience. Talk to her preschool teachers to find out how she's doing in the classroom once you're gone and how long it takes her to calm down and get involved. Talk to your child about it. Get her input: Ask her how she feels and whether she has fun even though she's sad to say good-bye to you. Remind her that you will *always come back* to pick her up. Watch her behavior in the mornings when you're getting ready to go to school. If she's really resistant, perhaps this is not the right time for her to go; perhaps she just isn't ready. Listen to her. Give her another year and try again. Sometimes that's all it takes, and the following year she'll happily wave good-bye to you as you walk out the school door.

3–4
years

9

Solving Problems and Negotiating Like a Pro

Exuberant. Imaginative. Energetic. That's how we'd describe your four- to five-year-old. Her language skills continue to expand at an incredible rate, and she is becoming a great conversationalist, rarely needing a prompt from adults to include all the pertinent details in her stories. (It may be more common that she needs a prompt to leave out a few details!) She is on a quest for information and under-standings; she wants to know how the world and everything in it works. This is also a great year for physical mastery. You will be amazed at how much your child can learn, understand, and remember at this age. And you'll probably laugh at every other sentence that comes out of her mouth. She sees the world in such a different way from adults— full of innocence, curiosity, and creativity.

As you read through this chapter on the general development of four- to five-year-olds, remember that each child is unique. Your child will develop at his own pace, and though you can certainly create environments and opportunities to enhance his development, you cannot actually speed it up. He'll do things when he's ready to do them. Your child may be right on target with the information we present here, or he may be ahead of or behind it. If you are concerned about your child's development, please speak with your family physician or pediatrician. But remember that children will develop in their own time. Relax and enjoy your child's journey through childhood!

DEVELOPING BODY

Your Child Is More and More Physically Coordinated

Your four- to five-year-old loves active play. He is full of energy, and he will enjoy long periods of activity on a daily basis. His large motor skills are growing along with his body. He can run, jump, and hop on one foot. He can learn to skip, gallop, and march. Given the opportunity (or if the thought merely occurs to him), he will jump over and off things. Everything!

He can now walk in a straight line and down a flight of stairs alternating feet while holding on to the handrail. It's fairly easy for him to kick, throw, and bounce a ball, and he can catch a thrown or bounced ball as well. He loves outdoor play—any play that involves big movements—and especially loves playing with you. If he's had access to a tricycle or bicycle with training wheels, he will be pedaling and steering like a pro. He may learn how to swing by himself, pumping to swing higher and higher, or it may not happen until next year.

You may be surprised at all the physical things your child can do and will learn to do this year. Mastering the monkey bars is a great feat, taking coordination, strength, and a whole lot of self confidence.

Your Child's Physical Development Leads to Greater Independence

Physically, your child can take over some of his personal care, because he can now go to the bathroom alone and wash his body in the bath or shower. He's not quite old enough to brush his teeth entirely on his own. He'll still need you to brush his teeth at least once or twice a day to make sure all of his teeth are properly cleaned. He can dress and undress himself, and he may have the dexterity to fasten his buttons and work his zipper, though he may still need help for a little while longer. He is adept at using utensils at mealtimes and can feed himself quite neatly.

At this age, your child can help set the table, arranging the plates and silverware. He is able to pour water from a small pitcher to fill everyone's water glass at the table. He loves to help! He also loves to use tools, such as hammers and screwdrivers. In fact, if he has battery-operated toys, he can unscrew the battery door to remove the dead batteries, put in fresh or recharged ones, and close it back up by screwing the door shut. Your child can cut along a straight line with scissors, and he is a great help at cutting out coupons (regardless of whether you use them).

Children love to help out in any way they can. Setting the table and helping to prepare meals is also a great way to get a picky eater involved and more likely to try the foods you prepare together.

4–5
years

Your Child's Inner Artist Emerges

Artistic abilities really blossom at this age. Your child can form objects—animals, insects, shapes, etc.—out of clay or play dough. He enjoys threading beads onto a string, and he can build more elaborate structures out of wooden or Lego-like blocks.

Your child may be drawing simple shapes such as circles, and many of those circles will turn into faces. These faces will gain more definition and more details as he grows.

At this stage, your child draws by moving his whole arm instead of making small hand movements. This makes for writing that is quite large, and he'll have trouble writing smaller letters. But the letters he writes are well formed and clear, and he may even start to use lowercase letters. He may be able to hold a pencil correctly in the tripod position, or it may take more time for him to adopt that position. He will enjoy writing words, and he can probably write his own name.

Activities to Enhance Your Child's Physical Development

Keep activities fun for everyone. If you find that you're pushing your child to do something he doesn't want to do simply because you think it's good for his physical development, then it's time to find a new activity. He only wants to do something if he's enjoying himself. If it's not fun, or if he just doesn't like what you're doing, don't force it. It doesn't mean he won't acquire whatever developmental skills are involved. He will, but by doing something else. A quick glance at the list of activities below shows that there are plenty of different things you can do with your child that will enhance his development.

Activities for Large Motor Skills Development

- Give your child at least an hour of physical activity most days.

- Visit playgrounds to help your child develop large motor skills such as balancing, running, climbing, and jumping. Go up and down the slides.

Your child may have been drawing faces for a while, or he may just be starting to do it now. It's amazing to watch the progression of details in his drawings of faces and bodies as your child grows and develops.

- Play catch with various size balls. Play baseball with your child, giving him practice at hitting a ball with a bat.

- Create an obstacle course in your yard that includes balancing, running, going under and over things, climbing, and jumping. Don't make it competitive; just do it for the pure fun of it.

- Play soccer! Run around and kick balls to each other in your yard or at the park or playground to improve your child's coordination.

- Play follow the leader on the playground, through your obstacle course, and even in your home. Include skills like hopping, skipping, jumping, walking, running, and turning in circles. Alternate being the leader so your child gets a chance to lead you!

- Do forward rolls on a mattress on the floor, on a gym mat, or outside on the grass.

- Hit balloons with a badminton or tennis racket. Bounce balloons off different parts of the body. Practice keeping the balloon in the air without letting it touch the ground for as long as possible.

- Have child-size tools available (gardening tools, snow shovel, etc.) so your child can help you while learning how to use tools that fit his hands and stature. He'll also love helping you with adult-size tools such as a broom and vacuum. After grocery shopping, ask your child to help carry in the light bags and unpack the items.

Activities for Fine Motor Skills Development

- Do puzzles that offer a little challenge, but not so much that your child loses interest.

- Play board games.

- Provide a small table and chairs for your child to use for playing, drawing, and eating. Find play dishes for him to pretend with.

- Increase hand-eye coordination by building cities with blocks, stringing beads onto pipe cleaners, doing various puzzles, using scissors, drawing, spreading jam on bread, and pouring liquids from a small pitcher into cups.

- Develop strength, dexterity, and control by cutting with scissors; using a stapler, hammer, or hole punch; squeezing water out of a washcloth; squeezing balls or soft bath toys; and drawing.

- Ask your child to cut out coupons. This is a great activity to do together because you can let him know which coupons you would like to use, and he'll feel proud when you use the ones he snipped out.

4–5
years

- Have glue, scissors, paper, stickers, markers, and crayons always on hand. Store them on a low shelf that your child can reach, so he can get what he needs independently. He'll also like to use his hands with play dough, clay, and paints. (Look for washable finger paints, watercolors, and acrylics.)

- Make paper airplanes or learn origami. Search online for different designs of paper airplanes and instructions for making them.

- Supervise your child's use of a computer keyboard and a mouse, which can improve his dexterity and hand-eye coordination. There are numerous free preschooler game websites on the Internet, or you can purchase games to load onto your computer. Your local public library may have a children's computer with access to many educational computer games.

- Thread small beads onto string or pipe cleaners.

- Put small pegs in holes.

- Use tools. Pound several nails partially into a board as a start for your child. He can pound them in the rest of the way. Start screws and give your child a screwdriver to screw them in farther. Or if your child has battery-operated toys, give him the screwdriver to open the door to replace the batteries.

- Pour sand or water from container to container. Your child can play with water either outside or in the bath. It's an all-weather activity. Provide several small containers for your child to use.

- Build together with blocks and let your child have time to build alone. Create complex structures, make shapes, and spell your child's name with blocks.

- Draw with your child. He'll sometimes try to draw what you draw. If he asks, lead him through step-by-step so he understands how to draw a certain object.

- Your child can help you cook by spreading butter and jelly on toast, cutting vegetables for a salad or stir-fry with a child-safe knife, or measuring and mixing ingredients (all under supervision, of course). He wants to do everything you do. Ask for his help setting the table, stirring the iced tea, or carrying the bread to the table.

- Your child can learn to fold clothes and hang them up or put them away in his drawers.

4–5
years

Healthy foods are an important part of your child's overall development. Fresh whole foods like fruits and vegetables are the best nutrition—especially if they come straight from your garden or are grown locally.

DEVELOPING MIND

Your Independent-Minded Child Solves Problems and Negotiates like a Pro

A four- to five-year-old child is very curious and eager to learn. He will want to try out new experiences that he hears about from others. ("Mom, can we do that, too?") He will want to know what will happen next during daily activities, and he will ask about future events. ("Hey, Dad, when can we go to a hot air balloon festival again?") He may be very talkative and is getting to the age where he enjoys serious conversation. He'll even *start* conversations with others!

Your child is becoming his own person more and more each day. **He likes to make his own decisions about what he wears, what he eats, how he plays, and what he wants to play with.** You're often likely to hear "It's my choice, not yours." This surge in independence is good, though it may make things a little more challenging for you. **Give your child as much autonomy as you can. If it really doesn't matter, then let him make the decision. He needs the practice as well as the freedom.** Much of his life is not under his control at this age, so give him control whenever you can.

With your child's blooming independence comes the ability to empathize. Your child will begin to recognize situations that he senses could lead to anger, happiness, or sadness. He'll be able to look at the world and identify with others. He'll know why someone is crying, if he saw what happened. This will affect his pretend play, and his scenarios will become longer and more complex. You'll see his understanding of cause and effect in his play. **He'll use make-believe to work through strong emotions, or to work through something he's experienced. He may play the same scene over and over again, which is a healthy way for him to process his emotions.** And it gives you insight into what he's absorbing from his interactions with you and others, and which things in his daily life upset him.

Being a natural scientist, your child will ask lots of questions at this age. Who? What? When? Where? And, especially, Why? His problem solving becomes more creative, as he tries different tactics and looks to others to figure out a solution. He wants to problem solve on his own, but he'll also seek help from adults or peers when he needs it. He is very imaginative when trying to figure out how to do something or how to make something. You'll be surprised at his ingenuity! **Try not to direct how he does things—even if you "know" it won't work. Let him discover it on his own. Let him figure it out. The lesson he learns is more powerful if he does it himself.** He'll learn how to do whatever it is he's trying to do, and he'll learn that you believe in his ability to do it on his own.

Since his ability to focus on a task is stronger, you may find your child concentrating on his drawings for longer periods of time or doing puzzles with much more focus than he used to.

Your child's focus is lengthening. **He can concentrate on a single activity for ten to fifteen minutes, and he is better able to ignore distractions and interruptions** that previously would have caused him to run off on another tangent. You are likely to find that his focusing skills support his talent for negotiation. Kids at this age are great negotiators! (So good, in fact, that you might think you have a future lawyer on your hands.) Your child will try to negotiate virtually everything. That's wonderful—and exhausting at times. But it's a great skill for him to hone. If something is nonnegotiable, then tell him upfront, but if it really doesn't matter, let him negotiate a deal. This is another chance for him to exert some control over his life. He needs that because it boosts his self-esteem every time he negotiates for something he wants. And he may offer a great solution to what you thought was a problematic situation. **His negotiation tactics are important to his development as a confident, responsible, and independent adult.**

Your child may negotiate everything from which color cup he wants to whether he can have a goldfish as a pet, but your child is able to follow directions very well by now. He's also taking turns without needing to be reminded constantly. Once the turn-taking pattern is set up for a particular activity, he sticks to it. You'll see this trend during playdates and time spent at the playground, or when he's playing with his sibling(s). This shows that he's becoming more aware of others' needs and wants.

4–5
years

Reading, Writing, and Organizational Skills Bloom

You may notice your child's growing interest in learning letters and numbers. He probably recognizes several letters of the alphabet, perhaps all of them, and he may be able to write his name. He also may recognize simple words. He might surprise you at the grocery store one day with, "Hey, Dad, that says 'dog'!" Your child enjoys counting various items—pictures in a book or objects around the house—and can count to seven or higher.

Your child's organizing and sorting skills are getting refined. He can order objects in a line from largest to smallest, or he may sort objects by shape or color. He's starting to understand that you can group things differently based on common traits. He also understands the concepts of tallest, biggest, smallest, same, more, on, in, under, and above. And he can name at least six colors and three shapes by now.

Your child's awareness of patterns, common traits, and organization means he knows the order of his daily routines very well, starting with breakfast in the morning, followed by lunch and then dinner in the evening, and bedtime. This also ties into his desire to know what comes next, and to know future plans. He appreciates having a reliable organization to his day—whether it is loosely defined around meals or more structured with household or school routines—because it gives him a sense of what his day will entail.

Activities to Enhance Your Child's Cognitive Development

- Play games with your child that require thinking. He may enjoy matching games, board games, card games, dominoes, or tic-tac-toe.

- Do puzzles together, and let him do them alone. Find ones that give him a little challenge, but are not overly difficult. If they are too easy, they won't hold his interest.

- Practice the alphabet with your preschooler. Sing the ABCs, read books that highlight the alphabet, and regularly write it out for him to help him recognize the letters as well as see how to write them. Discuss what sounds the letters make. Ask him about the sounds of letters: "What does *m* say?"

Your child's sorting skills can be put to work to help the environment. Enlist his help in organizing and sorting the recyclables into containers and carrying them out to be picked up on recycling day.

- Practice numbers and counting whenever you have the opportunity. Read counting books. Count everything! Ask your child to pick out five apples at the grocery store. See if he can find a bunch of three bananas. Ask him to count the number of dinosaurs on a book page, the number of chairs you need when friends stay for lunch, or the number of cupcakes for a birthday party. Write down the numbers 1 through 10 so he will learn to recognize them. Count higher as he shows proficiency.

Talk numbers whenever you can. Count things all day long, look at a calendar together, talk about the numbers on the face of a clock and how the position of the hands tell you what time it is.

- Encourage your child's mathematical thinking by asking him to count, sort, match, group, sequence, and recognize patterns in everyday situations. Have him help sort the dirty laundry into lights and darks. Ask him to sort the clean socks and put them in matching pairs. When your child helps you set the table, ask him to count how many forks, spoons, knives, plates, and glasses you'll need, then have him arrange them in a place setting pattern.

- Read to your child as often as you can and make it a part of your daily routine. Read books on his favorite subjects. Go to the library together so he can find books he wants to read. He will memorize text as you read books repeatedly, and he will also start to recognize some words on the page.

- Sing songs with your child. Listen to music in the house and when driving. (Be sure to have music that you won't mind listening to repeatedly.) He'll memorize song lyrics, though he won't always come up with real words for what he hears. It doesn't matter to him. He'll sing them anyway!

- Encourage the magic of make-believe play with building blocks and make-believe play materials such as scarves, hats, old clothes, shoes, recyclables for creating fantastical costumes and props, blankets for building forts, and anything else you can think of. You can step into your child's make-believe worlds as a character he wants you to play to learn more about the way your child thinks and feels. Follow his lead and rules of play; don't try to direct the show. Just play along.

- Host a tea party your child's his beloved stuffed animals.

- Make a grocery store in your home with old pasta boxes, bags of dried fruit, and household supplies like clean sponges or rolls of paper towels. Let your child decide who gets to be the cashier and who will play the customer.

4–5
years

DEVELOPING LANGUAGE

Your Child's Vocabulary Grows by Leaps and Bounds

By the age of four, your child knows about 2,500 to 3,000 words, and he will learn another 2,000 in the coming year. (Isn't that amazing? How many new words did you learn last year?) Given the right opportunities, your child can learn up to six new words each day. Read to him! Talk to him like he's an intelligent person, not a child with limited understanding. He understands (and *can* understand) much more than you think.

Your child is speaking in complex sentences by now, and using good grammar. He is also adept at using the regular past tense of words. **We cannot stress enough the importance of speaking correctly around your child. Remember to use**

Read, read, read to help your child's language development. Go to the library and let her browse the bookshelves to find books that look interesting to her. Set the example by reading yourself in your child's presence during quiet times.

proper grammar and correct pronunciation when you talk with him. Model for him how it's done, and he will learn through your example. You do not need to correct his grammar or pronunciation, but model it, and he will self-correct in time. Trust that he will learn it without correction. (Who wants someone constantly pointing out that you're doing something wrong?)

Your child is beginning to understand that letters grouped together represent words, and he can actually identify the beginning and ending sounds of words. This new attention to the sounds of letters means that he can use invented spelling when he wants to write words that he doesn't know how to spell. He'll guess at the spelling, based on his knowledge of letter sounds. This is normal development, and it does not call for correcting his spelling mistakes. That will come as he learns to read. If he asks you how to spell something, spell it for him out loud or write it down for him on a separate piece of paper. His knowledge of letters, also means he knows that numbers (numerals) are not letters, and they do not appear in words.

Your child is learning time words, including *yesterday, today, tomorrow, morning,* and *afternoon.* He might learn money words if you talk about money with him by pointing out the names of the different coins and bills. He is also gaining an understanding of figures of speech, such as "hold your horses." Your child is becoming more precise in the words he uses to describe things, putting his rapidly expanding vocabulary to good use.

Your child is asking more direct questions and wants to know "why?" and "how?" He is figuring out his world—how things work, why things happen—with every question he asks. Answer his questions truthfully, and if you do not know the answer, say so and then look it up together in a book, at the library, or online. **Model for him that it's okay not to know the answer to everything and that you should either ask someone else for the answer or look up the information yourself.**

RED FLAG!

If you are concerned with your child's pronunciation or worried that he may have a speech impediment, ask your physician for a formal evaluation as soon as you can. Early intervention is best.

At this age, your child will probably love to sing songs. He'll learn lyrics quickly, though he doesn't limit himself to real words when he repeats lyrics. (He most likely still uses nonsense words when he plays sometimes, so singing nonsense words is not out of the ordinary for him.) He'll sing what he hears, regardless of whether it makes sense. As his vocabulary continues to grow, he'll start to hear and internalize the correct words. He likes rhymes, and can even identify rhyming words. In fact, he'll enjoy coming up with a whole list of words that rhyme—some real, some made up.

Use Your Child's Memory and Conversational Skills to Keep Him Safe

Your child is at the perfect age to teach him his full name, home address, and phone number. He is a gifted memorizer, so take advantage of that to help keep him safe. When teaching him his address and phone number, discuss who would be a good person to talk to if he were lost. If he's lost in a store, tell him to find an employee for help and to stand in the aisle so he can see you and you can see him when you're looking for each other. (And next time you go shopping, point out store employees, telling him what clues to look for, such as a uniform, ID tag around their necks, etc.) If you are not convinced that your child can tell the difference between an employee and a shopper, consider teaching him that if he is lost, to look for a mother with a child to ask for help. Talk about how police officers, EMTs, paramedics, and firefighters are safe people to seek help from as well.

4–5
years

Your child loves a good conversation, and he is better at waiting for his turn to talk while he listens to someone else. He can describe a simple experience he had recently and will initiate conversations with adults and peers alike. His phone skills are improving, so he can have longer, more in-depth and complete conversations. He's using appropriate tone, volume, and inflection more consistently, which makes his speech very clear to anyone he speaks with.

Talking on the phone is so much fun. And with the development of his conversational skills he's much more talkative on the phone with grandparents and family friends. He has a lot to say!

Reading and Writing Skills Increase

With your child's ability to concentrate on tasks for longer periods, he now has the necessary focus to listen to longer stories. His memorization skills have allowed him to commit his favorite books to memory, and he can recite them while "reading" the books or whenever he pleases. If you've talked about the authors and illustrators of his favorite books, he may recognize them. He certainly knows the book titles very well and will ask for them by name!

When you read to your child, he will probably begin to ask where a word appears in the printed text: "Where's *quiet*?" He'll want you to point to the printed word so he can see what it looks like and how it's spelled. He may also ask you to read signs that he sees when you're out and about, or headlines in magazines or newspapers. He's becoming more and more curious about words and the magic of reading. He's also developing a flair for telling fictional stories of his own, which he's happy to share with anyone who will listen.

Your child doesn't always plan for enough space when he's writing words on paper. When he comes to the edge of the paper, he'll simply place the remaining letters wherever there is space on the page, which may be above, below, or to the left of the word. He hasn't figured out spacing between words, either, so he'll usually run words into each other. This will work itself out naturally as his writing skills progress. Eventually and without instruction, he'll start planning for the appropriate amount of space when he writes.

With her increased awareness of the written language, your child will ask for you to point out words on the page when you are reading to her. She may even start to recognize those same words when she sees them in other places.

Activities to Enhance Your Child's Language Development

- Read every day, several times a day if you can. Talk about the characters in the stories. Read alphabet books to help your child learn the ABCs and letter sounds.

- Practice the alphabet and sing the ABCs. Write the alphabet out for him regularly to help him identify the letters as well as see how to write them. Talk about what sounds the letters make. Ask him about the sounds of letters: "What does the letter *b* say?"

- Write out your child's name. If he's ready to write it himself, he will!

- Treat your child like he's an intelligent person. (He is!) Talk with him. Have conversations in which you ask for his opinions and discuss his likes and dislikes. Listen closely when he talks to you and respond to him in a way that shows you heard him and understood what he meant.

- Always use correct grammar when you speak to model it for your child. He is learning to speak (and write) from the way you speak.

- Joke with your child, and he'll learn to joke, too. He loves to laugh, and he will enjoy playing with language.

- Tell your child stories. Talk about your experiences or make up stories with your child(ren) as the leading character(s). Those may become his favorite stories.

- Ask your child to tell you stories. Encourage him to describe something that happened to him or something he saw. He'll also enjoy telling completely imaginative tales.

4-5
years

- Spell words for your child if he asks you how to spell something. If you are not sure how about a particular spelling, look it up in the dictionary. That way you'll make sure you're giving him a correct spelling, and you'll also model how to find information when you don't know the answer.

- Point out words that begin or end with the same sound when you are talking or reading to develop your child's awareness of letter sounds.

- Listen to music and sing! Your child will love singing along, and he'll quickly memorize song lyrics.

- Read rhymes. Talk about rhyming words, and ask your child for rhymes. "What rhymes with *hat*?" Write rhyming poems.

- Collect items suitable for make-believe play, like puppets and dolls and materials such as old clothes, hats, scarves, and shoes, recyclables for creating costumes and props, blankets for building forts, etc. Craft hand puppets out of paper bags decorated with markers, paper, felt, and glue, or out of socks decorated with buttons, yarn, fabric, and thread. (Your child will love to make puppets, and it's wonderful for his fine motor skills.)

- Have alphabet puzzles, games, and magnetic refrigerator letters for your child to play with.

Playing with letters is a great way to improve his language skills. Talk about the sounds the letters make, spell words, and show how to sound them out one letter at a time.

DEVELOPING PERSON

Your Child Pretends, Converses, and Participates in Household Activities

Your four- to five-year-old child is very imaginative. His pretend play is becoming much more elaborate, and it may include imaginary friends and objects. It most certainly will involve impromptu costumes. Your favorite salad bowl may be his new hat, and he'll be delighted if you give him access to dress-up clothes so he can turn into whatever he desires. He'll pretend that he's working in an ice cream store or that he's a delivery person or going grocery shopping. He's not just playing "house" anymore.

Make believe play now becomes more elaborate with costumes usually required and more complex story lines, scenarios, and themes. Help her become whoever she wants to be in her pretend play.

> **TIP**
>
> ### Make It Routine to Help around the House
>
> When household tasks become a normal part of your child's day, it's good for everyone in the family. Ideally, you should start as soon as your child is able to help and shows interest, which is usually around age two. But if you haven't done so until now, it's certainly not too late. Encourage his involvement, and it will become habit once he's been helping out for a while. Try to find things that your child enjoys doing. If he loves to vacuum, let him vacuum. It doesn't matter if he doesn't get every speck of dirt off the carpet; what matters is that he's willingly helping. In another year or so, he'll have watched you vacuum enough to do a thorough job of it himself.

4–5
years

Your child will happily create complex make-believe scenarios and act them out by himself, with siblings, or with friends. Or he may ask you to pretend with him. (It's a great way to better understand which events in his life are meaningful to him, as well as how he perceives them.) He's still at the age where he may not always know the difference between make-believe and reality. That'll come over the next few years.

Your child is a budding conversationalist who enjoys serious talks, constantly asks "why?" and does his best to comprehend the world around him. He's trying to make sense of all he sees, hears, and experiences. He'll start to show off, here and there, and brag about his accomplishments, be they large or small. "Dad! I ate my whole sandwich!" "Mom, watch me swing!" He may start to tell jokes, if he's been hearing them, though they may not always make sense. He'll find them hilarious regardless. You probably will, too!

At this age, your child may become more involved in the household caretaking, especially if he's been allowed or encouraged to help when he was younger. He'll help clean up when asked. He'll enjoy being entrusted with an important task, such as taking out the compost container to empty it into the compost pile. He'll help set the table, and he can clear his place after a meal.

How You Handle Tattling May Encourage Your Child to Lie or Keep Secrets

Your child is at the point where he understands and follows the rules most of the time. He'll also be very concerned when someone is not following the rules, especially when it's something he has been told not to do, and he will tell on the other child. Be very careful how you handle tattling.

We caution against telling your child "Don't be a tattletale" for a couple of reasons. First, you are calling him a name, and most parents don't want their children to engage in name-calling. And second, we assume you want to have a close, honest relationship with your child, one in which he would come to you when he needs you, would tell you the truth, and would seek your help if someone were in danger. **If you tell him to stop tattling on others, then you are sending him the wrong message about honesty and safety.**

It is a fine line on which you will have to find your own position. If what's going on is a matter of safety, then it's essential that your child report to you. If it's a case of children fighting over something, can you sit down with them and have a discussion in which they work it out themselves? You should listen and encourage them to find a solution that is fair to everyone without injecting your own opinion or advice. That's not always easy to do, especially because we as parents tend to try to fix everything. The larger goal is teaching your children how to work out a problem by talking it through, allowing each person time to speak, listening to each other, brainstorming a solution, and trying to make it fair for everyone involved. That's a lifetime skill!

TIP

What to Do When Your Child Swears

Swearing, like name-calling, is a learned trait. Children who have been exposed to adults or other children who swear will pick it up quickly. It's best to ignore swearing (so don't give a huge reaction when he drops the F-word) and to discuss it casually: "Oh, love, let's not use that word. I think you meant ___. That's something you can say."

Just like anything else, if you make it a big deal, your child will continue to do it. If you react with vigor, he may enjoy triggering that response. It's like power in his hands. (It also satisfies his scientific streak and his fascination with cause and effect: If I say this, wow, that happens. What happens if I say it again?) What you focus on is what you will get from your child. Ignore it whenever you can and it will go away. Remember to give your child examples of what he *can* do when you are telling him something he can't do.

If the situation involves one sibling doing what another sibling was told not to do, you can gently suggest to the child who told you that his job is to worry about himself, not about his sister. Worrying about his sister is your job. Then you can speak to his sister about not doing something she just heard you tell her brother not to do. No one should be made to feel bad for telling. **No one should be called a tattletale and shamed. That doesn't benefit anyone. It simply begins to teach your child to withhold information and lie to you.**

Even if you avoid using "tattletale," it's possible that name-calling will start at this age if your child has learned it from others. If your child is name-calling, tell him calmly and seriously, "Let's not call each other names because it hurts people's feelings, and that is not how we treat people. We are kind and gentle. If you are mad at someone, you can simply tell her you are mad without name-calling."

New Fears Erupt at Four or Five Years Old

Don't be surprised if you find your child suddenly becoming afraid of things that didn't frighten him before. Movies he's seen many times may suddenly scare him, and he won't want to watch them anymore. He may become afraid of the dark or worry about monsters in his closet or under his bed. If he's been exposed to death, he may worry that you are going to die. These new fears come with his increased understanding of danger.

4–5
years

Be assured—your child will grow out of them, but it is important for you to acknowledge the fears and talk about them with him. You might have to ask leading questions to understand his fear. You might not see the connection at first between seeing a dead bird in the park and acting clingier and having difficulty falling asleep that night. By gently asking him what he is worried about, you might discover that he is thinking about death, his own and yours. He might be worried that he is not going to wake up in the morning. By understanding his fears, you will be able to more directly reassure him.

Your Child Relates More to Other Children

Sometimes your child will prefer to play with other children, and sometimes he'll prefer to play alone. He will really enjoy having regular playdates with friends, and you'll notice that he's become more and more social. He will approach a group of familiar or unfamiliar children to play with. He will share and take turns most of the time when asked, and he'll try to negotiate or bargain with his friends, siblings, and parents or other adults. He cooperates with his peers at times, although he still can be bossy or aggressive.

You will notice occasions when your child works to please other children, and to comfort them when they are in need, hurt, upset, or mad. He is beginning to identify what causes feelings and to learn that people sometimes feel differently from him: "I'm having fun, but Jillie isn't." He starts to compare himself and his experience to others at this age: "Why can Audrey do that, but I can't?"

When trying to figure out a solution to a problem, your child will start to work with other children rather than immediately seeking out an adult's help. He will still ask for an adult to help when necessary, but he's more apt to try to take care of it on his own and with his peers first.

Your Child Needs Freedom and Your Continual Support

Like everyone else, your child needs to feel important. He needs opportunities for greater independence, more chances to make his own decisions, and increased autonomy. Give these to him whenever you can. He needs to practice making decisions on his own. He needs the freedom to choose what he wants (and to face the consequences of his choice). It's fine to counsel him with your experience and to let him know if his choice might lead to a negative outcome. But ultimately, you should let him make the decision. This is how he learns to be his own person. This is how he learns to be independent.

Your child may start lying at this age, usually to protect himself. He may not entirely understand the concept of lying; it may be more the product of a vivid imagination. Emphasize the importance of telling the truth when he lies. This is not a phase that's best to ignore and to allow to go away on its own. When it comes to lying, your child needs to hear that it's unacceptable, and that you expect him to tell you the truth, even if it means he might get into trouble. Try to handle things gently when he's telling you the truth, so he knows that it's much better to tell the truth than to lie. For more on lying, read the section in Positively Parenting on page 264 at the end of this chapter.

When your child expresses himself, he is relying on adults as role models in the way he inflects words, the phrases he says, and the facial expressions or greetings he uses. You'll see yourself in so much of what he does at this age! As you model this skill for him and remind him to use it the next time he's angry, he is learning to express his anger in words rather than physically. Part of the time. He's not perfect at it, but he's making progress. Remember that it takes years before this skill becomes second nature.

Your child loves playing with friends and is very interested in other children. He'll even play with unfamiliar children at the playground or park. He's becoming much more social as he grows.

4–5
years

Your child may still throw tantrums over seemingly "minor" issues, but keep in mind that what's minor to you may *feel* major to him. Equate it to experiences in your life: Some days you are barely holding it together, and something as simple as spilling your coffee can set you off in a rage or a puddle of tears. An observer might think you're crazy to get so worked up over a cup of coffee. It's the same with your child. You are not witness to all that is going on inside him, so the seemingly silly thing that pushed him over the edge may have been the last straw in a long line of obstacles and frustrations. Treat him with kindness in those moments, and give him the support he needs to get himself back in emotional balance.

Your child has reached the age where he may be able to separate from you for a brief time without crying if he's in a familiar and comfortable environment. If your child cannot separate without crying, don't force him. When he's ready, when he feels safe being on his own, he'll do so easily and happily. He is coping better with his emotions these days, and he is able to use words more often and more effectively to express himself.

A child who will happily wave goodbye to you is ready to do things on her own without you around for a little while. Don't rush this milestone by forcing her. Let your child separate when she is ready.

Activities to Enhance Your Child's Emotional and Social Development

- Get out and about! Go to cafes and museums with your child. Show him how to be in the world. Run errands and do other everyday stuff that involves interacting with people to model how it's done and to give your child opportunities to practice it himself if he wants to. All on his own, he will start to interact with people of all ages when he's ready.

- Have fun with children of various ages (a great reason to join a playgroup). Allow your child plenty of chances to engage with adults of various ages as well. Give him the tools and practice time to become comfortable interacting with people of all ages.

- Go to playgroups and make playdates. Your child needs regular opportunities to be with others to learn the art of cooperative play. And remember: It is a gradual learning process.

- Play various games with your child: board and card games, dominoes, tag, hide-and-seek, etc. It's a fun way to learn to take turns.

- Stock up on make-believe play materials such as scarves, hats, old clothes, shoes, recyclables for fashioning fabulous costumes and props, blankets for building terrific forts, etc.

- Have conversations with hand puppets (you can make your own—a great activity for fine motor skills) where they discuss issues that may bother your child or problem solve something he's concerned about.

- Find noncompetitive team activities to do such as cleaning up the park or building a tree house.

- Give your child words he can say when he is upset, angry, or sad. Continue to remind him to express himself with words, not with pushes, hits, or kicks.

- Allow your child time to be alone if he wants it.

- Set aside an alone spot for your child where he can hide whenever he feels the need to. You can use a large cardboard box or a closet with pillows on the floor. (This is *not* a time-out spot.)

- Encourage your child to help plan activities, playdates, and parties. Ask for his input, preferences, and help. He loves to to be a part of such important tasks!

Join in social gatherings in your community like beautifying the local park or planting a community garden. Being around people and working cooperatively is great for your child's social development.

4–5
years

POSITIVELY PARENTING

Are You Teaching Your Child to Lie?

Children begin to lie around the age of four—most often to protect themselves from getting into trouble or to give you the answer that will not upset you. Imagine this scenario: "Did you draw all over this wall?" (He sees your stern face.) "No." Your child does not want to upset you, so he gives the answer he knows *will not upset you.* Except he doesn't realize that lying will upset you more. All he knows is that he doesn't want you to yell, so he gives the answer that logically should keep you from yelling. He gives you the answer he thinks will make you happy.

Children naturally seek out happiness. They live their lives for joy and in joy. (We could learn a lot from them on this, couldn't we?) Think about how you ask your child a question: "Did you draw on this wall?" or "Who drew all over this wall?" Are you prompting your child to lie by the question you ask? Instead of questioning your child, try describing what you see. (After all, it's clear to you who did it—or if you have more than one child, you have a short list of suspects and everyone should share in the lesson.) "Wow, I see that you drew on the wall. We draw on paper, not walls. Let's make sure you know where the paper is for when you want to draw. I wonder if you could help me clean this up. I would really like to have your help. And next time you know that walls are not for drawing on."

Another way that parents inadvertently teach their children to lie is by telling white lies or by encouraging them to do the same. Does your child ever hear you spare someone's feelings by lying? "I'm so sorry, but I can't make it to the meeting because I have other commitments." Or, after making faces and comments about a gift you received but didn't particularly like, has your child ever heard you tell the gift giver, "I just *loved* the _____ you gave me! Thank you so much!"

It may seem like innocent behavior, but when you demonstrate how to fake enthusiasm in front of your child, you are encouraging your child to lie (and feel proud of his ability to do so). If he receives a gift that he doesn't like, do you urge him to say more than "thank you"? A "thank you" is appropriate for every gift, liked or disliked, because it shows appreciation for someone's thoughtfulness. But gushing over a gift is unnecessary, and in this scenario, it is lying. Even if it is meant to protect the gift giver's feelings, it is still lying. And your child will recognize it as such and not make a distinction between these kinds of white lies and lies that are more serious.

When children are forced to lie to be "polite," you can see how uncomfortable they are being disingenuous. With practice, it becomes less uncomfortable and easier to pull off. Before you know it, they are lying to you with casual aplomb. Most parents would agree they do not want that!

So what should we do? We must tread carefully and become more aware of our own lying, eliminating it as best we can. Don't make an elaborate excuse when you can't do something. Simply say you are sorry, but you can't make it. Leave it at that. Teach your child to say "thank you" when he receives a gift and to smile or hug the gift giver. Teach him that the value is in the gesture, not in the material item. Talk to him about how much he is loved because someone gave him a gift, no matter what the gift was. Explain that a gift shows that someone thought about him and what he might like. Be truthful. It's kind to spare other people's feelings, but be truthful.

Teach your child that—liked or disliked—a gift is a sign that someone cares about you and it is appropriate to thank that person for his or her thoughtfulness. Gushing over a gift is not necessary and could lead to lying. A simple "thank you" suffices.

TIP	**Slow Down to Prevent the Quick Lies**

If your notice your child lying automatically, without thought, as if it's a reflex to give you the "right" answer, ask him to slow down before he answers. "Did you wash your hands?" "Yes!" If you are not convinced that he washed his hands because it didn't seem he was in the bathroom long enough or you didn't hear the water running, ask him to slow down. "Okay. Stop and think about what's true before you answer the question. What's true? *Did* you wash your hands?" This can inspire him to really think about what he did—and you'll be able to see on his face whether his first answer was a lie—and he may reply, "No, I didn't." "Okay, go back and wash your hands, please."

4–5
years

In the meantime, take every opportunity to stress to your child how important it is to tell the truth. When he lies to you, don't ignore it and expect it to go away. **If a child gets used to lying, gets good at it, and doesn't learn early on that it's an undesirable trait, he'll do it for a long time to come.** Teach your child that lying is not okay and that it makes people feel bad when you lie to them.

When your child lies to you, tell him you expect him to tell you the truth. Retrain yourself to avoid setting your child up to lie. Don't ask questions you know the answer to! Don't ask questions merely to force your child to admit his guilt. He'll probably lie to you. Don't set him up. Talk to him about what happened, describe what you see, talk about how he can do better next time, and enlist his help to remedy the situation. Turn his mistakes—and a lie at this age is a social mistake—into learning moments. Keep reinforcing your expectations for the truth, keep calm when he makes a mistake, and over time he will learn.

Well-Child Checks and Vaccines

Your child's birthday each year is the perfect time to schedule his annual well-child checkup. As in previous visits, he will be weighed and measured and his growth curves will be updated with the new information. Your doctor will discuss his development, paying less attention to his language and motor skills at this age and more attention to his social skills.

Two screening tests at the four-year well-child check are the vision and hearing tests. Your child may have attempted these last year but three-year-olds are often not able to complete them. It's not unusual for a child to not have 20/20 vision at this age. Many children do not achieve that goal until age six or seven. If there are any concerns with his vision or hearing, you will be referred to a specialist for more formal testing.

There are four vaccine boosters recommended between ages four and six. These include: the measles, mumps, and rubella (or MMR) vaccine; the varicella or chickenpox vaccine; the diphtheria, tetanus, and acellular pertussis (or DTaP) vaccine; and the inactivated polio vaccine (or IPV).

In addition, your child's doctor will recommend that your child receive the flu vaccine at the start of the flu season. In the Resources and Recommended Reading section on page 296, you'll find the most up-to-date list of recommended vaccines.

Health and Safety Tips

Your child should see the dentist every six months for dental checkups and cleanings. If your water supply doesn't contain fluoride, your doctor or dentist can give you a prescription for supplements in either drop or pill form, if you are interested in supplementation.

Excessive sun exposure is dangerous and should be avoided. Childhood sunburns are a primary cause of adult skin cancer. To avoid sun damage, keep your child out of the sun during the middle of the day, use sun-protective hats and clothing when dressing him, and apply sunscreen to any exposed skin when you need to be out in the sun.

A four-year-old child usually weighs close to 40 pounds (18 kg), the weight at which he can sit in a booster car seat using an adult seat belt across the shoulder. Remember that you don't have to transfer your child to the booster seat at 40 pounds (18 kg). The five-point restraint seats are safer, and some accommodate weights up to 50, 60, or even 80 pounds (23, 27, or 36 kg). The car's backseat is still the safest place for your child to ride.

Your child should wear a protective helmet while biking, in-line skating, or participating in other activities that carry a significant risk of head injuries, including skiing or snowboarding.

Remember to follow the basic ongoing safety precautions. Medications and unsafe home and garden products need to be safely kept out of your child's reach. Check your smoke detector batteries twice a year when the clocks change in the spring and the fall. When your smoke detectors expire, usually every ten years, install new ones. Place a carbon monoxide detector in your home if you use a woodstove or fireplace. Keep the poison control phone number prominently posted on or near every telephone in your house and programmed into your cell phones and handheld electronic gadgets. (You can find your area's poison control number listed in the Resources and Recommended Reading section on page 296.) Do not store guns in your home; if you do, keep them safely locked away and the ammunition locked in a separate location.

Nurture Yourself to Better Nurture Your Child

For you to be the best possible parent for your child, you need to make sure you are also taking care of yourself. Find the parts of life that enrich and restore you, and fit them into your schedule. Whether it is dinner with a dear friend, taking up jogging again, or joining a book club (or starting your own), make sure you take time for yourself.

Be sure to also make time for yourself as a couple. Nurture your relationship. Go out and spend time together as adults without your child, if you can and want to. Some parents don't want to leave their child behind, and that's fine. If you're not comfortable leaving your child or just don't feel it's necessary, then don't. You can spend couple time together in the evening after he has gone to sleep. Sit in front of a fire, watch a movie, talk, reignite your romantic flame. Some parents can't afford to hire a babysitter. If that is the case, ask relatives or find other young couples with children and arrange a babysitting swap. You'll feel good that you are leaving your child with a trusted caregiver, and your night out won't be too expensive.

Whatever you do, be sure to make time together to check in. Reconnect with each other and express your feelings of love and appreciation for your partner. Saying it out loud to each other is very important. We need to hear that we are valued, that we are good at what we do, and that someone acknowledges all that we do. Don't assume that your spouse knows how you feel. Take the time to tell him or her.

4–5
years

10

The Art of Self-Control

Your five- to six-year-old is an inquisitive, joyful person. She is a great thinker—figuring out different and creative ways to solve a problem, hypothesizing and testing, coming up with unusual ways of thinking about and doing things. Her imagination takes flight! She is also very physically active, still in possession of that seemingly limitless energy that we parents covet. She is able to maneuver more independently in social situations, occasionally displaying the skills she's learned in peaceful negotiation. It is a wonderful age!

As you read through this chapter on the general development of five- to six-year-olds, remember that each child is unique. Your child's development takes place at her own pace, and though you can certainly create environments and opportunities to enhance her development, you cannot actually speed it up. She'll do things when she's ready. Your child may be right on target with the information we present here, or she may be ahead of or behind it. If you have concerns about your child's development, please raise them with her pediatrician or your family physician. But remember that children develop in their own time. Relax and enjoy your child's journey through childhood!

DEVELOPING BODY

Your Child Is Energetic and Active

As your child moves through her sixth year, she'll become more and more physically coordinated. She's already got it together with balance, walking, running, and climbing. This year she may learn to use a swing all by herself, pumping her legs and upper body to swing higher and higher. She can ride a bike with training wheels, and she may even begin to show an interest in learning to ride without them. If shown how, she can learn to skip, gallop, and do broad jumps. At this age, she can throw a ball with a degree of accuracy, catch it a good amount of the time, and hit it with a bat. She may get a kick out of pounding nails into a heavy piece of wood with a hammer.

Your child can easily walk down a flight of stairs with alternating feet and without holding on to a handrail. She has a good sense of balance and can stand on one foot (and will love pretending to be a tree or a bird). She is also adept at climbing ladders. She has become more safety conscious and will usually look both ways before she crosses a street.

Riding bikes is a great activity for your child to do alone, with friends, or with you. Stick to bike paths or roads with very little traffic (only if you are with him, of course, and teach him to get off the road when a car is coming) and be sure he always wears a helmet.

Your Child Is Capable of Doing Many Things Independently

Your child's physical development gives her greater independence as she learns to brush her teeth fairly well on her own. That said, you should continue to brush her teeth at least once a day. (Remember that her teeth should be brushed at least twice a day for good dental hygiene.) Can you believe that she's reached the age when her baby teeth begin falling out? It's true. You may see her playing with a couple of wiggly teeth this year. Be sure to discuss it with her, letting her know that her teeth may begin to wobble and fall out as her bigger, adult teeth come in.

Your child is also at the age where she will be able to use the bathroom completely on her own, wiping herself appropriately and washing her hands afterward. She also may be able to wash herself independently in the shower or bath. She can certainly do a good job washing her face at this age.

Your child will be quite skilled at using a knife and fork when eating. She is very capable of making her own sandwich and cutting it the way she wants. She may also enjoy helping you cook meals. She can cut up vegetables for a salad with a child-safe knife, help mix ingredients together for baking, and roll out and cut dough. There's so much she can do!

Around the age of six, your child will start to lose her baby teeth. It can be a scary or unpleasant idea to your child, so you may want to start talking about the new adult teeth coming in. And point out any friends who've already lost teeth.

5–6
years

Fine motor skills undergo fine-tuning at this age. Your child enjoys cutting paper, and she can cut a straight line very well if you draw one for her to follow. She is taking more time and care in her coloring, being selective with her colors and staying inside the lines more consistently than she did previously. She is starting to print letters and can write her name. Her drawings become more complex. People have more features, animals are easier to identify, and the drawings are closer to scale and show a sense of composition. Also, her hand dominance is well established by this age.

TIP

Get Her Cooking!

It's a wise move to encourage your child to help out in the kitchen. If you have a picky eater on your hands, she may be more likely to try a variety of dishes when she's a part of the preparation and cooking process.

Your child can fold paper on the diagonal if you show her how. (It's a great time to teach her to make paper airplanes or to do origami together!) She will love to do fine-motor work, such as putting paper clips on paper, threading beads, even sewing, knitting, or crocheting. She may be ready to learn to tie her shoes (if you still find shoes that have laces instead of Velcro!). Her hands work so well that she can fasten her own buttons, zippers, and snaps, which means she can dress and undress herself. She is also old enough to hang up her own clothes, or fold them and put them away in her drawers.

Activities to Enhance Your Child's Physical Development

Activities should be fun for everyone involved. This is play! If your child isn't having fun, then switch to a different activity. Don't push your child to do something she seems reluctant to try or unhappy doing merely because you think it's necessary for her physical development. If she's enjoying herself, if it feels like play, she'll do it with enthusiasm. But if she doesn't like a particular activity, don't force it, and don't worry about it. It doesn't mean she won't gain those developmental skills; it just means she'll gain them through a different activity. There are so many ways to enhance your child's development. Check out the list that follows!

Activities for Large Motor Skills Development

- Make sure your child gets an hour or more of physical activity every day.

- Spend time at playgrounds to enhance your child's large motor skills such as balancing, running, climbing, and jumping. Go up and down the slides for a good physical challenge.

- Play catch with balls of different sizes. Play baseball, giving your child practice at hitting a ball with a bat. (Both are great hand-eye coordination activities.)

- Develop an obstacle course in your yard that has balancing, running, climbing, and jumping parts to it. It should be noncompetitive—just pure fun!

- Play soccer! Kick balls back and forth around your yard, park, or playground to increase your child's coordination.

- Play follow the leader. Try it at home, at the playground, or through an obstacle course. Include hopping, skipping, jumping, walking slow, running, turning in circles . . . anything you can think of. Take turns being the leader.

- Practice forward rolls outside on the grass, on a mattress on the floor, or gym mat.

Your child can do more than you think she can. Encourage her help in the kitchen, and give her opportunities to do more when she helps. She is eager to do it all, and with practice she'll be able to.

5–6
years

- Play with balloons. Hit balloons back and forth with a badminton or tennis racket. Hit balloons with various parts of the body. Try to keep the balloon up in the air without letting it fall to the ground for as long as possible.

- Find child-size tools (construction, gardening, cleaning, etc.) so your child can learn how to use tools that are appropriate for her size while helping you. She'll also enjoy helping with adult-size tools such as a broom and vacuum. She'll feel like a grownup if you let her help carry in the groceries and put stuff away.

Using scissors improves her hand-eye coordination as well as hand strength, control, and dexterity. Keep a stack of to-be-recycled paper that your child can cut up whenever she is in the mood.

Activities for Fine Motor Skills Development

- Do puzzles that are somewhat challenging but not so difficult that your child loses interest.

- Play various board games.

- Set up a small table and chairs in the dining room for your child to use for playing, drawing, and eating. Give her play dishes to pretend with.

- Improve hand-eye coordination by building various structures with blocks, stringing beads onto shoelaces, doing puzzles, cutting with scissors, drawing, spreading butter on bread, and pouring water or juice from a small pitcher into cups.

- Help your child increase strength, control, and dexterity through the use of scissors, a stapler, a hammer, and a hole punch, by squeezing water out of a washcloth or squeezing balls or soft bath toys, and by drawing.

- Clip coupons. This is a fun activity to do together because you can indicate which coupons you would like to use, and she'll feel proud when you use the ones she cut out.

- Have available for your child glue, scissors, paper, stickers, markers, and crayons. Place them on a shelf that she can easily reach, so she can get what she needs all by herself. She'll also like to work with her hands manipulating play dough, clay, and paints (finger paints or washable watercolors and acrylics with brushes).

- Make paper airplanes or learn origami. You can find different designs of paper airplanes and instructions for making them by searching online.

- Allow your child to use a computer keyboard and a mouse to increase her dexterity and hand-eye coordination. You can find free educational game websites online, or purchase games for preschoolers to load onto your computer. Your local library may even have a children's computer with many educational computer games on it to use for free.

- Thread small beads onto pipecleaners, shoelaces, or string.

- Teach your child to sew by hand, knit, or crochet.

- Put small pegs into holes.

- Use tools. Start nails in a board and let your child use a hammer to pound them in the rest of the way. Set up screws in a board the same way and let your child use a screwdriver to screw them in. If your child has toys that are battery-operated, give her the screwdriver to open the little door to remove the batteries herself.

- Pour sand or water from container to container. Provide several small containers for your child to use. Playing with water can be done outside or inside in the bath. It's a great activity for any season, and children love playing with water.

- Build with blocks with your child and give her time to build on her own. Create complex structures, fashion shapes, build favorite items such as airplanes or boats, and spell your child's name with blocks.

- Draw animals, plants, and people with your child.

- Encourage your child to write letters to people—especially people who will write back. Your child will find it very exciting to get a letter in the mail or an e-mail.

- Your child can help you prepare meals by spreading mayonnaise on sandwich bread, cutting vegetables with a child-safe knife for a soup or salad, or measuring and mixing ingredients (all under supervision, of course). Ask for her help with arranging plates on the dinner table, placing utensils next to the plates, stirring the batter, or carrying the milk to the table.

- Your child can learn to fold clothes and hang them up or put them away in her drawers. She loves to do what you do and wants to learn how to do everything.

5-6
years

DEVELOPING MIND

Your Preschooler Branches Out in Thinking, Solving, and Playing Skills

By this age, your child can identify basic colors such as red, blue, yellow, green, purple, and orange. She can count to at least ten and knows the alphabet. She loves to trace or copy letters and shapes. She can write her name quite legibly, and she will draw pictures of familiar people, animals, and objects.

With your child's developing mind comes the desire to do larger projects. She will really get into creating an elaborate scene for a play, with a detailed plot, costumes, and props planned out. She may build more complicated structures with blocks or create a fort with blankets, chairs, and handmade signs. If interrupted in her work, she can come back later to pick up where she left off. She will even resume work on her projects on subsequent days. Her focus and concentration have improved so that she is more able to accomplish long-term tasks.

Your child has an amazing memory. She's quick to pick up song lyrics and memorize books that you read to her. Make a point of reading to her on a daily basis and involve her when picking out books to borrow from the library. This is a great age to branch out from children's books to reading children's classics such as *Little House on the Prairie,* *Charlotte's Web,* and *The Jungle Book,* to name a few. She might enjoy listening to you read or to a recording of a book on tape. Your local library should stock a number of audio books that you can borrow for free.

Your child understands that stories have a beginning, a middle, and an end. She can even sequence events of a story by arranging three pictures in story order. From all the time you've spent reading with her, she now knows that one reads from the left to the right side of the page and from top to bottom. She is a voracious learner at this age! She wants to know what unfamiliar words mean and will ask every time she hears one. She can define some words as well, and she will tell you how they are used. She understands the meanings of *more, less, same, before, after, above,* and *below.* She has also figured out *first, second,* and *third.*

Your little learner can sort objects by size, recognize categories (such as which items are toys, which are animals, which are food), and order objects from shortest to tallest. She knows which is the front and back of her clothes, and she may be able to identify common coins such as pennies or quarters. She is fascinated by cause and effect, and she will conduct little experiments on a daily basis. *That made a cool noise when I dropped it. Will it make that same noise when I drop it again? What about if I drop it one more time? What happens when I go down the slide backward?*

Activities to Enhance Your Child's Cognitive Development

- Play games of strategy with your child. She may enjoy board games, various card games, dominoes, or tic-tac-toe. You can even start to teach her how to play chess at this age.

- Do puzzles with your child, and let her try them on her own. Select ones that present her with a little challenge, but not too much. If they are too easy, she can lose interest fairly quickly.

Puzzles are great for cognitive development as well as for improving fine motor skills. They can be done alone, with a sibling or friend, or as a family activity.

- Practice the alphabet by singing the ABCs, reading alphabet books, and writing it out for her on a regular basis. This helps her identify the letters and see how to write them. Review the sounds the letters make. Ask her about the sounds of letters: "What does *k* say?"

- Practice numbers and counting throughout the day. Read counting books. Count everything! Ask her to pick out seven potatoes at the grocery store. See if she can find a bunch of five bananas. Ask her to count the number of dogs in the pet-store window or how many cupcakes you'll need to make for a birthday party. Write down the numbers 1 through 10 so she can identify them. Go higher in your counting as she shows proficiency.

- Enhance your child's mathematical thinking by asking her to count, sort, match, group, sequence, and recognize patterns all around her. Ask her to help sort the dirty laundry into lights and darks. Have her match the clean socks and put them in pairs. When your child helps you set the table, ask her to count how many forks, spoons, knives, plates, and glasses you'll need, and have her arrange them in place settings.

- Read stories or nonfiction books on your child's favorite subjects. Go to the library together and have her select books she's interested in reading. She will memorize text as you read books over and over, and she will also start to recognize certain words on the page.

5-6
years

- Sing songs and listen to music in the house and in the car. Choose music that you will enjoy listening to again and again (and again). You'll be amazed at how quickly your chld picks up song lyrics.

- When you are looking at the world or at books, discuss with your child how things are alike and different. Ask her thought-provoking what-if questions: "What if you were a bird?" "What if you could understand dolphins?"

- Encourage make-believe play by filling your house with make-believe play materials such as scarves, hats, old clothes, shoes, recyclables for creating costumes and props, blankets and chairs for building large or small forts, whatever you can think of. Join your child in her make-believe world some of the time to learn about the way she thinks and feels. Make sure you follow her lead and rules of play; don't try to change or "fix" things. Just go with her flow.

- Set up a slumber party for all of your child's stuffed animals.

- Create a store in your home stocked with old cereal boxes, plastic fruit, and household supplies. Your child can choose whether she wants to be the customer or the cashier.

DEVELOPING LANGUAGE

Your Child May Double Her Vocabulary

By the age of five, your child likely speaks between 4,000 and 5,000 words! This year she will almost double that number, gaining about 4,000 more words. **Your child can learn eight or nine new words a day, given the exposure.** She can define familiar words and will ask the meaning of unfamiliar words whenever she hears one. She may be developing a command of specialized terminology in whatever interests her—birds, dinosaurs, flowers, construction vehicles, marine animals, etc. She is on a quest for knowledge right now, eager to learn and know everything.

Your child is also better at inferring the meaning of unfamiliar words, relying on contextual clues. You might say, "See that blue and white bird? The kingfishers found near water eat small fish they catch by diving." She may not have heard the word *kingfisher* before, but from the context you've provided, she's likely to grasp that it is the name of the blue and white bird. She's starting to understand the meaning of common phrases, such as "keep an eye out" and "take it easy." She's recognizing rhyming words, so you'll be likely to hear such statements as "*Band* rhymes with *sand, stand,* and *land.*" Many of the rhyming words may not be actual words, and you can help her by giving her real words that rhyme.

Your preschooler will try out new words and phrases every day. Her vocabulary continues to grow each week, and her words are becoming more complex. **She now speaks in at least six-word** sentences, and will use *and, but,* and *then* to make her sentences longer. She's also starting to use past and future tenses appropriately most of the time. Her sentences are grammatically correct, with words in the right order.

Your child is discovering the fun of language by inventing stories and telling jokes and riddles. She likes to sing little songs—some she makes up, some she has memorized. She is attracted to rhyming verse; in fact, books with rhyming text may be her particular favorites at the moment. She may sing songs and replace some words with her own lyrics—to be funny or because it's what she feels like doing. She is a creative thinker at this age, and it shows in her language development.

TIP

Help Your Child Learn to Read

As your child begins to show an interest in reading, scan the children's section at the library for their collection of easy reader books. Choose books that have only a few words on each page with good context clues in the illustrations. Your child may surprise you (and herself!) by being able to read some of these books with very little help from you on her first try. Success breeds motivation to keep learning and improving.

Reading and Writing Skills Begin to Emerge

You have a pre-reader on your hands. Your child is able to recognize some words, such as her name, and she will "read" them when she sees them. She knows most, if not all, the letters of the alphabet, is familiar with both upper and lowercase (though lowercase is more difficult and usually gets mastered later), and can identify some written numbers. With her memorization skills working brilliantly, this is a great time to begin talking about the sounds each letter makes, preparing her for sounding out words as she learns to read. Your child may start to show a preference for fiction or nonfiction at this age, or she may alternate between the two. She may also show a preference for a particular author.

Your child's growing language skills, including reading, leads to writing skills. Your child can probably write her name and other familiar words. She may use inventive spelling, or she may ask you to spell words for her if she's starting to read at this age. (She'll ask for correct spelling because the words won't look right to her if they're spelled wrong, even though she may not know how to spell the words yet.)

5–6
years

Your child is likely to sit down and look at books all on her own at various times of the day if she's been read to regularly. She may be looking at only the illustrations or she may be looking for words she can read.

Activities to Enhance Your Child's Language Development

- Read, read, read, read! Discuss characters and why they do the things they do. Model sounding out words. Point out words your child might recognize and ask her what they are. (She might surprise you with how many words she knows!) Encourage your child to read to you, but don't push if she's reluctant.

- Play with alphabet puzzles, games, and magnetic letters.

- Practice the alphabet with your preschooler by singing the ABC song and reading books that highlight the alphabet. Regularly write out the alphabet for her so she can identify the letters and see how to write them. Talk about what sounds the letters make. Ask her about the sounds of letters: "What does *d* say?"

- Make sure to speak using proper grammar to model it for your child. She'll learn to speak (and write) the way you do.

- Write out your child's name. She'll be writing it herself very soon, if she isn't already.

- Talk with your child like she's an intelligent person. (She is!) Be sure to ask her opinions, likes, and dislikes whenever you can. Listen carefully when she talks to you and respond in a manner that shows you heard her and understood.

- Joke around with your child, and she'll learn to joke, too. She loves a good laugh and will have fun playing with language.

- Tell stories to your child about your life experiences or make up stories that include your child(ren) as character(s). She's likely to ask you to repeat those stories for several days.

- Encourage your child to tell stories. Ask her to tell you about something that happened to her or something she saw. She'll also love telling you completely imaginative tales.

- Ask your child what-if questions: "What if you lived on a boat?" "What if you could run faster than a horse?"

- Encourage your child to write—her name, the dinner menu, notes to friends or family, labels for her drawings, short stories, etc.

- Spell words for your child whenever she asks you how to spell a specific word. If you don't know how to spell a word, look it up in the dictionary. That way, you'll get the correct spelling, and you'll also be showing her how to find information when you are unsure of the answer.

- Sing songs with your child and listen to music together. She'll quickly memorize song lyrics.

- Talk about words that rhyme. Make up rhymes with your child. "What rhymes with *day*?" Write rhyming poems.

- Point out words that begin or end with the same letter sound when you are talking or reading to help your child become more aware of letter sounds.

- Provide your child with pretend play materials such as feather scarves, hats, old clothes, shoes, recyclables for making costumes and props, blankets for building forts, etc. Create hand puppets out of paper bags decorated with markers, paper, string, and glue, or out of socks decorated with buttons, yarn, fabric, and thread. (She'll have fun making a puppet, and it'll enhance her fine motor skills.)

5-6
years

DEVELOPING PERSON

Your Child Recognizes Differences and Similarities

Your child is at the age where she has greater curiosity and interest in other people. Her world still revolves around herself, but to a lesser degree. She is more sensitive to other people's feelings, and she will show concern and sympathy. She is more aware of the differences between big kids and little kids and will speak differently to a younger child than she does to an elder. She will also try to protect younger children. You may see her walking alongside a toddler with the intent of making herself a safe barrier between the smaller child and the rock wall that surrounds the playground, or she may pick up a toddler who is getting too close to the street and bring him back to a safe spot.

This is the age when your child may begin to invent her own games, including specific rules of play. She may like to organize other children and props when she's setting up a make-believe play, and she can come across as bossy sometimes.

Your child is adept at taking turns and sharing, but she'll still have moments when she doesn't want to. That's okay. We all have moments when we don't feel like sharing, don't we? If she's taking turns and sharing most of the time, then it's important to respect her choice not to occasionally.

Your Child Thinks She's Five Going on Thirty-Five

Encourage her to do things herself. If she's enamored with the vacuum cleaner and begs for a turn every time you get it out; let her vacuum! Yes, it will slow down your cleaning routine, but it will expand her skills while enlisting her as an active participant in the caretaking of your home and family. **Your child likes to feel big, as if she's on the verge of being grown up. She wants to do everything herself and help with everyday tasks. Let her!** Teach her how to fold laundry; she's likely to enjoy folding clothes with you. Allow her to help wash or rinse dishes in the sink or load the dishwasher with

Your child takes more care with a younger child, is gentler in her play with him, and protective of his safety. She may be fascinated with babies as well.

you. Encourage her involvement as much as you can. Not only does it boost her self-confidence to be a contributing member of the household, but it also encourages her to be independent by gaining important life skills and learning that everyone in a house is responsible for taking care of it. Plus her participation makes your life easier as she grows up and learns to automatically clean up after herself and take on some of life's daily tasks.

Your child's sense of being big (and her strong desire to be grown up) means she likes to make her own decisions. You'll probably hear "I want to choose" when it comes to everything, whether it's what's for lunch or what clothes she will wear. Allow her to make the choice as often as you possibly can. There are still so many things beyond her control—just imagine how frustrating that must feel—so give her the freedom to choose whenever you can. If the decision is one that's not up for debate, then tell her so. "I'm sorry, love, but you have to brush your teeth. I don't want your teeth to hurt. We need to keep them healthy and strong. But you can decide what kind of toothpaste you'd like to use."

Also, when she's making a choice that can potentially have unpleasant consequences, tell her so. She doesn't have the wealth of experience that you have. Let her benefit from your experience by explaining what the consequences of her actions might be. "If you choose not to let Tommy play with you, he might not want to play with you the next time you want to play with him. How would you feel if Tommy didn't want to play with you? Do you think that's how Tommy will feel if you don't let him play this time?"

Get your child involved in the daily care of the family and house. He wants to help at this age, so take him up on his offer. He'll learn that in a family everyone pitches in, and it gives him valuable life skills for when he's older and living on his own.

Your child is old enough to talk about how she feels, and to express in words that she is mad or upset about something rather than acting out physically. However, don't expect her self-control to be consistent at this point. She may still respond physically when she's overwhelmed with feelings, but she's gradually learning to get it under control. Keep reminding her of the appropriate way to handle situations, and tell her what she *can* do next time.

By this age, your child understands and respects rules, and she will ask permission to do things. She also has a basic understanding of right and wrong. Along the same lines, she is much more aware of which behaviors garner approval from important adults in her life and which do not.

5-6
years

Understanding Self-Control

When you find yourself becoming exasperated with your child's tendency to react physically when she's mad, rather than expressing her feelings with words, take a moment to think about how you handle strong emotions. Imagine you've been lectured by your boss in front of your colleagues. Imagine the embarrassment and anger you feel as a result. Imagine that feeling stewing all day, building up as you relive the moment over and over again in your mind. By the time you get into your car to drive home, you're ready to blow. Imagine, then, someone carelessly cuts you off in traffic, and the kind of language that might erupt from your mouth (assuming the kids are not in the car, of course!). Imagine how strongly you'd like to ram your car into theirs. Maybe you flash your lights to express your anger, or honk your horn, or drive very close behind them, or even give them certain hand signals.

Think about how, at times, you become a slave to your emotions, even though you like to think of yourself as being in control. You are an adult, and you rein yourself in most of the time. (And it took you many, many years to be able to do that.) But there are still times when you simply snap.

Now think about the times when your child reacts physically. Remember how overwhelming feelings can be and how difficult it can be to keep yourself in check. Think about how much more difficult it is for a child to control herself without the inner discipline, knowledge, or experience you possess. She doesn't know how to calm herself, take deep breaths to regain her equilibrium, or let off steam by going for a jog or using another stress management technique. Don't be surprised when she reacts physically. Don't be punitive. And whatever you do, don't lose your cool! (We're modeling how to handle anger here, right?) Help her understand that her reaction is unacceptable, and give her examples of what she can do next time. Remind her to express herself in words. Offer specific words she might use: "Next time, instead of pushing, you can say, 'I don't like that. It makes me really mad when you do that.' Say it in words next time, because pushing hurts, and we do not hurt each other." Remind her she can ask for help, walk away, or hit a pillow if she feels like getting out her frustration.

And remember that learning self-control takes a long time.

By the age of six, your child will like to try new skills—insisting that she do so all by herself from the start—and will take new risks. She may branch out socially, all of a sudden becoming interested in playing with the new kids she meets on the playground. She enjoys giving to others, as well as receiving; it's exciting either way for her at this age. And she may start collecting things. You may find her focusing on a category of items—rocks or seashells, for example—that she'll pick up whenever she has the opportunity.

Although your child may show signs of being more social and perhaps more focused on other people, she still needs time to herself. You may find her alone in her room playing with her toys or reading the books you brought home from the library. Or perhaps she wants to spend time playing a computer game by herself or watching a video. Give her time to be by herself if she wants it. It allows her to recharge her batteries and begin to get to know who she is. It is healthy and normal to want time alone.

Activities to Enhance Your Child's Emotional and Social Development

- Head out! Take your child on errands and to stores and restaurants. Carry on the kind of everyday activity that brings you into contact with people to model how to interact and give your child opportunities to practice it herself if she wants to. She will start to interact with people of all ages when she's ready.

- Make playdates and keep going to playgroups. Regular exposure to other children helps your child learn the art of cooperative play, which is a learning process.

- Play with children of various ages (one of the perks of a playgroup). Let your child engage with adults of various ages as well. Give her plenty of opportunities to become comfortable interacting with anyone of any age.

- Play games together that your child enjoys playing: board games, card games, dominoes, tag, hide-and-seek, etc. Your child can even start to learn chess at this age. Games help your child learn to take turns.

- Give your child materials such as scarves, hats, old clothes, shoes, recyclables for making costumes and props, blankets for building forts, etc., to encourage make-believe play.

- Play with puppets to help your child work through some emotions or to figure out how to do better next time. The puppets can discuss issues that are bothering your child.

- Participate in noncompetitive team activities such as planting a community garden, painting a mural, or planning a block party.

- Encourage your child to write thank-you notes or letters, especially to someone who will write back. There is nothing more exciting for a child than getting a letter in the mail!

5-6
years

- Continue to give your child words to use when she gets upset, angry, or sad. Keep reminding her to say it in words, not in pushes, hits, or kicks. Remember that self control takes a long time to master.

- Allow your child alone time whenever she wants or needs it.

- Create a spot for your child to be alone where she can hide whenever she needs to, such as a large cardboard box or a closet with pillows on the floor. (This is *not* a time-out spot.)

- Invite your child to help plan activities, playdates, and parties. Welcome her input, preferences, and help.

POSITIVELY PARENTING

Treat Mistakes as Teaching Moments to Help Your Child Do Better Next Time

As your child gets older, it is easy to assume that she knows more than she does. It is easy to assume that she knows what will happen when she does something or that she can predict outcomes or consequences. **It may feel natural to expect more adultlike behavior from your child, but it is not a reasonable expectation for a five- or six-year-old.**

When you find yourself face to face with a teaching moment—when your child has done something inappropriate or unacceptable—approach the situation as a chance for your child to learn how to do better next time. If you have steam coming out your ears, you need to gather yourself and calm

down before talking to your child; she won't learn anything if you're yelling at her. She *will* learn if you speak honestly, calmly, and gently about what she did, how it made someone else feel, how she might feel if it happened to her, and what she can do differently next time.

Kids make mistakes all the time. So do we! As parents, we make mistakes on a weekly, if not daily, basis. We are learning how to be parents. And just when we figure out how to parent a five-year-old, she turns six, and we have to shift gears and learn how to parent a six-year-old! Similarly, kids are learning how to be who they are, how to get along with others, how to empathize, how to be kind, how to stick up for themselves, how to get mad without hurting someone, and so much more. We all make mistakes, and our home is the one place where we should be able to make mistakes safely. **Treat your child gently when she makes a mistake, talk to her as if she is an intelligent person, explaining why what she did is not okay, and help her learn from her mistakes.**

If you've made a mistake, you can model for your child how to do better by doing it over right away. Perhaps you've come home in a foul mood, and as soon as you're in the door, you snap at your child "Just give me a minute!" before you look at

the drawing she is so excited to show you. Her face crumples, tears gather, and she runs off to her hiding spot. You feel like an utter monster. Instead of beating yourself up or maintaining a rotten attitude, do it over. Go see your child, tell her you're sorry you snapped, and that you'd like to start over. Tell her you're going to come in the front door again as if you're just arriving home, and ask if she'd please show you her drawing when you do. Come in the door. Get down and hug your child when she comes over to you. Focus on her, drink in her good energy, and allow it to lift your energy so you're genuinely feeling good. And admire her drawing.

When Your Child Makes a Mistake, Give Her the Chance to Do It Over

Let's say your child lies to you about washing her hands after using the bathroom. She's made a mistake by lying, so give her a chance to do it over. Ask her to stop and think about what's true, and then to tell you whether she washed her hands. She'll probably look at you and admit that she did not wash her hands. You can thank her for telling you the truth, remind her how important it is to always tell the truth, and then ask her to go wash her hands.

When your child makes a mistake or when she does something unacceptable, talk with her about it in a calm and gentle voice. She won't learn anything if you're yelling at her. Tell her what was inappropriate and how she can handle it differently next time.

As Your Child Changes, So Must the Rules

As you journey along the parenting path, make sure you check in with yourself periodically to determine whether your rules are still reasonable given your child's age, abilities, and level of responsibility. The rules should change as your child grows. At what age is your child no longer required to hold your hand while walking through a parking lot? When is she old enough to cross a street on her own? At what age will you let your child play outside in your yard unsupervised? For each parent, the answers will be different because they depend on the particular child, the parent's comfort level, and the environment in which they live.

The point is that rules have to change as your child changes. When you are taking a mental inventory of all your rules (or when you encounter one during an interaction with your child), you may discover that a rule is no longer reasonable for your child. That's when you should change it—and tell your child you are changing it. Let her know that because she's older and more responsible or capable, the rule is no longer necessary. Let her feel big and grown up. Empower her in her natural development toward independence.

Children Cooperate More When You Ask Nicely

Children are people, too, and just like you, your child does not like to be bossed around. Consequently, you are likely to come up against a child who refuses to comply or acts defiant if you regularly bark out commands. In the same way that children need to learn how to ask nicely to get what they want, parents need to learn that approach, too. (And think of what a great model you are when you do!)

Take a step back from a situation that has made your child defiant. Look at your own actions. How are you talking to her? What words are you using? What is your tone of voice? What does your body language convey? Are you delivering your request or demand in such a way that your child will *want* to comply?

If not, change what you are doing. (A golden rule in parenting: If it's not working, don't keep doing it.) How can you get your child to cooperate most of the time? (It won't happen all the time, and that's okay. Your child should have the right not to do something if she really doesn't want to—except where safety is an issue.) Be creative! Be positive! Present your request as a challenge. Or make it playful, make it fun. Request, don't command.

The goal is not to trick your child into doing something; you're just working with her natural inclination to do what is pleasurable and fun to gain her cooperation. And it's much more pleasurable and fun for you, as well, to have a willing, cooperative kid.

Well-Child Checks and Vaccines

You should schedule your child's annual well-child checkup soon after her birthday every year. She will be weighed and measured, and her measurements will be plotted on her growth curves. Your doctor will discuss her development with less attention spent on her language and motor skills and more on her social skills. She will have another vision test at this time. Don't be surprised if your child's vision is not 20/20, a target that many children do not achieve until age six or seven. If any concerns come up with your child's vision or hearing, you will be referred to a specialist for more formal testing.

Four vaccine boosters are recommended between ages four and six. These include: the measles, mumps, and rubella (or MMR) vaccine; the varicella or chickenpox vaccine; the diphtheria, tetanus, and acellular pertussis (or DTaP) vaccine; and the inactivated polio vaccine (or IPV). In addition, your doctor will recommend that your child get vaccinated for the flu when flu season begins during the winter. For information on where to find the most up-to-date list of recommended vaccines for children turn to the Resources and Recommended Reading section on page 296.

Health and Safety Tips

Your child should visit the dentist every six months for a checkup and cleaning. If your household water supply lacks fluoride, your doctor or dentist can give you a prescription for supplements in either drop or pill form, if you are interested.

It's important not to expose your child to excessive sunlight. Among the leading causes of adult skin cancer is childhood sunburns. Protect your child by avoiding the sun during the middle of the day, putting sun-protective hats and clothing on her, and using sunscreen on any exposed skin when you need to be out in the sun.

Your child should still be in some type of car seat. You don't have to transfer your child to a booster seat when she reaches 40 pounds (18 kg). The five-point restraint seats are safer and can accommodate weights up to 50, 60, or even 80 pounds (23, 27, or 36 kg). Having your child in the backseat of the car is still the safest place for her to ride.

Insist that your child wear a helmet while biking, in-line skating, or doing other activities with a high risk of head injuries, like skiing or snowboarding.

Remember the basic ongoing safety precautions. Keep medications and unsafe home and garden products safely secured out of your child's reach. Smoke detector batteries should be changed twice a year when the clocks change in the spring and fall. Install new smoke detectors when they expire, usually every ten years. Install a carbon monoxide detector if you use a woodstove or fireplace. Keep the poison control phone number prominently posted near every telephone in your home and program it into your cell phones and handheld electronic gadgets. (To find the poison control number in your area, check the Resources and Recommended Reading section on page 296.) Don't store guns in your home; if you have no choice but to store them, keep guns safely locked and the ammunition locked in a separate place.

5-6 years

SCHOOL READINESS, SCHOOL OPTIONS

Most parents prepare to send their child to school when she is around five or six. We've included information on various educational options, as well as how to determine whether your child is ready for kindergarten. This is general information to help you assess what is best for your child. Keep in mind that you know your child better than anyone. You are the expert on your child and therefore the best equipped to decide what is in her best interest when it comes to her education.

The Many Options for Your Child's Education

We are lucky to have choices when it comes to our children's education. There are many outstanding public schools, and if you are lucky to live in a town that has one, and you think your child will thrive in that environment, then your school decision is fairly easy. But it doesn't have to be a given that your child will attend the local public school for kindergarten and beyond.

School can be a great experience for a child who is ready to go off on her own. Kids are kept busy and engaged throughout the school day, which may be a big change for a child who has been home with a parent since birth.

Our objective is to cover educational opportunities beyond the public school system that you may not be aware of. There are charter schools cropping up all over the country. Charter schools are public schools, but they are less restricted than other public schools because they are exempt from most of the laws that school districts must adhere to, and they are held more accountable for student performance. Private school options are many, including Montessori, Waldorf, religious schools, and others. Each comes with its own educational philosophy and style of teaching, and is very worth looking into if you don't think a public school setting is best for your child. The tuition at private schools, however, can be quite expensive. Research the options available to you in your community and talk to parents with older children enrolled at the various schools. Armed with research, input from other parents, and your instincts and knowledge of your child, you will be in a good position to make an informed decision.

Certain children don't adapt well to a school environment, and for them, homeschooling can be the right path. More parents are choosing to homeschool every year, which means there is a wealth of support available for homeschoolers. You can find information online, in magazines published for homeschool families, and in the many books published on the subject. Homeschooling breaks down into a few options: distance learning via the Internet through established schools (which might offer regular teacher contact, tests, grades,

One of the great benefits of homeschooling is the one-on-one attention your child's education gets. He benefits greatly because you can mold your educational activities to suit his interests and strengths, while working to improve his weaker areas.

transcripts, and a diploma), curricula you can purchase that supply all the information your child needs to learn in every subject each year, or outlines of what children should learn each year for you to use as a guide as you create your own curriculum based on your child's interests. For an outline of what your child should learn each year, start by taking a look at your state standards (you can find them online), and then read through books on the subject that cover everything your child needs to learn from kindergarten through twelfth grade.

5-6
years

How to Determine Whether Your Child Is Ready for a Kindergarten Classroom

You want to give your child the best educational start possible. In that spirit, you wouldn't want to send her to school if she isn't ready yet. Your state has an age requirement that must be met before a child can attend kindergarten (e.g., a child must be five by December 1 of the year in which you plan to enroll her). The requirement differs by state and you can find your state's age requirement and cutoff date through your local school system. **If your child meets the age requirement, then you need to determine whether your child would benefit from heading into the kindergarten classroom, or whether it might be better to delay enrollment for a year.**

How do you make that call? First, if your child has been in preschool, talk to her preschool teachers. They have the most informed opinion on this matter because they've spent a year or two getting to know your child and seeing her work in a classroom setting. Next, if you're entering the public school system, you'll likely be asked to make an appointment for a kindergarten screening in which the kindergarten teachers will evaluate your child to see whether she seems ready. Finally, you can assess your child by going through the following checklist of kindergarten readiness skills.

This checklist is meant to help you determine whether your child is ready for kindergarten. If she can do most of the items on the list, she is probably ready for the classroom.

RED FLAG!

If you find yourself thinking that your child may not be ready for kindergarten, consider keeping her home for one more year. There is no benefit to sending her to school if she is not ready, and there is much to be gained from keeping her home until she is ready. She will have a much more positive experience in school if you send her when she is ready, which will hopefully lead to a lifelong love of learning. If she's enrolled before she's ready, a negative experience may cause her to dislike and resist school and learning. She will also benefit from spending more time and deepening her bond with you and strengthening her sense of security and a solid home base.

Your Child Is Ready for the Kindergarten Classroom If She . . .

- Has a long attention span and can sit still at a desk or table for stretches of time. Can your child focus on one topic for twenty minutes?

- Is very patient and can wait her turn when someone else is speaking.

- Can sit still through a story that she's not interested in. Can your child listen to a story without interrupting?

- Listens to instructions and follows them.

- Goes to the bathroom by herself and puts on her coat, hat, and mittens by herself. Is your child self-sufficient?

- Follows rules and respects authority and those around her. Does she respect other people's belongings?

- Knows the alphabet and can count to at least ten. (These will be covered in kindergarten, but most kindergarten teachers expect that children will already be familiar with letters and numbers.)

- Cuts with scissors and holds a pencil correctly. Can your child trace or draw simple shapes?

- Is interested in reading and shows a desire to read books by herself.

- Enjoys group settings and gets along with other children. Does your child take turns easily? Does she like to work together in a group? Can she compromise and go along with what others want to do even when it's not what she wants to do?

- Can separate from you without being upset.

- Speaks clearly and is easily understood by others.

Preparing Your Child for the First Day of School

Talk to your child about going to kindergarten. Tell her about the friends she will make, the fun she will have, and all she will learn. **Tour the school, check out the playground, meet with her teacher if you can.** Explore the classroom in advance so it seems more familiar on that first day. If you get a list of your child's future classmates from the school, arrange several playdates over the summer so she can meet some of the students ahead of time.

5–6
years

If your child has not been in day care or preschool, practice leaving her in a safe, comfortable environment without you. Arrange for her to play at a friend's house while you run an errand, or drop her at her grandparents' house for the afternoon. See how she handles being someplace without you. See whether the school your child will attend offers summer programming, such as a day camp. She might enjoy it, and it will introduce her to the school setting. It will also get her used to being in a safe place without you, and she will likely meet many kids who turn out to be some of the friendly faces in the classroom when school starts.

Be sure to stock up on all the school supplies your child will need; you'll either get a list from your school, or you'll find one posted at local stores that sell back-to-school items. Go shopping together and let your child pick out a first day of school outfit. Celebrate this milestone! On the morning of her first day of school, take pictures, make a special breakfast, and plan a favorite snack for when she returns home. Ask questions about her day and listen attentively. She has a new life now, a new journey ahead of her, and you'll need to reconnect with her every day to find out all about it.

As you watch your child get on the school bus, enter the school from where you dropped her off, or begin her learning from home, you may find it hard to believe that six years have already passed. Does it feel as if you've had her forever and yet she can't possibly be old enough for school already? Time passes so quickly when you're raising a child. Too quickly.

Pause for a moment and think about all that your child has learned and achieved in these six short years. She's grown from helpless infant to on-her-way-to-independent person. She still needs you, and she will for years to come. Hopefully she'll always need you in some way, but there is so much that she can do now on her own. So many skills that she has mastered. So many developmental milestones she has attained.

You and your child are beginning a new phase of your journey now, as she becomes more and more independent and self-sufficient. Many of the same ideas we've discussed still apply as you head into unknown territory: Spend time with your child, **show her through your actions that you love her unconditionally, respect her as a person, and most important, be the person you want your child to be**. Make the most of every day you have with your child, and don't forget to enjoy the journey along the way!

Celebrate your child's first day of school with a special outfit, her favorite foods, pictures, and an extra hug and a kiss. Be ready to reconnect with her when she gets home and share in her excitement over her day and the new life ahead of her.

RESOURCES AND RECOMMENDED READING

POISON CONTROL INFORMATION

In the United States: call **800-222-1222.** You can call it from home or when you're away and automatically be connected to the closest poison control center.

In Canada:
Calgary: **+1 403-670-1414** or **800-332-1414** (Alberta only)
Halifax: **800-565-8161** or **+1 902-470-8161**
Québec: **+1 418-656-8090** or **800-463-5060**
Regina: **+1 306-766-4545**
Saskatoon: **+1 306-655-1362**
Toronto: **+1 416-813-5900** or **800-268-9017** (Ontario only) www.ontariopoisoncentre.ca
Vancouver: **800-567-8911 (Vancouver only)** or **+1 604-682- 5050**
Winnipeg: **+1 204-787-2591**

In Australia: call the Poisons Information Centre at **13 11 26** (accessible 24 hours anywhere in Australia) or see the website: www.poisonsinfo.nsw.gov.au.

In the United Kingdom: the UK National Poisons Emergency number is **0870-600- 6266** (Outside the UK: **+44 870-600-6266**). From London you can call the local poisons information service at **+44 (0)20-7771- 5315** (Director), **+44 (0)20-7771-5310** (Poisons information service), or emergency telephone **0870-243-2241.**

CAR SEAT SAFETY INFORMATION

In the United States: Have your car seat reviewed by an expert. Many police or fire departments have car seat rodeos where you can have your installation inspected and adjusted if necessary. See the website at www.seatcheck.org, or call 866-732-8243 (866-SEAT-CHECK).

In Canada: Check with your local fire, police, or public health department to find out if they have a car seat clinic. See the Canada Safety Council website at www.safetycouncil.org/info/child/childcar.htm or at Caring for Kids, a website created by the Canadian Paediatric Society, at www.cps.ca/caringforkids/keepkidssafe/CarSeatSafety.htm.

In Australia: contact your local motoring authority for a list of approved fitters to professionally check your child restraint or visit your local ambulance station. Some safety organisations, like Kidsafe (www.kidsafe.com.au), and the Australian Red Cross will also check or fit seats. There may be a small fee for this service.

In the UK: Visit www.childcarseats.org.uk for information and laws on car seat safety.

VACCINE INFORMATION

In the United States: The most up-to-date information on vaccines can be found at the Centers for Disease Control and Prevention website. www.cdc.gov/vaccines

In Canada: Vaccine information can be found on the Public Health Agency of Canada website. The current recommended schedule is at the following website: www.phac-aspc.gc.ca/im/is-cv/index-eng.php

In Australia: The main website on vaccines below is where you will find a link to National Immunisation Program Schedule (NIPS) which is the current recommended vaccines. www.immunise.health.gov.au/

In the UK: This is the National Health Service Immunisation Information website in the United Kingdom. The most up-to-date recommended schedule can be found at www.immunisation.nhs.uk/Immunisation_Schedule.

PEDIATRICS

These websites offer many puplications with information ranging from baby safety and infant feeding to caring for your teenager.

American Academy of Family Physicians (AAFP) and American Academy of Pediatrics (AAP): www.aafp.org and www.aap.org

Canadian Paediatric Society (CPS): www.cps.ca A national organization made up of over 2,000 Canadian paediatricians. This website has information for parents and professionals about the health and safety of children of all ages.

BREASTFEEDING

La Leche League International: www.llli.org This nonprofit organization is dedicated to supporting breastfeeding internationally through educational meetings, phone support, and in-person support from trained leaders.

Australian Breastfeeding Association : www.breastfeeding.asn.au This nonprofit self-help group is one of the largest in Australia. The organization is dedicated to promoting and protecting breastfeeding through education of the larger community and offering mother-to-mother support.

GENERAL CHILD DEVELOPMENT

Mothering magazine, www.mothering.com

PediNeuroLogic Exam, http://library.med.utah.edu/pedineurologicexam/html/home_exam.html

National Network for Child Care, www.nncc.org

PBS Parents, http://www.pbs.org/parents/childdevelopment

What Can My Baby See?, www.ski.org/Vision/babyvision.html

BOOKS

Your Amazing Newborn by Marshall Klaus, M.D., and Phyllis Klaus

The Ultimate Breastfeeding Book of Answers by Jack Newman, M.D., and Teresa Pitman

The No-Cry Sleep Solution by Elizabeth Pantley

The Playskool Guide to Baby's First Year by Jamie Loehr, M.D., and Jen Meyers

The Baby Book: Everything You Need to Know About Your Baby from Birth to Age Two (Revised and Updated Edition) by William Sears, M.D., Martha Sears, R.N., Robert Sears, M.D., and James Sears, M.D.

The Vaccine Book by Robert Sears, M.D.

The Vaccine Answer Book by Jamie Loehr, M.D.

Raising Your Spirited Child by Mary Sheedy Kurcinka

Quirky Kids: Understanding and Helping Your Child Who Doesn't Fit In—When to Worry and When Not to Worry by Perri Klass and Eileen Costello

The Explosive Child: A New Approach for Understanding and Parenting Easily Frustrated, Chronically Inflexible Children by Ross W. Greene

You Can't Say You Can't Play by Vivian Gussin Paley

Starting Small: Teaching Tolerance in Preschool and the Early Grades by Vivian Gussin Paley

INDEX

PHOTOGRAPHER CREDITS

Sacha Ajbeszyc/gettyimages.com, 171

Alloy Photography/veer.com, 80

Altrendo Images/gettyimages.com, 58; 92

American Images Inc./gettyimages.com, 283

arabianEye/gettyimages.com, 255

Neil Beckerman/gettyimages.com, 154

Christopher Bissell/gettyimages.com, 163

Reggie Casagrande/gettyimages.com, 150

Ron Chapple/gettyimages.com, 168

Jay L. Clendenin/gettyimages.com, 22

Andy Cox/gettyimages.com, 54

Ellen Denuto/gettyimages.com, 98 (bottom)

Kevin Dodge/masterfile.com, 205

Laurence Dutton/gettyimages.com, 158

Courtesy of www.edmunds.com, 36

Fotolia/fotolia.com, 39; 40; 69; 106; 122; 148; 160; 249

Rene Frederick/gettyimages.com, 114

Michael Goldman/masterfile.com, 75

Charles Gullung/gettyimages.com, 74; 103 (top); 141

David Hanover/gettyimages.com, 218

Noel Hendrickson/gettyimages.com, 129

Frank Herholdt/gettyimages.com, 200

iStockphoto.com, 2; 5; 6; 8; 11; 12; 14; 16; 17; 18; 19; 30; 34; 37; 38; 44; 45; 47; 48; 51; 57; 59; 63; 64; 73; 76; 77; 78; 79; 84; 98 (top); 100; 120; 123; 125; 132; 133; 137; 146; 152; 153; 156; 157; 176; 178; 180; 185; 192; 196; 199; 201; 210; 214; 215; 217; 225; 232; 234; 240; 243; 244; 246; 251; 252; 256; 260; 262; 263; 268; 271; 272; 280; 290

Christina Kennedy/gettyimages.com, 183

Julia Kuskin/gettyimages.com, 184

Sarah Lawless/gettyimages.com, 188

Martha Lazar/gettyimages.com, 96

Martin Lof/ANYONE/gettyimages.com, 216

Marko MacPherson/masterfile.com, 195

Alex Mares-Manton/gettyimages.com, 274

Tony Metaxas/gettyimages.com, 23; 139

Tom Morrison/gettyimages.com, 111

Jeffry Myers/gettyimages.com, 181

Gen Nishino/gettyimages.com, 95

Stuart O'Sullivan/gettyimages.com, 277

Jose Luis Pelaez/gettyimages.com, 224; 265

Alan Penn, 83

Lisa Petkau/gettyimages.com, 250

Joe Polillio/gettyimages.com, 144

Erik Rank/gettyimages.com, 242

Rich Reid/gettyimages.com, 52

S. W. Productions/gettyimages.com, 91

Shinya Sasaki/NEOVISION/gettyimages.com, 187

Shutterstock images/shutterstock.com, 13; 25; 26; 28; 49; 50; 53; 67; 71; 72; 86; 99; 101; 102; 103 (bottom); 109; 113; 118; 126; 128; 131; 173; 175; 198; 212; 220; 229; 238; 254; 270; 282; 291

Ariel Skelley/gettyimages.com, 20; 97

Zia Soleil/gettyimages.com, 165

Carlos Spottorno/gettyimages.com, 233

Simon Stanmore/gettyimages.com, 104

Marla Sweeney/gettyimages.com, 257

Christopher Thomas/gettyimages.com, 124; 230

Donn Thompson/gettyimages.com, 286

Camile Tokerud/gettyimages.com, 42; 89

Jilly Wendell/gettyimages.com, 182

Ross Whitaker/gettyimages.com, 295